The Rent Curse

The Rent Curse

Natural Resources, Policy Choice, and Economic Development

Richard M. Auty and Haydn I. Furlonge

OXFORD
UNIVERSITY PRESS

OXFORD
UNIVERSITY PRESS

Great Clarendon Street, Oxford, OX2 6DP,
United Kingdom

Oxford University Press is a department of the University of Oxford.
It furthers the University's objective of excellence in research, scholarship,
and education by publishing worldwide. Oxford is a registered trade mark of
Oxford University Press in the UK and in certain other countries

© Richard M. Auty and Haydn I. Furlonge 2019

The moral rights of the authors have been asserted

First Edition published in 2019
Impression: 1

Published in the United States of America by Oxford University Press
198 Madison Avenue, New York, NY 10016, United States of America

British Library Cataloguing in Publication Data
Data available

Library of Congress Control Number: 2018945756

ISBN 978–0–19–882886–0

Printed and bound by
CPI Group (UK) Ltd, Croydon, CR0 4YY

Preface

More than two decades of statistical analysis have failed to resolve the causes of the resource curse or even determine whether the phenomenon exists or not. We employ rent cycling theory to undertake a more subtle approach to the resource curse than that achieved by statistical studies to date. We do so by analysing the political economy of windfall gains from natural resource exploitation in two case study countries and then applying the findings to the principal global developing regions. We construct two stylized facts models of rent-driven growth to show that: (i) the resource curse exists but that it is caused by policy failure, so that it is not a deterministic phenomenon; (ii) the global incidence of the resource curse varies over time and by commodity; and (iii) the resource curse is a variant of a wider rent curse that can be caused by windfall revenues from foreign aid (geopolitical rent), worker remittances (labour rent), or government manipulation of relative prices (regulatory rent).

The basic premise of rent cycling theory is that low rent incentivizes the elite to grow the economy in order to become wealthy, whereas high rent encourages the elite to siphon away rent for immediate self-enrichment at the expense of long-term economic growth. The contrasting incentives trigger systematic divergence in policy that results in two distinctive trajectories for structural change. More specifically, low rent encourages the elite to grow the economy by allocating inputs efficiently, which aligns the economy with its comparative advantage in labour-intensive exports and drives rapid and relatively egalitarian economic growth along with incremental democratization. In contrast, high rent elicits contests among the elite to capture the rent for immediate personal enrichment and discourages the distribution of wealth in a fair and sustainable manner. This causes the high-rent economy to absorb rent too quickly and to experience Dutch disease effects, which lead to the expansion of a subsidized urban sector whose burgeoning demand for rent eventually outstrips supply and causes a protracted growth collapse, with attendant political destabilization. The resulting high-rent staple trap trajectory fails to achieve competitive diversification and consequently intensifies rent dependence.

Our findings carry significant implications for development research. We trace rent flows from their extraction, through their deployment, to their impact on the political economy. We thereby respond to recent calls by leading economists such as Stiglitz to study the distorting impacts of rent on economic growth. Our low-rent model identifies the importance to sustainable (productivity-driven) long-term development of: rent scarcity in incentivizing the elite to pursue growth-oriented policies; Lewis's labour market turning point, in triggering self-sustaining competitive diversification of the economy; and early passage through the demographic cycle, for achieving rapid and egalitarian per capita GDP growth. In contrast, the high-rent staple trap trajectory risks incentivizing contests among the elite for rent that cause over rapid domestic rent absorption and Dutch disease effects. This postpones the labour market turning point and precludes the benefits that the low-rent economy derives from its singular pattern of *competitive* structural change. Instead, the high-rent economy diversifies into rent-subsidized activity, which is not sustainable.

Our two basic stylized facts political economy models of low-rent and high-rent growth usefully complement statistical studies of the resource curse. The statistical studies pursue rigour at the cost of oversimplifying the factors at work, whereas case studies allow for a more nuanced explanation of resource curse effects. For example, we identify significant fluctuations in the global intensity of resource curse effects, linked to historical changes in development policy fashions since the 1950s. We also show that resource-poor economies can exhibit 'resource curse symptoms' due to flows of geopolitical rent, labour rent, and regulatory rent that can rival resource rents in their magnitude and consequences. Moreover, commodities differ in their vulnerability to rent curse effects.

Our research identifies the misallocation of inputs arising from the widespread post-war policy bias in favour of manufacturing-driven growth, which invariably occurred at the expense of the potential contributions to economic development from the agriculture and service sectors. The policy was especially disadvantageous for small economies, which lacked sufficient domestic demand to sustain factories of minimal viable size. Invariably, rent was deployed to protect inefficient import substitution industry rather than the dynamic and competitive manufacturing that low-rent economies achieved. Instead, import substitution policies invariably degenerated into a source of regulatory rent that consolidated rent-seeking constituencies that locked the economy into a staple trap. Finally, scholars of development have frequently underestimated the flexibility of the plantation as an institution, which in countries as diverse as Malaysia, Mauritius, and Guyana has proved to be adaptable to major changes in the political economy.

We draw upon Mauritius and Trinidad and Tobago to illustrate the argument because they exhibited remarkably similar initial conditions at independence in the 1960s, apart from their mineral endowments. We demonstrate that Trinidad and Tobago has experienced resource curse effects: its high-rent economy traced a staple trap development trajectory and experienced a protracted growth collapse through 1981–93. Moreover, Trinidad and Tobago has yet to diversify away from rent-driven growth into productivity-driven growth, upon which sustainable long-term gains in welfare depend. Trinidad and Tobago shares this unsatisfactory outcome with other rent-addicted economies including the Gulf States, Russia, and Venezuela. We use Mauritius as a counterfactual to illustrate the low-rent trajectory that is also associated with the four Asian Dragons, as well as China, Bangladesh, and Vietnam, and is likely to be pursued by sub-Saharan African economies as more and more of them are rendered land-poor by population growth.

We trace the origins of Trinidad and Tobago's strong addiction to rent to its early reliance on sugar. We also demonstrate the risks to Trinidad and Tobago of relying upon its current strategy of gas-based industrialization, which is a minimal diversification from dependence on hydrocarbon rent. Rather, we propose reform of the political economy to capitalize on recent global growth in sophisticated service exports and value chains, which offer new opportunities to achieve productivity-driven development that is sustainable. But a precondition for success is that politicians must build a coalition of pro-growth interest groups to promote a competitive non-hydrocarbon sector. The final chapters apply the models to interpret structural change in five global developing regions with reference to: agricultural involution in sub-Saharan Africa; premature deindustrialization in Latin America compared with East Asia; and the potential for absorbing surplus labour into export services in South Asia and the Gulf states.

We gratefully acknowledge the hard work of Adam Swan, Katie Bishop, and Catherine Owen at OUP in guiding this book to fruition, and the subsequent tireless help of Julie Musk with copyediting and Alamelu Vengatesan in shepherding the book through the publication process. We are also much indebted to the constructive comments of five reviewers who offered extremely helpful suggestions regarding the overall structure of the book as well as some details. In particular, the reviewers provided the push that we needed to shift the final sections of the book towards the implications of our findings for the principal global developing regions.

Contents

Contents

List of Tables

List of Abbreviations

ANC	African National Congress
bl	barrel
CBD	central business district
CEPEP	Community-based Environmental Protection and Enhancement Programme
CSA	Commonwealth Sugar Agreement
DRI	direct-reduced iron
EPZ	export processing zone
EU	European Union
FDI	foreign direct investment
GATE	Government Assistance for Tuition Expenses
GDP	gross domestic product
GNI	gross national income
GNP	gross national product
IADB	Inter-American Development Bank
ICOR	incremental capital output ratio
ICT	information and computer technology
IFI	international financial institution
ILO	International Labour Organization
IMF	International Monetary Fund
IOC	international oil company
ISCOTT	Iron and Steel Company of Trinidad and Tobago
IT	information technology
LNG	liquefied natural gas
MIT	Massachusetts Institute of Technology
MMM	Mauritian Militant Movement
MNC	multinational corporation
MRSF	mineral revenue stabilization fund
NAR	National Alliance for Reconstruction

List of Abbreviations

NASSCOM	National Association of Software and Services Companies
ODA	overseas development assistance
OECD	Organization for Economic Co-operation and Development
PMSD	Parti Mauricien Social Democrate
PNM	People's National Movement
PPP	purchasing power parity
REER	real effective exchange rate
TCS	Tata Consultancy Services
UAE	United Arab Emirates
UNC	United National Congress
WTO	World Trade Organization

Section 1
Context

1

Aims, Approach, and Structure of the Study

1.1 Aims and Approach of the Study

Economists expect resource-rich economies to grow faster than resource-poor economies if their governments take advantage of the natural resource rent[1] to raise the rate of investment compared with low-rent economies and to increase the level of imported goods that are required to build a modern infrastructure. This appeared to be the case for the developing countries before the 1970s: the mean per capita gross domestic product (GDP) of the resource-rich developing economies was 50% higher than that of the resource-poor economies (Auty 2001: 5). However, Table 1.1 shows that during the period of heightened commodity price volatility of 1973–85 and on into the late-1990s most resource-rich economies grew slowly, if at all, before recovery belatedly commenced. By then, however, the mean per capita income of the resource-poor developing economies exceeded that of the resource-rich ones.

Table 1.1 also shows that at the outset of the period analysed (the early-1960s when the World Bank (2017a) began to compile comparative data) most developing economies were resource-rich and also small. The increased incidence of growth collapses in resource-rich economies through the 1970s and 1980s stimulated case study research (Gelb and Associates 1988; Auty 1993; Karl 1997). Subsequently, Sachs and Warner (1995, 1999) triggered a surge of statistical research into the resource curse, which after a promising start gave way to contradictory claim and counter-claim that has failed to

---

[1] Rent is defined here as the surplus revenue after deducting all production costs including a risk-related return on investment. Philip Crowson (personal communication), former chief economist of RTZ, argues that revenues from foreign aid (geopolitical rent) and the adjustment of relative prices (regulatory rent) are more accurately conceptualized as supernumerary government revenues. Basically, the phenomenon is a revenue stream within an economy that in aggregate can be 20–30% of GDP or more, and which is detached from the activity that generates it and is up for grabs.

Table 1.1 Per capita GDP growth by country resource endowment, 1960–2015 (%/year). Growth rates are simple averages

Economic phases	Preshock global growth 1960–73	Acute commodity price shocks 1973–85	IFI-backed reforms 1985–97	Post-reform recovery 1997–2015
Resource-poor[1]				
Large[2]	2.4	3.7	4.7	3.9
Small	3.5	1.8	2.4	2.4
Resource-rich				
Large[2]	2.7	0.7	1.9	2.3
Small, nonmineral	1.6	0.7	0.9	2.1
Small, hard mineral	2.2	0.1	−0.4	2.1
Small, oil exporter	4.0	2.3	−0.7	1.6
All countries	2.7	1.6	1.5	2.3

[1] Resource-poor = 1970 cropland per head < 0.3 hectares.
[2] Large economy = 1970 GDP > US$7 billion (proxy for domestic market size).
Source: World Bank (2017a).

determine whether a resource curse exists or not (Lederman and Maloney 2007; Cavalcanti et al. 2011). Part of the reason for this impasse is that, as Table 1.1 demonstrates, the intensity of the resource curse effects eased through the commodity boom of the 2000s, which has limited further widening of the income gap between resource-poor economies and resource-rich ones.

This book argues that the resource curse is more complex than initially thought, so that the parsimonious silver bullet explanations that characterize much statistical analysis neglect important features. There are four key aspects to this extra complexity. First, symptoms of the resource curse may be associated with streams of rent other than that from natural resources, principally foreign aid (geopolitical rent), government manipulation of prices (regulatory rent), and worker remittances (labour rent). The resource curse is therefore part of a wider rent curse, which the statistical studies largely ignore. Moreover, each rent source can generate 10% or more of GDP, so that in aggregate the potential rent that can be allocated outside competitive markets for political goals can be on a scale that is sufficient to profoundly distort the economy.

Second, the global incidence of the resource curse fluctuates over time: it intensified through the 1970s and 1980s before easing in the late-1990s and 2000s. This trend reflects in part major shifts in global development policy whereby many developing countries that gained independence in the 1960s initially favoured state intervention to force industrialization. Their governments subsequently relaxed this policy through the 1990s as a condition for receiving loans from the international financial institutions (IFIs) with which to stabilize their economies.

Third, the risk posed by rent streams varies with their size relative to GDP, volatility, and distribution: the risk is higher the larger and more volatile the revenue stream and the greater its concentration on a few economic agents. For example, resource curse symptoms appear stronger in small economies than large ones, and especially in mineral-driven economies, most notably oil exporters (Table 1.1). During 1973–85 the mineral economies generated the highest resource rent relative to GDP but the slowest GDP growth, with the oil exporters having the highest rent and weakest growth of all.

Fourth, the rent curse has not only economic causes (the prime ones being Dutch disease effects and volatile revenue) but also institutional and political ones (Acemoglu et al. 2001). Subsequently, attention turned to policy failure (Glaeser et al. 2004), notably the consequences of the trade policy closure of the 1960s and 1970s (Lal and Myint 1996). Importantly, these causal factors are not mutually exclusive, but interact systematically, as we demonstrate through two rent-driven models. We contend that there is a rent curse, but that it is not deterministic and results from political contests over rent, which can cause policy failure that leads to a protracted growth collapse.

In order to achieve a more nuanced explanation of the rent curse than the statistical analyses provide, we examine the political economy of rent deployment. We also adopt a case study approach with an historical perspective that is nevertheless rooted in theory. In doing so, we trade some loss of rigour for greater analytical flexibility, which is necessary because measurement of cropland rent and regulatory rent relies on either case study estimates or proxy indices such as, respectively, export share and degree of trade policy closure.[2] More specifically, we draw upon rent cycling theory (Auty 2010) to trace how rent impacts: the economic incentives of the elite; the choice of development strategy; and the resulting development trajectory with particular emphasis on structural change. The book draws upon two stylized facts models of rent-driven growth that between them explain the growth trajectories of most developing countries since the 1960s. The models are the low-rent competitive diversification model and the high-rent staple trap model. They start from the basic assumption that low rent incentivizes the elite to improve its welfare by efficiently growing the economy, while high rent deflects elite effort into extracting and deploying rent for immediate enrichment at the expense of long-term economic growth.

Efficient growth requires the pursuit of comparative advantage, which in low-rent economies lies in the expansion of labour-intensive exports. This triggers a singular pattern of structural change that is self-sustaining and drives rapid GDP growth along with an incremental shift towards a self-reliant form of social capital and towards political pluralism. In contrast, high-rent economies absorb windfall rent too quickly in response to political pressures,

---

[2] The World Bank is developing time series for crop rent from 1995 (Lange et al. 2018).

which triggers Dutch disease effects that impede competitive diversification and encourage subsidized employment creation. This locks the economy into a staple trap of increasing reliance on rent to subsidize protected urban activity. The burgeoning rent demands of the subsidized activity eventually exceed the capacity of the rent to meet them, triggering a growth collapse that is protracted because rent recipients resist reform. A dependent form of social capital also emerges while the polity may veer towards an autocracy that is brittle.

We illustrate the two trajectories with case studies of high-rent Trinidad and Tobago and low-rent Mauritius, which provide an instructive comparison because prior to independence in the 1960s, the two shared much in common, apart from their mineral endowments. They were both British colonies with parliamentary governments elected by an ethnically diverse population totalling nearly one million in each case, which relied heavily for employment on sugar plantations that were running short of land. As small island economies, their diversification options were somewhat constrained (Demas 1965), but the prime difference was that Trinidad and Tobago had access to hydrocarbon reserves, which Mauritius lacked. In fact, Mauritius's economic prospects were viewed as Malthusian: its per capita income lagged that of Trinidad and Tobago and contracted through the late-1950s, stoking social tensions (Findlay and Weitz 1993). Yet Mauritius subsequently made a successful transition from rent-driven growth to productivity-driven growth that still eludes Trinidad and Tobago. Mauritius's development trajectory therefore provides a low-rent counterfactual to help explain why Trinidad and Tobago, like many high-rent economies, struggled to diversify away from rent dependence (Warner 2015).

Trinidad and Tobago presents an instructive case study of the rent curse. Commencing in the 1970s, its economy has periodically generated large hydrocarbon rents, driven first by the 1974–78 and 1979–81 oil booms and subsequently by large inflows of foreign direct investment (FDI) in liquefied natural gas (LNG) that exploit hydrocarbon reserves that are high for a country of its size. However, the origin of its reliance on rent can be traced back much earlier, to the introduction of sugar plantations in the late-eighteenth century. The rent from sugar cane can be classified as geopolitical rent because it arose from changes in trade concessions by the colonial government in London. The reliance of Trinidad and Tobago on rent was strengthened in the mid-twentieth century, first by much-improved trade preferences for sugar exports and then by the positive hydrocarbon price shocks of 1974–78 and 1979–81.

Although small country size somewhat constrains development options compared with large economies, we show that the development trajectory of small countries (as opposed to micro states) is not significantly different from that of larger economies. The small size of the case study economies therefore does not limit their capacity either to illuminate the two basic post-1960 development trajectories or to explain broader development themes in the major global regions. We demonstrate that Mauritius's development trajectory is basically similar to those of the four Asian Dragon economies, Hong Kong, Singapore, South Korea, and Taiwan. China's development path has also paralleled Mauritius's low rent trajectory in key respects.[3]

Manufacturing played a key role in the rapid development of the low-rent East Asian economies and Mauritius, but it proved a double-edged sword in most high-rent economies. We argue that the prioritization of manufacturing by high-rent developing economies through the early post-war decades represents a major policy error. This is because whether governments pursued industrialization by import substitution or by resource-based industry, the manufacturing sector invariably degenerated into a vehicle for rent-seeking on a scale that distorted the economy and led to protracted growth collapses.

This was not the case in the low-rent East Asian economies and Mauritius, and the competitive diversification model explains why. The singular pattern of low rent structural change elicited by their initial comparative advantage in labour-intensive manufactured exports was what drove their rapid economic development. It was not the result of an interventionist industrial policy as argued by Amsden (1992) and Wade (1990). Rather, Stern et al. (2005) and Noland and Pack (2003) convincingly critique the efficacy of aspects of the East Asian industrial policies, whose varied levels of intervention also suggest that industrial policy played a secondary role to that of self-sustaining structural change. We identify numerous instances of the adverse impacts of interventionist industrial policies on rent cycling throughout this book.

Most high-rent economies in Latin America, the Gulf states, and sub-Saharan Africa experienced a staple trap development trajectory, like Trinidad and Tobago. The widespread espousal of activist industrial policies steadily distorted these economies through the 1960s and 1970s, after which intensified commodity price volatility triggered a series of growth collapses. The growth collapses first hit the least credit-worthy states (mainly sub-Saharan African oil importers) through the mid-1970s. They then impacted other economies in sub-Saharan Africa and Latin America in the early-1980s that had earlier been judged sufficiently credit-worthy to borrow recycled petrodollars for economic adjustment. Finally, growth collapses hit the oil exporters in the mid-1980s as energy prices collapsed when cumulative energy conservation curbed global oil demand.

---

[3] Like Mauritius, China eliminated surplus labour via diversification into labour-intensive exports, and relied on dual track reform to manage the political opposition to the reform (from state enterprises in China's case) that were the likely losers from reform (Lau et al. 2000).

Although the assistance of the IFIs with stabilization eventually revived economic growth, the high-rent economies remain vulnerable to revenue volatility and rent-seeking activity. Policy lapses during the commodity super-cycle of 2004–14 suggest that in some cases lessons were only partially learned and that rent-dependent development persists (Cherif and Hasanov 2016). Hausmann et al. (2007) convincingly argue that rent-dependent economies need to produce goods and services that have ever weaker direct links to rents and exhibit ever more sophistication. Fortunately, emerging trends in global demand for goods and services are expanding scope for lagging economies to supply these products (Mckinsey 2012; Ghani et al. 2012; Loungani et al. 2017), as India (and Mauritius) demonstrate. Loungani et al. (2017) suggest that lagging developing countries might leapfrog industrialization.

The development literature warns that rent-driven growth can raise incomes without establishing the social, human, and capital resources to maintain them in the absence of rent (Cherif and Hasanov 2016). This is especially true for high-income energy-rich economies, notably those of the Gulf states. One variant of the rent curse is associated with economies that become ever more dependent on the rent. In fact, some researchers identify an even more acute condition (Gaddy and Ickes 2010). They argue that countries like Saudi Arabia and Russia are not just dependent on oil rent but 'addicted' to oil, a much more difficult pathology to treat. Their economies require constantly rising energy prices and/or expanding energy output just to maintain fiscal balance and meet existing social entitlements like energy subsidies, upon which government survival comes to depend.

We argue that diversification away from rent dependence should be the priority, especially by hydrocarbon exporters because changes in technology are weakening prospective LNG exports, while deepening concerns about global pollution pose the risk that both oil and natural gas reserves may become stranded. For example, Trinidad and Tobago faces the prospect of a steady decline in hydrocarbon output that could terminate production within two decades, unless significant new commercial discoveries are made in deeper waters or from cross-border fields. Yet gas from fracking diminishes the incentive to search for gas from traditional fields. This unexpected acceleration in the pace of maturation of the hydrocarbon sector calls for speedy economic reforms so as to establish the productivity-driven economy that is needed to sustain incomes, let alone to enhance them.

Rodrik (2015) argues that far from diversifying, many developing countries are experiencing premature deindustrialization as their manufacturing sector contracts relative to services. We argue, however, that this trend is more accurately regarded as an adjustment to the earlier overexpansion of manufacturing that resulted from the prioritization of industrialization. The relative decline in manufacturing is associated with IFI reforms aimed at removing the cumulated economic distortions of the 1960s, 1970s, and 1980s and realigning economies with their underlying comparative advantage.

Two other factors are at work in making Rodrik's prognosis less ominous. First, the long-running process of business specialization continues, as productive businesses like farms and manufacturing firms contract out tasks previously performed in-house, often services, to specialist firms (Haig 1926). This implies that part of the contraction of manufacturing is more a book-keeping adjustment than a significant loss of manufacturing output (McKinsey 2012): support services are transferred from the manufacturing column into the services column. Second, and more recently, the diffusion of Information and Communication Technology (ICT) has expanded scope for productive service exports that exhibit significant potential to boost labour productivity and economic growth as manufacturing has done in the past (Loungani et al. 2017).

These trends strengthen the case for pursuing sector neutral development policies that focus on creating an enabling environment for investment that is rooted in prudent macroeconomic policy and supportive institutions. Sector neutral policies recognize the risk of policy capture by rent-seeking interests, which this book argues has severely damaged economic growth within the developing countries and remains a threat.

1.2 Structure of the Study

1.2.1 *Literature Context*

The book is structured into four sections. Section 1 explains the objectives of the research and sets them in the context of the literature on economic development and, in particular, the rent curse. More specifically, Chapter 2 draws upon the literature on natural resources and economic development to explain the circumstances under which high rent can either drive sustained economic growth or become a curse. It notes that an initial surge in statistical research through the 1990s focused mainly on economic factors as the explanation for the resource curse, such as Dutch disease effects (Sachs and Warner 1995), commodity price volatility (Cashin and McDermott 2002), and over-rapid domestic rent absorption (Gelb and Associates 1988). Subsequently more prominence was given to political factors, notably the quality of institutions (Acemoglu and Robinson 2008) and policies (Glaeser et al. 2004). Most recently, political contests for rent have attracted attention (Mehlum et al. 2006; Holcombe 2013). In fact, these explanations are not mutually exclusive and the two rent-driven models from rent cycling theory explain how they systematically interact in response to the initial conditions of either rent abundance or rent paucity (Auty 2010).

Chapter 2 then examines the two rent-driven models in more detail. We briefly outline them here. The low-rent competitive diversification model is associated with sustained rapid economic growth, whereas the high-rent staple trap model leads to a growth collapse, recovery from which is protracted. More specifically, the low-rent model posits that low rent incentivizes the elite to enrich itself by growing the economy, which requires the pursuit of the low-rent economy's comparative advantage in cheap labour to export labour-intensive goods and services. The low-rent model explains how rapid progress in absorbing surplus rural labour speeds both the demographic transition and the onset of Lewis's (1954) labour market turning point, which triggers a singular pattern of self-sustaining structural change that drives rapid economic growth and political maturation.

The low-rent development trajectory produces self-reinforcing virtuous economic and sociopolitical circuits. First, an early start on competitive industrialization accelerates urbanization, which advances the demographic cycle so that a lower ratio of dependants per worker reduces the share of consumption in GDP and increases that of saving and investment, which spurs per capita GDP growth. Second, the rapid expansion of labour-intensive exports speedily absorbs surplus labour so that the labour market rapidly reaches its turning point, causing real wages to rise, which drives rapid structural change into more skill-intensive and capital-intensive manufacturing in order to boost productivity and maintain competitiveness. Third, the singular pattern of structural change in low-rent economies also promotes the formation of a self-reliant social capital and the proliferation of social groups ready and able to challenge policy capture by any one group. Together these social forces drive an incremental shift towards both higher mean incomes and political pluralism.

The low-rent model forms a useful counterfactual with which to explain the underperformance of the high-rent model. High rent incentivizes the elite to compete to extract rent for immediate self-enrichment or political gain, which results in overrapid domestic absorption of the rent that engenders Dutch disease effects. The resulting strengthening of the real exchange rate causes the high-rent development trajectory to omit labour-intensive industrialization and forgo the associated benefits that flow from eliminating surplus labour and embarking on rapid structural change. Consequently, both competitive diversification and the incremental shift towards political pluralism are retarded. Rather, in the absence of policy reform, which rent-seeking interests often oppose, governments in high-rent economies deploy rent to alleviate unemployment by subsidizing urban activity in protected manufacturing and government bureaucracy. This is the antithesis of the competitive economic diversification that is required. The subsidized urban sector's burgeoning rent requirements eventually outstrip the capacity of the economy to supply them. This triggers a growth collapse that is protracted because rent-seekers resist reform. The essence of the staple trap trajectory is therefore the diversification of the economy into a rent-dependent urban enclave whose demands for subsidies from the rent outstrip the supply.

1.2.2 Rent-Driven Development in Trinidad and Tobago and Mauritius

Section 2 provides detailed case study evidence, which first evaluates the legacy of the plantation economy with reference to Trinidad and Tobago in Chapter 3. The legacy includes establishing an initial reliance on rent. In contrast, the dependency theorist Best (1968) identifies the prime legacy of the plantation system as a strong external dependence in his model of the plantation economy. In fact, the plantation has proved more flexible than either the dependency theorists or mainstream economists like Baldwin (1956) have assumed. It has exhibited a capacity to promote domestic development, encourage small farm expansion, and sustain a basic standard of living for the workforce (Graham and Floering 1984). During the settlement of the sparsely populated islands of Trinidad and Tobago from the late-eighteenth century, the plantation dominated the economy. It established an ethnically mixed society due to the importation of indentured labour from South Asia after the abolition of slavery. The plantation was also associated with a marked skew in income distribution, rooted in differences in access to land and the wage-depressing effects of the Asian labour surplus (Lewis 1978).

We argue that the emphasis placed by dependency theorists on the plantation's external dependence obscures the more fundamental factor of rent dependence, which initially arose out of British colonial trade preferences for sugar. Paradoxically, as independence approached, the rent dependence intensified as an unintended consequence of British reforms to raise living standards. The reforms responded to the unacceptable levels of poverty caused by depressed sugar prices in the 1930s, which led to a Royal Commission of Inquiry that proposed a new trade deal. The resulting Commonwealth Sugar Agreement (CSA) guaranteed higher sugar prices so as to attract investment by efficient international companies in large modern factories. The investment aimed to boost productivity and thereby furnish living standards, equivalent to those of farm workers in the UK but for a smaller workforce.

Consistent with rent cycling theory, the higher rent elicited contests among plantation owners, unionized workers, cane farmers, and the government to capture the extra revenue. Consequently, although the CSA succeeded in improving living standards through the 1950s, the unions subsequently blocked labour-saving productivity advances in order to maintain employment, which eroded the return on capital and motivated the international companies to withdraw. The government of Trinidad and Tobago then

11

deployed hydrocarbon rent to subsidize the uneconomic plantations as an important source of rural employment. However, radical restructuring was forced on the industry in the mid-2000s when the World Trade Organization (WTO) removed trade preferences like the CSA. But significantly, whereas the elimination of sugar rent caused the plantation to collapse in Trinidad and Tobago, it thrived in Mauritius.

Chapter 4 analyses the impact of hydrocarbon rent on the economy of Trinidad and Tobago. After independence in 1962, Trinidad and Tobago initially pursued cautious economic policies for the deployment of its modest oil rent. The long-serving first independent government modified this stance in response to an extra-parliamentary challenge in 1970 by espousing an ambitious state-led industrialization strategy to accelerate economic growth and employment creation (Mottley 2008). The government established a consensus in favour of gas-based industrialization and drew upon the 1974–78 and 1979–81 oil rent windfalls to accelerate the strategy.

Gas-based industry was expected to be the catalyst for private sector investment in downstream materials fabrication, but, as elsewhere, resource-based industrialization produced few manufacturing jobs, whether direct or indirect (Auty 1990). Rather, in line with the staple trap model, it was associated with persistent unemployment that was masked by deploying rent to subsidize an expansion of the bureaucracy and extensive make-work schemes. The rent absorption also raised consumption by expanding subsidies to energy and food as well as housing and employment. The resulting increased rate of domestic rent absorption outstripped the absorptive capacity of the economy and fed Dutch disease effects that, as the staple trap model predicts, triggered a growth collapse when oil prices faltered, in this case through 1981–93. The growth collapse cut per capita income by one-third and boosted open unemployment to one-fifth of the workforce.

The economic recovery was lagged due to the opposition of rent-seeking interests to reform. The reforms were eventually implemented with IFI assistance and they reduced the role of the state in productive activity. However, when economic growth finally revived, it was due to the expansion of LNG rather than to investment in nonenergy activity, which has remained muted for more than three decades. Moreover, completion of the LNG complex coincided with the 2004–08 energy boom, which sharply boosted the rent stream. Despite initial caution, the LNG rent was absorbed too rapidly into the domestic economy, thereby further intensifying rent dependence at the expense of competitive diversification.

Section 2 concludes in Chapter 5 by posing the question: How might Trinidad and Tobago have developed in the absence of large hydrocarbon rents? It analyses Mauritius as a low-rent counterfactual for high-rent Trinidad and Tobago. Prior to independence in the 1960s the two colonies had much in common, apart from their mineral endowments. The development trajectory of Mauritius follows the low-rent competitive diversification model. In 1961 a Royal Commission on the economy of Mauritius recommended rapid implementation of birth control and industrialization by import substitution. However, the country's first independent government promoted birth control but, impressed by progress in Taiwan, quickly demoted import substitution policies in favour of encouraging private investment in an export zone.

Despite its potential disadvantages—a remote, small monocrop economy running short of land, and with an ethnically diverse population—Mauritius achieved sustained economic development and diversification. A key element in its success, which is often neglected, is the incentive that low rent conferred on the elite to build a political coalition to promote economic growth. But we identify a second critical element in Mauritian success, namely the elite's politically sensitive approach to economic reform. More specifically, Mauritius's elite built a political coalition to promote economic growth through a dual track strategy of reform (Lau et al. 2000). This strategy pursued the emerging comparative advantage and developed a dynamic labour-intensive market economy in an export processing zone (Track 1). It postponed reform of the residual rent-dependent sector (Track 2) until Track 1 had grown to dominate the economy, when it could absorb and neutralize rent-seeking groups in Track 2. The dual track strategy initially nurtured competitive industrialization via exports of textiles and then electronics, followed by tourism and financial services. Although Mauritius's mean per capita income remains below that of Trinidad and Tobago, the gap has narrowed since independence (World Bank 2017a). Moreover, the Mauritian economy relies on productivity-driven growth rather than rent, and has significantly improved social welfare. Most importantly, it has done so in a sustainable manner.

1.2.3 *Differential Rent-Driven Development in Global Developing Regions*

Section 3 applies the two rent-driven models to explain the development trajectories of five global developing country regions, namely sub-Saharan Africa, Latin America, East Asia, South Asia, and the Gulf, and analyses a systematic theme of importance to each region. For example, Chapter 6 focuses on sub-Saharan Africa and the consequences of agricultural neglect. Sub-Saharan Africa appeared initially to face favourable development prospects arising from the predominance of land-rich peasant farmer economies with diffuse linkages beneficial to economic growth and competitive structural change (Baldwin 1956).

However, ethnic diversity sparked political contests for rent among the elite that distorted most economies and deflected them from their comparative advantage. Crop marketing boards were abused to extract not only crop rents from peasant farmers but also returns to capital and labour. This was ostensibly done to sustain a policy of industrialization by import substitution that was ill-suited to the small domestic markets of most newly independent countries and quickly degenerated into a rent-cycling mechanism. Even the resource-poor economies of the Sahel espoused the policy, drawing upon regulatory rent that was augmented by geopolitical rent following the drought of the early-1970s. Whatever the rent source, the resulting misallocation of capital and labour led to protracted growth collapses that required IFI assistance, buttressed by geopolitical rent, which was not always directed at economic recovery.

More homogenous societies might be expected to pursue a third development model of staple diversification through diffuse linkages (Baldwin 1956; North 1955; Mellor 1976), which starts from the premise that small farms respond to modest increments of capital and labour by steadily intensifying yields. This expands incomes. It also increases taxes, which farmers accept because they benefit directly from public services such as improved transportation, education, and health care. Rising farmers' incomes also expand the domestic market for locally produced manufactures of household goods and farm equipment as well as services, thereby diversifying the economy away from staple dependence. Yet although the staple diversification model appeared well adapted to propel peasant farm economies, the factional politics in sub-Saharan Africa precluded its espousal. Instead, political contests and associated rent-seeking led the strategy of industrialization by import substitution to degenerate into a mechanism for rent cycling with long-lasting detrimental effects for agriculture, upon which a majority of the population continued to rely.

Chapter 7 focuses on the role of industrialization and draws upon the two rent-driven models to explain how the East Asian economies overcame Latin America's head start on development. Most Latin American countries adopted industrialization by import substitution in response to the disruption of global trade through 1913–45 (Lewis 1978). Crucially, their governments persisted with the strategy when global trade re-expanded from the 1950s, despite the failure of the protected infant industry to mature and become internationally competitive. The region's economic growth was punctuated by shortages of foreign exchange and public revenue because protected manufacturing failed to generate sufficient exports to purchase imported inputs, while recurring fiscal deficits fed debt accumulation, inflation, and protracted growth collapses commencing in 1979–82.

In contrast, elites in East Asia faced an existential threat from the deterioration of the US position in Vietnam and diminishing geopolitical rent. They built on a comparative advantage in cheap labour to pursue competitive industrialization. They deployed regulatory rent through low-interest loans to grow the economy efficiently under hard budget constraints by making future access to loans conditional on rapid maturation. The East Asian economies experienced rapid growth in per capita GDP and swiftly narrowed the productivity gap on the advanced economies, whereas Latin American economies fell back, leading to fears of premature deindustrialization (Rodrik 2015). However, as noted earlier, Latin American structural change may be conceptualized more accurately as the correction of earlier policies of subsidized industrialization.

Chapters 6 and 7 both query the strong bias in development policy towards industrialization since the 1950s and its corollary of neglect of the rural economy and export services. Chapter 8 examines scope for diversification into increasingly sophisticated export services with reference to the contrasting labour surplus economies of low-income South Asia and the high-income Gulf. Recent trends in demand for services and manufactured goods are increasing scope for mid-income developing countries to supply niche markets by participating in global value-added chains (Economist 2013). This creates new opportunities for developing countries to provide both the services that modern customer-tailored products increasingly require (which do not incur freight charges) and high-value industrial components capable of bearing high freight charges (McKinsey 2012).

Chapter 8 draws upon India, where the service sector outcompetes manufacturing in driving economic development. It contrasts the dynamism of the Indian service sector with the disappointing performance of Indian manufacturing, which was heavily distorted under the Licence Raj by the extraction and deployment of large regulatory rents to promote heavy industry. The corollary was prolonged neglect of labour-intensive agriculture and manufacturing, in which India held a comparative advantage at independence. The rapid rise of export services since 1990 reflects the exploitation by expatriate Indian private firms in North America of links with ICT clusters in India. We draw upon Indian experience to argue that the hydrocarbon-dependent Gulf governments can make the required transfer of nationals from rent-subsidized public sector jobs into more productive and sustainable private sector employment by exporting increasingly sophisticated services. As Loungani et al. (2017) argue, industrialization may not be essential for economic development.

Finally, Section 4 summarizes the research findings. It restates the case for conceptualizing the resource curse as part of a broader and richer rent curse; analyses the strengths and weakness of the two basic rent-driven models; reviews the consequences of prioritizing industrialization for economic development; sets out the principal requirements for the effective pursuit of a sector neutral development policy; and considers aspects of future research.

15

2

Natural Resources, Country Size, and Development

A Review of the Literature

2.1 Introduction

More than two decades of statistical research have struggled to establish the causes of the resource curse, and even the existence of the curse remains disputed (Lederman and Maloney 2007; Brunnschweiler 2008; Alexeev and Conrad 2009; Torres et al. 2013). Statistical analyses usually search for a dominant causal factor and deterministic laws. For example, Frankel (2012: 9) evaluates six monocausal explanations for the resource curse, namely long-term declining commodity prices, commodity price volatility, permanent crowding out of manufacturing, oligarchic institutions, institutional failure, and Dutch disease effects. In fact, all six factors, and more besides, appear to shape the outcome and there is also evidence of systematic interaction between some factors.

We argue that the statistical studies are usefully complemented by a nuanced, historically grounded, interdisciplinary approach that focuses upon case studies rooted in rent cycling theory. We distil two stylized facts rent-driven models from the literature to explain the global development trajectories summarized in Table 1.1. To reiterate from Chapter 1, our approach contributes four insights to the resource curse debate. First, the symptoms of the resource curse can be generated by other forms of rent in addition to natural resources, notably geopolitical rent, regulatory rent, and to a lesser degree labour rent. This implies that the resource curse is part of a broader rent curse. Second, the global intensity of the rent curse varies over time in response to changing fashions in development policy, and industrial policy in particular. Third, vulnerability to the rent curse varies with the source of the rent, which governs its size relative to gross domestic product (GDP), its volatility, and its distribution across economic agents. Fourth, explanations for the rent curse have not only economic causes, such as Dutch disease effects and rent volatility, but also institutional and policy causes. We argue that there is a rent curse, but that it is not deterministic and results from political contests over rent, which can cause policy failure that cumulatively distorts the economy and leads to a protracted growth collapse.

We also find that country size affects rent curse outcomes, although this aspect is contested (Alouini and Hubert 2012). Table 1.1 shows that small economies have performed less well than large ones, especially the small high-rent economies. The limited population and land area of small countries have constrained prospects for capturing the economies of scale, both the internal economies of scale and agglomeration economies (Demas 1965; Jorgensen 2013). Small size also reduces the economies of scope by shrinking diversification options and thereby heightening the risk that the economy is overreliant on one or two activities (Alesina et al. 2005). Finally, Jahan and Wang (2013) noted that small *island* states are more vulnerable to storm-related natural disasters. Nevertheless, we show that apart from the micro-states, small developing countries share fundamental developmental features with larger economies, including most critically the pattern of structural change. Moreover, the disadvantage of small size is eroding through the proliferation of global value added chains together with the rise of service exports (Ghani et al. 2012).

This chapter is structured as follows. Section 2.2 analyses the evolving explanations for resource curse symptoms, which initially prioritized economic factors and subsequently institutions and then policy. It shows how an appreciation of historical trends and the multiple sources of rent can explain some contradictions among the statistical studies. Section 2.3 explains in depth the two stylized facts political economy models of rent-driven development: the low-rent competitive diversification model and the high-rent staple trap model. Section 2.4 addresses country size, with particular reference to its implications for industrialization. Manufacturing was widely assumed to be essential for rapid economic development (Syrquin and Chenery 1989). This led the governments of small countries, which comprised the majority of developing countries, to espouse industrialization by import substitution, despite the fact that it was especially inappropriate for small economies due to their limited domestic demand. In contrast, industrialization through the export of labour-intensive manufactures was practical for small economies, but few of their governments pursued it. Section 2.5 summarizes.

2.2 Resource Endowment, Rent, and Economic Development

Sachs and Warner (1995) triggered a surge of statistical analyses of the resource curse from the mid-1990s, which after a promising start lapsed into contradictory claims as to whether the resource curse exists or not.

2.2.1 *Inconclusive Results from Statistical Studies of the Resource Curse*

The statistical studies initially focused on economic explanations as the driver of the resource curse, notably the 'Dutch disease' effects and macroeconomic instability (Stevens 2003). In this explanation, booming commodity revenue strengthens the real exchange rate, which causes the nonbooming tradeable sectors (agriculture and manufacturing) to contract, so that when commodity prices eventually fall the economy may be less prosperous than it was before the boom occurred. This arises because the adjustment to shifts in the exchange rate is asymmetric: tradeable activity is rapidly destroyed in booms but revives much more slowly when a boom subsides (Gelb and Associates 1988). Sachs and Warner conclude from data for 1970–89 that most governments of natural resource-rich countries closed their trade policy as their dependence on primary product exports increased in order to counter the employment-diminishing effects of Dutch disease.

Lal and Myint (1996) explain the consequences of such protective trade policies: the policies repress markets, distort the economy, and cause growth collapses. The growth collapses tend to be triggered by commodity price volatility, which heightened through 1973–85 due to three major oil price shocks, two positive and one negative, which severely tested macroeconomic policy (Cashin et al. 2000; Cashin and McDermott 2002; van der Ploeg and Poelhekke 2009). The governments of resource-rich economies invariably absorbed rent windfalls into their economies too rapidly during booms, making spending commitments that were politically difficult to cut back through downswings. This led to the accumulation of debt to levels that proved difficult to service (Gelb and Associates 1988).

The economic explanations are deterministic, yet resource-rich economies as diverse as Botswana, Malaysia, and Indonesia, as well as earlier mature resource-driven economies like Australia, Canada, and the US, managed to avoid prolonged growth collapses and to sustain rapid per capita GDP growth. This led researchers to query the choice of index of resource abundance (export dependence or resource stock) and also to favour panel data over cross-sectional data (Torres et al. 2013). The increased focus on methodology, however, risks bogging down the debate in discussions over definitions and techniques while neglecting the bigger picture identified from case studies.

The case studies suggest that economists tend to downplay the political dimension (Deacon 2011), although there are exceptions such as Mehlum et al. (2006) who link the resource curse to inadequate constraints on rent-seeking.

Case studies show that high rent creates contests for its capture, which can cause political objectives to override economic ones, so that the resulting rent deployment weakens the economy instead of strengthening it (Gelb and Associates 1988). In fact, Khan (2000) notes that the *political* rationale for choosing policies that are economically suboptimal is often compelling: governments in many newly independent countries find it necessary to deploy rents to secure political cohesion without which economic activity struggles. Similarly, North et al. (2009) model most developing countries as Limited Access Order Societies within which rent is deployed primarily to limit potential violence by co-opting into the elite those deemed capable of wielding violence. Such societies contrast with the Open Access Order Societies of the high-income OECD (Organization for Economic Co-operation and Development) countries.

These considerations nurtured political explanations for the resource curse, focusing initially on the role of institutions. Acemoglu et al. (2001, 2002) argue that the quality of institutions is more important than natural resources per se in determining whether resources are a blessing or a curse. In particular, they identify as detrimental to economic growth those extractive colonial institutions associated with tropical lands that were too unhealthy for significant European settlement. The flawed institutions, according to Engerman and Sokoloff (2012), include slavery, autocratic governance, and state control. The tropical plantation is another institution that Baldwin (1956) contrasts unfavourably with the yeoman farm, which prevailed over the plantation in the resource-rich temperate regions of the Americas and Oceania. Baldwin (1956) argues that yeoman farming exhibits a more flexible production function than the plantation and spawns more inclusive institutions, both of which are strongly beneficial for economic development.

Yet Glaeser et al. (2004) relegate institutions to secondary status: they find that institutions improve as a consequence of rising incomes but do not cause that rise, which is explained by human capital accumulation and policy choice. It seems likely that, consistent with North et al. (2009), institutions in *low-income* economies bend to accommodate political incentives rather than mould those incentives. For example, Schlumberger (2008) identifies a patrimonial form of capitalism in oil-exporting countries (with wider geographical applicability), the primary feature of which is the deployment of informal institutions to repress formal ones rather than strengthen them. Many developing countries may score favourably in respect to the quality of governance or business environment, but informal rules bend the formal rules to the advantage of the elite. More specifically, patrimonial capitalism: (i) prefers nondemocratic governments so as to sustain a 'shadow' political system that overrides the formal rules; (ii) concentrates rent-seeking opportunities on a favoured subset; (iii) guarantees property rights through patronage rather than law (demanding social investment by participants); (iv) emasculates competition policies and blocks reforms that constrain elite rent extraction; and (v) applies formal rules to discipline elements disloyal to the regime, a strategy that weakens respect for the rule of law.

Acemoglu and Robinson (2008) back-track on their earlier findings and recognize the ability of the elite in developing countries to manipulate institutions. The World Bank (2009a) provides further evidence of such manipulation. It reports that almost two-thirds of a sample of Middle East and North African civil servants view the private sector as rent-seeking and corrupt, dominated by a handful of well-connected firms that sustain quasi-monopolies by barring new entrants, bribing civil servants, lobbying for privilege, and underreporting earnings. For their part, a majority of (excluded) businesses view regulation of the business environment as arbitrary and biased in favour of politicians and a relatively small number of privileged businesses. In summary: institutions in Limited Access Order Societies are malleable. The key question is therefore under what circumstances will elites be motivated to prioritize economic growth over immediate enrichment through rent-seeking activity?

Robinson et al. (2006) usefully theorize on how rent incentivizes elites to capture it for both political gain and self-enrichment, which results in rent deployment that damages long-term growth. Our two rent-driven models start from this proposition. Nevertheless, some researchers like Di John (2011) remain sceptical of assigning rent-seeking the dominant role in causing the policy error that triggers resource curse effects. He cites the anomalous performance of some resource-rich economies to argue that policy choice counts. Although Di John is correct to stress the key role of policy in rendering resources a blessing or not, he errs in dismissing the impact of rent-seeking on policy *formation*. By so doing, he dismisses a more subtle explanation for the resource curse and instead locks the debate into a sterile search for silver-bullet explanations, which the constraints imposed by statistical proofs tend to encourage.

Summarizing, two decades of statistical research have failed to provide a definitive explanation for the resource curse, and its very existence is contested (Lederman and Maloney 2007; Brunnschweiler 2008; Cavalcanti et al. 2011). This partly reflects an overly-narrow perspective in statistical studies hitherto, which neglects the fluctuating global intensity of the resource curse over time and the major shift in economic policy that lies behind it. Such studies neglect additional sources of windfall revenue that replicate symptoms of the resource curse. They also miss the contrasting development outcomes associated with concentrated and diffuse natural resource rent streams. We examine the implications of these neglected issues in more depth.

2.2.2 Temporal Variation in the Incidence of the Resource Curse

Global shifts in economic policy underlie temporal changes in the incidence of the resource curse. Statist policies gained favour through the immediate post-war decades. They extended state intervention and with it the capacity of governments to distort the economy. The initial rise in statist policies followed the termination of Lewis's (1978) first golden age of economic growth (1870–1913), during which many primary product exporters had prospered as global trade expanded. Two World Wars and the Great Depression then disrupted global trade and inflicted volatile prices and limited market access on commodity-exporting countries. Many Latin American countries underwent forced industrialization by import substitution through the 1930s, a policy they voluntarily retained when global trade links reopened after World War II.

The interventionist policy was backed by influential development economists like Prebisch (1950) and Singer (1950) who argued that through the long term, the terms of trade were moving against developing country commodity exporters, requiring them to export greater volumes of commodities to pay for a constant volume of industrial goods from the advanced economies. Since the industrial countries' first-mover advantage impeded industrial diffusion, developing country governments should override markets to promote domestic manufacturing. The favoured strategy was industrialization by import substitution, which requires the government to identify imported products for which domestic demand can support a local factory of minimum viable size and to licence local production behind import tariffs that are lowered when the infant industry matures (i.e. achieves international levels of competitiveness and ability to manipulate technology). The policy was widespread in Latin America and also appealed to newly independent countries in Africa and Asia as a means of complementing their political independence with economic independence.

In practice, however, infant industries had little incentive to mature because their infant status conferred rent on investors and workers who could pass on the costs of their inefficiency to the captive domestic market. Actual factory maturation rates typically measured several decades rather than the five to seven years regarded by Krueger and Tuncer (1982) as the maximum if the discounted costs of infant support were to be compensated by the discounted benefits from the policy (Auty 1994a). The Achilles' heel of industrial policies, whether import substitution, resource-based industrialization, or an industrial big push is therefore policy capture (Auty 1994b). Import substitution policies invariably degenerate into vehicles for rent extraction by unions, managers, and, if privately owned, shareholders of the protected factories at the expense of domestic consumers who pay higher prices than imports for shoddier goods. Consumers also face higher tax bills to offset the tax revenue foregone on potential imports of the now protected and locally produced product.

The statist policies of the initial post-war decades ultimately relied on rents, usually from the resource-based sector, whether farms or mines, to subsidize the unprofitable urban activities. The resulting transfers from competitive primary activity to inefficient urban activity cumulatively undermined the resilience of the economy through the 1960s and into the 1970s in most high-rent economies, rendering them vulnerable to a growth collapse when commodity price volatility increased through 1974–85. This two-stage process of weakening and then collapse explains why per capita GDP growth rates show little evidence of a rent curse in the 1960s (Table 1.1), although case studies confirm that during that decade statist policies were distorting high-rent economies (Krueger 1992). The growth collapses initially hit the least credit-worthy states through the mid-1970s, mainly sub-Saharan African oil import-ers; then spread in the early 1980s to other economies in sub-Saharan Africa and Latin America that had earlier been judged sufficiently credit-worthy to borrow recycled petro-dollars to facilitate economic adjustment; before hit-ting the oil exporters in the mid-1980s when energy conservation nurtured by sustained high energy prices curbed global oil demand and caused energy prices to collapse.

Many rent-rich governments initially resisted economic reform because it threatened the interests of politically powerful rent-seekers. They accumulated further debt until they were forced to turn to the international financial insti-tutions (IFIs) for assistance. The IFIs made trade liberalization and market reform a condition of their loans, while aid donors pushed for political plural-ism. The hardship of economic reform and structural adjustment hampered reform implementation, so some adjustment programmes failed, delaying recovery and feeding accusations that the IFI policies were unsound. In fact, both IFI policies and the associated surge in foreign aid were frequently manipu-lated by the domestic elite so as to substitute for lost rent (Djankov et al. 2006), further postponing reform and economic recovery into the mid-1990s. Many rent-rich developing country governments, but not all, did eventually stabilize their economies and restore GDP growth from the late-1990s (Table 1.1).

The period 1960–97 proved to be a lengthy policy learning curve for the developing economies. One implication is that research using data from 1970–90, like that of Sachs and Warner, covers the years of maximum global incidence of resource curse effects, whereas later studies extending into 1990–2010 track a marked diminution in the frequency of resource curse cases (Gerelmaa and Kotani 2016). Consequently, statistical analyses that neg-lect the shift away from statist policy, risk overestimating the incidence of the resource curse if they stress early decades like Sachs and Warner (1995) or else discounting its significance if they focus on later years (Brunnschweiler 2008).

2.2.3 Different Rent Sources Have Different Economic Linkages

A second factor influencing the incidence of the resource curse that has received inadequate recognition arises from additional sources of windfall revenue. The additional sources of revenue include regulatory rent and labour rent as well as geopolitical rent, all of which can match natural resource rent in scale relative to GDP. In addition, natural resource rent itself can be differentiated into at least two categories according to its distribution across economic agents, with potentially quite different development outcomes (Isham et al. 2005). Basically, the dispersed crop rent associated with peasant farming is potentially more beneficial to economic development than the concentrated rent associated with modern mining.

Table 2.1 identifies the principal categories of rent in developing countries and compares them in terms of their key characteristics, which are: size relative to GDP; dispersal across economic agents; revenue volatility; and developmental impact. Rent that is high, volatile, and concentrated (Isham et al. 2005) carries the greatest risk of maladroit deployment. It is strongly associated with mineral economies and especially the oil exporters. These

Table 2.1 Stylized rent stream properties and predicted political and economic impacts, by rent source[1]

	Concentrated natural resource rent	Diffuse natural resource rent	Regulatory rent	Labour rent (remittances)	Geopolitical rent (foreign aid)
Rent stream properties					
Scale (% GDP)	8–20+	5–15	5–20+	2–10	2–10+
Degree of rent concentration	High	Low	High	Low	High
Volatility (standard deviation)	High	Moderate	Moderate	Moderate	Low
Potential rent impacts: economic					
Investment efficiency	Falling	High	Low	High	Equivocal
GDP growth	Decelerating	Rapid	Decelerating	Moderate	Equivocal
Dutch disease effects	High	High	Moderate	Moderate	High
Market repression and corruption	High	Low	High	Low	Equivocal
Potential rent impacts: political					
Self-reliant social capital	Low	High	Low	Moderate	Equivocal
Proliferation of social groups	Constrained	High	Constrained	High	Equivocal

[1] Most economies generate more than one rent stream.

23

features result from mining's remarkable capital intensity and large-scale operation, which together ensure the rent is large relative to GDP; concentrated on large mining companies and governments; and also volatile. The revenue volatility reflects lumpy investment and long investment lead times that retard adjustment to glut and shortage alike, and so make them both more likely to occur. In contrast, rent that is dispersed across many economic agents on an individual small scale, such as rent from peasant cash crops, is likely to be saved and invested more carefully and flexibly, thereby reducing the boom and bust risk compared with rent that accrues to governments (Bevan et al. 1987; Baldwin 1956). Dispersed rent is also less vulnerable to theft under developmental governments.

The recognition of multiple sources of rent allows for the possibility that resource-poor countries like those of the Sahel can exhibit symptoms of the resource curse. For instance, during the first forty years of independence, Mauritania consistently generated rent of around two-fifths of GDP, at least half of which comprised foreign aid, with the remainder split between natural resource rent from fisheries licences sold to the European Union (EU) and an iron ore mine on the Moroccan border (Auty and Pontara 2008). Boone (1996) confirms that foreign aid can replicate resource curse symptoms. In the countries he studied using data for 1970–90, foreign aid did not increase the investment rate in recipient countries but went mostly into consumption and expanded government activity. Moreover, the increased consumption did not benefit the poor in any of the three types of political state that he analysed (autocratic, egalitarian, and oligarchic laissez-faire).

Rajan and Subramanian (2011) found that domestic expenditure of aid within the public sector triggers Dutch disease effects that stifle labour-intensive manufacturing. Foreign aid has also been abused by the elite both for personal enrichment and to maintain political power by biasing public expenditure towards targeted goods, which deliver political support, rather than towards universal public goods that benefit supporter and foe alike. Yet, Table 2.1 suggests that overall the development outcomes from flows of aid are equivocal due to variations in the rigour of donor aid supervision. Donors became more discriminating in allocating aid in the 1990s (Collier 2006).

Regulatory rent is created by governments manipulating relative prices to favour one group over another (Tollison 1982). It is associated with trade policy closure and increased state intervention within the economy, which expand scope to extract regulatory rent. In contrast, economic reform shrinks rent by expanding competitive markets. Regulatory rent tends to be concentrated and therefore easy to steal (Table 2.1). Moreover government price manipulation may extract not just the rent from economic activity but also part of the return to capital and labour. The revenue so extracted represses producer incentives and all too often is expended to subsidize activity that markets would not support, a situation that is unsustainable, as the staple trap trajectory shows.

Regulatory rent is challenging to measure, however. For example, Krueger (1992) reports that governments in sub-Saharan Africa in the 1970s and 1980s abused crop marketing boards to transfer rent from peasant farmers to urban elites without fully comprehending the consequences of their intervention. In the context of rent cycling theory, such policies transformed beneficially diffuse crop rent into concentrated rent that was deployed inefficiently and contributed to protracted growth collapses, as discussed in Chapter 6. Case study estimates of the scale of regulatory rent include 20% of GDP in Brazil in the 1960s (Bergsman 1970); 30–45% of GDP in India during the 1970s (Mohammad and Whalley 1984); and 40% of GDP in Iran in the 1980s (Esfahani and Taheripour 2002).

Finally, wage remittances are a diffuse form of rent that boosts domestic consumption, often of the poorest, and funds local investment where financial systems are underdeveloped (Giulano and Ruiz-Arranz 2009). Wage remittances also tend to be less volatile. These positive impacts on economic growth attenuate as incomes rise, however, because the adverse effects of remittances on work incentives tend to strengthen and also financial intermediation improves. Moreover, as with resource rent and geopolitical rent, large remittance flows can trigger Dutch disease effects and depress GDP growth (Rajan and Subramanian 2011).

Each rent source can comprise 10–20% of GDP or more (World Bank 2006; Svenssen 2000; Krueger 1992), potentially taking the *total* rent within the economy to one-fifth to one-third of GDP or more. It is therefore not surprising that rent has the capacity to distort the economy and profoundly affect development outcomes. Moreover, rent on this scale is sufficient to suggest that statistical studies of the resource curse that ignore rent streams other than natural resources are at best impaired by background noise and at worst flawed in their conclusions. There is, therefore, a case for formulating a theory of rent cycling so as to capture the complexities associated with temporal shifts in the timing of the resource curse, the presence of additional rent streams, and the contrasting features of different types of rent.

2.3 Stylized Facts Models of High-Rent and Low-Rent Development

2.3.1 *Rent Cycling Theory, Elite Incentives, and the Resource Curse*

Rent cycling theory (Auty 2010) is rooted in the interaction between the rent (its scale, volatility, and concentration) and elite incentives, structural change, social capital accumulation, and political maturation. Such interaction systematically shapes the development trajectory. The basic premise of rent cycling theory is that low rent incentivizes elites to create wealth efficiently, whereas high rent encourages the elites to compete to extract rent for immediate enrichment to the detriment of long-term economic growth. The theory assumes that, in the presence of low rent, the elite promote policies to accelerate economic growth as the fastest route to personal enrichment, since rapid economic growth increases all incomes but raises the incomes of elite owners of wealth the most. These features are captured by the low-rent competitive diversification model (Table 2.2), which matches the development trajectory of the Asian Dragons (Hong Kong, Singapore, South Korea, and Taiwan) as well as Mauritius and China.

Table 2.2 Principal features of two stylized facts rent-driven development models

	Low-rent competitive diversification model	High-rent staple trap model
Elite incentive	Form developmental state to grow the economy Hard budget constraints to curb rent-seeking Promote public goods and efficient markets Align economy with comparative advantage	Elite compete to siphon rent for personal gain Lobby for and exploit soft budget constraints Press for rapid domestic rent absorption Lobby to sustain patrimonial capitalism
Economic growth	Export labour-intensive goods and service exports Early onset of labour market turning point Rapid and competitive structural change Early onset of demographic dividend Rapid, sustained, and equitable per capita GDP growth	Overrapid rent absorption fuels Dutch disease Rent subsidizes employment and consumption Expand inefficient protected urban industry Erratic rent-dependent growth and rising inequality Rent demands exceed supply, so growth collapses
Social capital	Market encourages self-reliant social capital Social capital switches from bonding to linking Increasing reliance on institutional safeguards	Rent fosters dependent social capital Reliance on political links, not rule of law Politicized application of institutional safeguards
Political change	Structural change proliferates social groups New social groups help resist policy capture Taxation feeds demands for accountability Firms lobby for strong institutional safeguards Incremental consensual democratization	Slow structural change constrains social change Rent-dependence blunts accountability demands Elite factions capture and abuse government policy Oligarchs slant policy to sustain rent siphoning Authoritarian tendency of government, but brittle

The high-rent staple trap model helps to explain why so few resource-rich economies managed to sustain rapid economic and political maturation through the initial post-war decades (Table 2.2). A handful of high-rent economies did avoid the rent curse (including Botswana, Chile, Indonesia, and Malaysia), while some (the Gulf economies) raised incomes but without embedding sustained productivity growth into their economies. Most rent-rich economies, however, struggled to overcome growth collapses of varying degrees of severity (Auty 2001). Rent cycling theory posits that high rent elicits contests among the elite for its capture, which confer immediate personal wealth on the elite, in contrast to the deferred gains from promoting long-term economic growth, which risk capture by political rivals. The contests for rent, akin to the process of 'grabbing hand' in the face of inadequate institutional safeguards (Mehlum et al. 2006), exert pressure for rapid domestic absorption of the rent, which is politically difficult to resist and encourages channelling the rent through patronage networks at the expense of markets. The combination of Dutch disease effects and politically driven rent allocation distorts the economy and locks it into a staple trap trajectory. Each model is now explained in more detail.

2.3.2 The Low-Rent Competitive Diversification Model

The initial condition of resource paucity limits scope for the elite to expand primary product exports and extract rent. Instead, to create wealth the elite must grow the economy and taxes, from which it derives the most benefit due to an initial favourable distribution of assets. In effect, low rent motivates the elite to establish a developmental political state, which according to Lal (1995) has both the aim of raising social welfare and the autonomy with which to achieve it. Economic growth requires the efficient allocation of inputs under hard budget constraints so that the economy pursues its comparative advantage, which in a low-income, low-rent economy initially lies primarily in labour-intensive manufactured exports, the global demand for which expanded rapidly during the post-war decades. The resulting competitive industrialization requires governments to provide infrastructure and competitive domestic markets, which constrain scope for extracting regulatory rent.

More specifically, the early pursuit of competitive industrialization brings early urbanization, which confers three economic benefits. First, it accelerates passage through the demographic cycle because an urban environment encourages reduced family size by: offering a wider range of employment than the rural economy; facilitating rising family incomes; and placing a higher premium on space than rural living does. Slowing population growth advances the onset of the demographic dividend as the dependent/worker ratio falls. A lower dependent/worker ratio reduces expenditure on consumption, leaving more for saving and investment. The higher investment is efficient in an export economy that is exposed to global competition, so it generates high per capita GDP growth. The demographic dividend persists until the workers in the expanded cohort begin to retire, when each worker must support a growing number of dependents, so that a worsening dependent/worker ratio becomes growth depressing (Bloom and Williamson 1998).

Second, early industrialization rapidly absorbs surplus rural labour, which advances the arrival of the Lewis (1954) labour market turning point. Taiwan and South Korea suggest the labour market turning point can arrive within a decade of launching competitive industrialization. The onset of labour shortages boosts wage costs economy-wide, which encourages government and employers to invest in improving worker skills so as to maintain competitiveness by raising productivity. In this way, rising wages propel a sustained diversification into the production of more skill-intensive and capital-intensive goods and services, which drives rapid growth in per capita incomes. This is the critical developmental benefit of the low-rent model, which the high-rent model fails to emulate. The elimination of surplus rural labour also allows farm consolidation that permits the more efficient use of rural land and labour, raising agricultural productivity and rural incomes, in contrast to the outcome in many land-rich economies.

Third, GDP growth in the low-rent economy is not only rapid but also relatively egalitarian because the elimination of surplus rural labour puts a floor under the wages of the poorest, while the rapid diffusion of technological skills caps the skill premium (Londono 1996). The resulting egalitarian and high per capita GDP growth can transform a low-income economy into a high-income economy within two generations. The rate of per capita GDP growth may exceed 8% per annum through mid-income levels, which is sufficient to more than quadruple per capita income within twenty years.

The low-rent development trajectory accumulates a self-reliant form of social capital. At low income levels, most transactions occur over short (i.e. local) distances (Woolcock and Narayan 2000) and are facilitated by bonding social capital that insures individuals against risk. However, bonding social capital can stifle innovative and entrepreneurial activity (Stiglitz 1995) because it carries group social obligations that require any gains accruing to an individual, whether from luck or diligence, to be shared among the group, hampering wealth accumulation. Early urbanization permits individuals to reduce their dependence on local groups by extending social links through regional associations, which build *linking* social capital that reduces risk but imposes fewer redistributive claims than bonding social capital. As development proceeds further, formal legal institutions gain in importance over linking social capital because large anonymous markets are more effective than (informal) networks, since the 'best' buyer or seller may not be part of the network (Serageldin and Grooteart 2000, 213). The more anonymous markets require effective institutions, notably a reliable legal system and property rights, which businessmen have a strong interest in promoting in the competitive markets that characterize low-rent economies.

Finally, the rapid structural change of the low-rent model encourages an incremental political maturation because it strengthens sanctions against antisocial governance (Lizzeri and Persico 2004). It engenders new professions and social groups that can and do contest policy capture by any single group. In addition, the egalitarian income distribution of low-rent economies helps cement social solidarity and limit political polarization, in contrast to the income skew of most resource-rich economies. Income equality also eases pressure for redistribution, so that changes in government tend not to result in sharp changes of economic policy that can be wealth-destroying. A diversifying social structure also encourages democratization by strengthening three sanctions against antisocial governance as private firms lobby for property rights and the rule of law (Li and Li 2000); competitive urbanization strengthens self-reliant civic voice and social capital (Isham et al. 2005); and government reliance on taxes rather than rent spurs demand for transparent public finances (Ross 2001). The net result is an incremental political maturation in low-rent economies with rising per capita income. A caveat is in order, however, because East Asia provides evidence that populations experiencing sustained and rapid rises in personal incomes may forgo some political freedoms for longer than those populations where rising living standards become insecure.

2.3.3 *The High-Rent Staple Trap Model*

A high-rent economy risks falling into a staple trap of dependence for economic growth on expanding rent rather than on raising productivity. This is basically because high rent fuels political pressure for the rapid disbursement of rent, which governments find difficult to resist (Table 2.2). Consequently, rent deployment invariably exceeds the absorption capacity of the domestic economy and stokes inflation. This causes an appreciation of the real exchange rate which strengthens Dutch disease effects, whereby the nonboom tradeables contract unless they are given protection and soft budget constraints. Meanwhile, limited international competition accommodates price rises in the service sector. The change in relative prices triggers a resource movement effect that shifts capital and labour out of the struggling tradeables sector and into more profitable services.

Historically, most governments responded to Dutch disease effects by closing their trade policy to protect domestic producers of tradeables, especially manufacturing, whose urbanized presence strengthens its political influence compared with dispersed rural activity like farming. But import barriers reduce incentives to compete, since domestic producers can pass increased costs on to their captive domestic market. The policy therefore shifts the internal terms of trade against agriculture, mining, and competitive manufacturing in favour of *protected* manufacturing, which is the very opposite of the required competitive diversification of the economy. Although agriculture generates the most employment at low incomes, in the high-rent economy it invariably functions as a reservoir of cheap labour, a supplier of cheap food, and a potential source of rent, rather than an engine of economic growth. The resulting neglect of agriculture squanders its considerable potential to stimulate growth at low income levels through its role as a market for domestic goods and a buoyant source of tax revenue (Mellor 1995).

Dutch disease effects and protection preclude labour-intensive export-led manufacturing, so the high-rent economy foregoes all three of its beneficial effects on development. First, surplus labour persists and mutes the impulse from rising real wages for rapid and sustained productivity-driven structural change. Second, the labour surplus depresses the wages of the rural poor, while urban workers in protected activity tap rents to boost their wages, amplifying income inequality. In addition, fears of urban unemployment encourage the government to expand jobs in protected manufacturing and unproductive bureaucracy that markets would not support. Third, lagging urbanization postpones the emergence of the demographic dividend and its associated boost to saving, while protection depresses investment efficiency, which slows economic growth. The policy quickly degenerates into a vehicle for rent-seeking and government corruption, which makes increasing demands for subsidies from the rent that eventually outstrip the capacity of the economy to sustain them (Gelb and Associates 1988), due either to declining prices or resource exhaustion. This is the essence of the staple trap: the economy displays an increasing dependence on rent that is unsustainable, and without reform leads to a growth collapse that is protracted because rent recipients are powerful and oppose reform.

In respect to the sociopolitical circuits, household subsidies funded by rent foster a dependent form of social capital reliant on government largess, while retarded structural change impedes the emergence of self-reliant social groups that contest political power and drive an incremental shift towards political pluralism. Rather, all three sanctions against antisocial governance that strengthen under low-rent competitive diversification weaken in the high-rent staple trap model. Protected businesses find it more profitable to lobby politicians and bureaucrats for favours rather than to invest in boosting productivity; social capital is dependent because of reliance on government subsidies and employment; while the dependence of public finance on rent rather than personal taxation blunts incentives for accountability.

In summary, the high-rent trajectory forfeits the six developmental benefits that the low-rent model confers, namely:

(i) alignment of elite and majority interests in prioritizing GDP growth;

(ii) early reliance on labour-intensive exports that trigger competitive diversification;

(iii) early passage through the demographic cycle and capture of the demographic dividend:

(iv) rapid absorption of surplus labour and skill diffusion that constrain income inequality;

(v) accumulation of self-reliant social capital;

(vi) strengthening political competition and sanctions against antisocial governance.

The high-rent staple trap model is inherently unstable: it creates a burgeoning parasitic urban sector that relies increasingly on transfers of rent (as well as some of the returns to capital and labour) that a weakening primary sector can ill-afford. The eventual growth collapse is protracted because elites seek to perpetuate rent-seeking by capturing the reforms and turning them to advantage by, for example, promoting privatization to secure favourable terms for buying privatized industry but then obstructing trade liberalization that would threaten their newly secured monopolies.

2.3.4 *Some Variations around the Basic Development Trajectories*

Some refinement of the two rent-driven models is in order. First, rent cycling theory predicts that a growth collapse in a high-rent economy is self-correcting. This is because the development trajectory retards the demographic transition, which prolongs relatively high population growth and thereby steadily shrinks per capita rent. Second, the specific nature of the natural resource can mediate outcomes. In particular, the risk of a growth collapse is heightened: (i) the higher the ratio of rent to GDP; (ii) the more concentrated the rent on a handful of economic agents; and (iii) the greater the volatility of commodity prices. This implies that mineral-driven economies are most at risk, and the oil-exporting economies most of all (Table 2.2). The governments of oil-exporting economies with the largest reserves can deploy more rent to buy the support of their citizens, wealthy and poorer alike, but abundant rent merely perpetuates rent dependence and blunts the incentive to switch to productivity-driven growth. Saudi Arabia provides a stark example: the 2004–14 commodity boom was associated with the rapid expansion of subsidies, so that by 2014 Saudi Arabia required oil prices above US$95/bl to balance its budget, compared with US$40/bl ten years earlier (IMF 2017).

In contrast, crop-driven economies can more easily harness the potential benefits of rent. There are three reasons for this. First, crop rent is usually a smaller fraction of GDP than mineral rent (Auty 2001: 131). Second, the volatility of soft commodity prices is less than that of hard commodities like minerals, where long lead times on large investments hamper matching supply and demand (Cashin and McDermott 2002). Third, the commodity linkages disperse rent across many economic agents, namely peasant cash crop farmers, who tend to save and invest rent more effectively than governments do (Baldwin 1956; Bevan et al. 1987; Bevan et al. 1999).

Finally, rent cycling theory recognizes that specific initial conditions exacerbate the risk of a growth collapse, notably youthful democracy, statist policies, and high ethnicity. The nature of government has emerged as an initial condition exacerbating the rent curse: Collier and Hoeffler (2009) find that in the presence of high rent, autocracies outperform democracies in terms of economic growth, whereas the reverse is true in the presence of low rent. They suggest with regard to mineral rent that high rent makes it politically more profitable for democratic governments to channel public revenue through patronage networks to secure the support of swing voters, rather than into providing public goods, which confer no electoral edge since they benefit supporters and opponents alike. Keefer (2007) found that the age of a democracy is significant: young democracies are less successful than either autocracies or more established democracies because they are unable to make credible pre-election promises to voters.

Finally, statist ideology amplifies the adverse effects of high rent and youthful democracy by boosting scope for rent-rich governments to override markets and prioritize political goals over economic goals in the allocation of expenditure (Van de Walle 1999). Ndulu et al. (2007) identify regulatory regimes as the principal antigrowth syndrome behind the disappointing performance of sub-Saharan Africa since independence. Ethnic tension also reinforces incentives to use rent to win political support. Bridgman (2008) identifies a strong statistical link between low growth in ethnically diverse economies and redistributive pressure that deflects resources away from welfare-enhancing activity. Montalvo and Reynal-Querol (2005: 294) find ethnicity is negatively associated with the rate of investment, the rate of economic growth, and the quality of government.

2.4 Country Size, Manufacturing, and Economic Development

The low-rent model attributes the success of the resource-poor economies to early entry into competitive manufacturing under hard budget constraints. Without sizeable primary product exports or other forms of rent, the elites in small rent-poor economies are incentivized to eschew trade policy closure and export into global markets so as to overcome the constraint of limited domestic market size. In contrast, prior to the IFI-backed reforms of the 1980s, most rent-rich economies deployed their rent to pursue industrialization by import substitution. This entailed closing their economies and promoting infant industry, which took decades to mature, if it ever did. The smaller rent-rich economies were particularly handicapped by this strategy because the size of their domestic markets was often insufficient to support plants of minimum viable size, let alone capture localization economies or agglomeration economies. Small rent-rich economies have therefore struggled to industrialize efficiently, because unlike the competitive structural change of the small low-rent economy, their structural change is hampered by unproductive investment, excessive rent-seeking, a dependent form of social capital, and faltering steps towards political pluralism.

The International Monetary Fund (IMF) defines small economies as having fewer than 1.5 million people. Globally they comprise nineteen small states plus fifteen microstates (population less than 200,000) and range from upper middle-income Barbados, Mauritius, and Trinidad and Tobago, through lower mid-income to low-income Bhutan, Belize, and Guyana (Jahan and Wang 2013). The stylized facts indicate that small states exhibit higher expenditure on government, due partly to diseconomies of scale in government services, and greater dependence on one or two sectors of the economy (either on commodity exports or tourism or financial services). Their financial sectors tend to be underdeveloped and lack depth, competition, and adequate regulation[1] so that capital markets are thin. Jahan and Wang (2013) found that increased commodity volatility has been the prime reason why small states have tended to grow slower than larger ones since the late-1990s, but a brain drain to larger economies and the termination of favourable trade deals by the World Trade Organization (WTO) were additional factors (Auty 2017a).

---

[1] The Trinidad insurer CLICO collapsed in 2009, having met its commitments by relying heavily on real estate, which foundered through the financial crisis and left a shortfall in excess of 12% of GDP that was met by government intervention (IMF 2013b: 9).

2.4.1 Overview: Manufacturing, Country Size, Trade Policy, and Structural Change

Chenery and Syrquin (1975) and Syrquin and Chenery (1989) draw upon data for more than one hundred countries over the period from 1950 to 1983 to analyse how country size, natural resource endowment, and trade policy interact with structural change and per capita income. They confirm the central role of manufacturing during those years in driving structural change, which conferred stronger gains in productivity than either agriculture or services. Table 2.3 shows that the share of agriculture in GDP declines from one-half at low-income levels to below one-fifth at mid-income levels, when it is overtaken by manufacturing. Within manufacturing, scale-sensitive heavy and chemical industry outstrips light industry in importance at the mid-income level. Further rises in incomes see agriculture contract towards 5% of GDP or less (albeit becoming increasingly productive), while manufacturing shrinks towards 10% of GDP. McKinsey (2012) updated the Syrquin and Chenery data and showed that manufacturing typically peaks at 25–35% of GDP but then declines to average in the advanced economies 16% of GDP and 14% of employment.

The changing structure of production as per capita income rises has implications for the rate of per capita GDP growth because agriculture, manufacturing, and services have *historically* made differing contributions to productivity growth. The rise of manufacturing at mid-income levels and its subsequent relative decline meant that the rate of economic growth first accelerated and then slowed down at higher income levels (Table 2.4). The

Table 2.3 Per capita income, structural change, and domestic absorption, post-1973 (share of GDP)

	Income per capita (US$, 1980[1])						
	<300	300	500	1,000	2,000	4,000	> 5,000
Production							
Agriculture	0.48	0.39	0.32	0.23	0.15	0.10	0.07
Mining	0.01	0.05	0.07	0.08	0.08	0.06	0.01
Manufacturing	0.10	0.12	0.15	0.18	0.21	0.24	0.28
Construction	0.04	0.04	0.05	0.06	0.06	0.07	0.07
Utilities	0.06	0.07	0.07	0.08	0.09	0.09	0.10
Services	0.31	0.32	0.35	0.38	0.41	0.45	0.47
Final demand							
Private consumption	0.79	0.73	0.70	0.66	0.63	0.60	0.60
Government consumption	0.12	0.14	0.14	0.14	0.14	0.15	0.14
Investment	0.14	0.18	0.21	0.23	0.25	0.26	0.26
Exports	0.16	0.19	0.21	0.23	0.23	0.26	0.23
Imports	0.21	0.25	0.25	0.26	0.27	0.28	0.23

[1] Since 1980 the US GDP deflator has risen by 1.92, so the income range rises from < US$575 to > US$9,600.
Source: Syrquin and Chenery (1989: 20).

Table 2.4 Per capita GDP and economic growth (Syrquin and Chenery aggregates[1])

Per capita GDP (US$, 1980[2])	Net investment (% GDP)	ICOR	Population growth (%/year)	Per capita GDP growth (%/year)	Value added growth (%/year)	Labour productivity growth (%/year)	Duration (years)
100–140	8	2.2	2.6	1.3	3.8	1.3	27
140–280	10	2.3	2.8	2.0	4.8	1.7	35
280–560	13	2.4	2.5	3.2	5.7	2.8	22
560–1,120	15	2.5	2.2	4.1	6.3	4.0	17
1,120–2,100	16	2.4	2.0	4.6	6.6	4.8	14
2,100–3,360	16	2.4	1.5	4.7	6.2	4.8	10
3,360–5,040	14	2.4	1.0	4.6	5.6	4.1	9

ICOR, Incremental capital output ratio.

[1] The numbers are synthetic ones, designed to represent a likely pattern over the very long run (M. Syrquin, personal communication).

[2] The advanced economies' GDP deflator for 1980–2010 is 2.52, which, applied to the Syrquin and Chenery data, lifts the income range in 2011 dollars from < US$300 to > US$4,000 and from < US$750 to > US$11,000 (IMF 2013a).

Source: Syrquin (1986: 233).

deceleration in economic growth at higher income levels reflected not only structural change but also the need of mature economies to devote capital and labour to research and development in order to maintain productivity growth. In contrast, with little cost of technological innovation, low-income economies can grow faster than mature economies. This is because they can benefit from their technological lag to apply existing global technology to boost their productivity.

The literature initially established that manufacturing drove faster economic growth than other sectors due to strong externalities arising from learning by doing (Matsuyama 1992; Sachs and Warner 1997). For example, Echevarria (1997) found that manufacturing displayed the fastest rate of productivity growth, and services the slowest. She concluded that changes in the sectoral composition of GDP explain more than one-fifth of the observed variation in economic growth among countries. Wood and Berge (1997) also found that manufacturing drove rapid economic growth during the middle stages of development. One consequence has been that countries that exported manufactured goods (resource-poor countries) grew faster than countries that exported primary products. Wood and Berge (1997) concluded that manufacturing was more skill-intensive and so accelerated human capital accumulation. Finally, McKinsey (2012) noted that although manufacturing contributes negatively to employment growth in the advanced economies (−24% in 1996–2006), it continues to make a higher contribution than its sector share of GDP to productivity growth (37%), total exports (70%), and private research and development (77%).

Importantly, however, the historical data may overstate the importance of manufacturing for economic growth, due to a post-war historical policy bias towards industry at the expense of agriculture, especially in resource-rich economies. During the immediate post-war decades, many developing country governments promoted manufacturing and neglected agriculture and to a lesser extent services. In economies characterized by such a pro-industry policy bias, resources were misallocated, while slow-maturing infant industry overexpanded and degenerated into a device for extracting rent (Auty 1994a). The corollary is that agriculture experienced relative neglect and underperformed in most developing countries, often significantly.

Mellor (1995) drew on extensive empirical evidence to show that in the early stage of development of a well-managed economy, agriculture can grow at 4–6% annually, a rate that can propel total GDP at 7.5% annually. Unfortunately, agriculture rarely fulfilled its growth potential in the post-war decades due to the pro-manufacturing policy bias. This implies that the Syrquin and Chenery data on structural change overstate the historical importance of manufacturing in economic development compared with the outcome under more rational sector neutral economic policies. This undermines the speculation by Rodrik (2015) of premature deindustrialization in Latin America and sub-Saharan Africa: the contraction in manufacturing's share of GDP reflects in part a realignment of an overexpanded manufacturing sector with underlying comparative advantage.

2.4.2 Country Size, Structural Change, and Development

Large economies, whether resource-poor or resource-rich, have tended to achieve significantly higher rates of per capita GDP growth than smaller economies (Table 1.1). Following Syrquin and Chenery, the criterion used in Table 1.1 to identify a large country is a GDP in 1970 above US$7 billion, which they judged sufficient at that time to furnish domestic demand to support larger industrial plants of minimum viable size. Resource-abundant economies are defined as having more than 0.3 hectares of cropland per capita in 1970, with small resource-rich countries further classified as oil exporters or mineral exporters if these commodities exceeded 40% of their exports.

The large economy has superior diversification options to the small economy, due not only to its usually greater geographical area, which widens the range of resources and export opportunities, but also from the greater scope that a large domestic market affords to capture the internal and external economies of scale. This allows the large economy to competitively diversify into a wider range of manufacturing activity and from a lower per capita income than the small economy. Large economies also tend to be more self-sufficient than small ones, so that they exhibit a lower ratio of trade to GNP and are less vulnerable to external shocks. Importantly, however, Alesina et al. (2005) noted that the post-war trend towards trade liberalization had the potential to help small economies to overcome the diseconomies of scale by serving large global markets, and thereby grow faster. Unfortunately, many small economies pursued closed trade policies that squandered this potential.[2]

Certainly, the large resource-poor economies as a group avoided the protracted growth collapses that befell so many other developing countries through the 1970s and 1980s. (The large resource-rich economies also experienced less protracted growth collapses than the small ones.) The large resource-poor economies doubled the share of manufacturing in GNP across the income range shown in Table 2.3 to almost 30% of GNP, compared to barely 22% in the large resource-rich economies (Fig. 2.1). Interestingly, although the large resource-poor economies could pursue *competitive* import substitution (including heavy industry) earlier than small economies, light

---

[2] Moreover, they noted that the same process may encourage homogenous regions within large economies to secede and form new independent small countries.

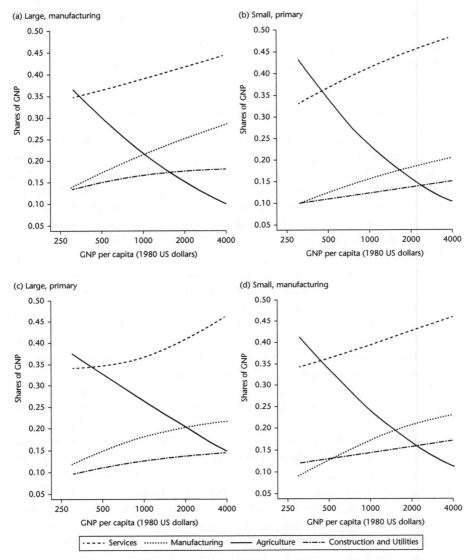

Fig. 2.1 Structure of value added in GNP by natural resource endowment.
Source: Syrquin and Chenery (1989: 56–7).

industry generated a higher share of GNP in large resource-poor economies than in any other endowment group.

In the large resource-rich countries, manufacturing expanded its share of GNP more slowly than in the smaller countries, albeit from a higher initial level, and its composition was skewed towards capital-intensive industry (Fig. 2.1). Early industry (including labour-intensive textiles and agro-processing) and middle industry expanded their share of GNP more slowly. Consequently, manufacturing in the large resource-rich economies was more capital-intensive and employed fewer workers than manufacturing in either large or small resource-poor economies. The large resource-rich countries' manufacturing was also less efficient and required protection prior to the 1990s' economic reforms, reflecting a previously strong policy bias towards self-sufficiency discussed in Chapter 7 that ran counter to their comparative advantage. Syrquin and Chenery suggest that even as global trade re-expanded during the post-war years, the share of exports in the GNP of large resource-abundant countries *shrank* with rising per capita income.

Among the small resource-rich economies, most increased their dependence on primary product exports through 1970–89. But their economies were relatively closed: the share of exports in GNP for small resource-abundant countries was barely one-fifth. This was similar to the ratio of the large resource-poor economies, but barely half the two-fifths ratio of the small resource-poor economies which pursued more open trade policies. The trade policy closure by small resource-rich economies occurred despite high self-sufficiency being less feasible for small countries than for the larger ones (reflecting their greater import dependence and constrained opportunity to capture the economies of scale). The principal exception was a handful of small resource-rich countries with unusually high resource rents like Saudi Arabia and Botswana, which retained more open trade policies (Sachs and Warner 1999). Overall, consistent with the staple trap model, small resource-abundant economies struggle to diversify into manufactured exports: even at a per capita income of US$4000, manufactured exports remained less than 4% of GNP and less than one-quarter of all exports in the small resource-abundant economies (Syrquin and Chenery 1989). Consequently, smaller resource-abundant countries frequently relied on a single primary product export, rendering them vulnerable to external shocks. The small mineral-driven economies were most vulnerable of all.

Many newly independent governments of resource-rich economies viewed agriculture as a reservoir of cheap labour and a source of rent rather than a dynamic agent of economic growth. Most abused crop marketing boards to extract rent, and more besides, whereas governments of small resource-*poor* countries tended to nurture farming through land reforms (to widen access to land), investment in rural infrastructure, and productivity-enhancing inputs.[3] The consequent rise in farm productivity in resource-poor economies furnished extra government revenue without depressing farm incentives and incomes. The revenue was invested to stimulate

---

[3] The small resource-poor economies comprise El Salvador, Haiti, Hong Kong, Jordan, Kenya, Mauritania, Mauritius, Nepal, Singapore, Somalia, Sri Lanka, Taiwan, and Tanzania (Auty 2001: 4).

competitive manufacturing. For example, Tomich et al. (1995) estimated that the government of Taiwan extracted one-fifth of farm income during the 1950s, when agriculture generated more than one-third of GDP, without impairing GDP growth. In contrast, land-*abundant* Thailand developed less-beneficial agricultural linkages. Siamwalla (1995) attributed this to the low demand for both domestic manufactured goods and skill acquisition that *extensive* agricultural expansion (i.e. land colonization) provided in cropland-rich Thailand compared to the intensive agricultural expansion in land-scarce economies like Taiwan.

Manufacturing and construction double their share of GNP in small resource-poor economies as incomes rise, whereas the small resource-rich economies see a more modest rise from just 20% to 36%. The difference is made up by extra services in small resource-rich economies, an outcome consistent with Dutch disease effects. Interestingly, the high share of manufactured exports in the small resource-poor economy exists alongside a high share of manufactured imports, which comprise inputs for domestic firms, and also goods for final consumption. Small resource-poor economies achieve a higher degree of specialization and greater integration into the world economy than the resource-rich economies (Syrquin and Chenery 1989: 50). At higher income levels, the composition of manufacturing in small resource-poor economies converges on that of the large resource-poor economies (Syrquin and Chenery 1989: 43). In contrast, but consistent with the staple trap model and the failure of import substitution policies, most small resource-abundant economies remain commodity-driven and vulnerable to external shocks.

2.4.3 *Prospective Role of Service Exports*

The rise of services in recent decades, including service exports, promises to help further reduce the country size constraints associated with manufacturing. The search for flexible production systems, which increasingly contracts out former in-house tasks to specialist suppliers, of both physical goods and services, should augment this favourable development. Small firms in small economies that are remote can compete to be part of the new flexible global manufacturing and service product chains. The more innovative manufacturing sectors rely heavily on service sector firms. For example, McKinsey (2012) identified the largest global manufacturing subsector as the application of global technology to produce goods for regional markets (including chemicals, automobiles, other transport equipment, machinery, and electrical engineering). It accounts for 34% of global industrial output, of which *services* comprise two-fifths of value added. Services comprise an even higher share (over 55%) of output for industries that supply global technologies to innovators (computers, electronics, and medical products), which represent 9% of global manufacturing output. The remaining three subsectors, which together produce 57% of global industrial output, generate 30% of that output from services.[4] Interestingly, the inclusion of outsourced service jobs within US manufacturing pushes the service component to more than half the total jobs within the sector, exceeding employment in manufacturing *production* on its own.

As discussed in more depth in Chapter 8, the experience of India since the 1980s suggests that services can increasingly match manufacturing for dynamism even at mid-income levels. Although India conformed to the Syrquin and Chenery pattern of structural change through 1950–90, during which years it prioritized industrial self-sufficiency, the share of manufacturing in Indian GDP has since stabilized. Expanding services have subsequently compensated for the continued shrinkage of agriculture in GDP. By 2005, services generated 50% of GDP (World Bank 2009b), but employed only 26% of the workforce, a ratio implying similar productivity to industry which by then generated 32% of GDP with 18% of employment.[5] Further research suggests that the rate of productivity growth in services is accelerating, while that of manufacturing is slowing (Ghani et al. 2012). The rise of services and service exports appears to offer much greater scope to diversify into productive activity than is captured by the Syrquin and Chenery data. Services also incur minimal transportation costs, which eases any disadvantages hitherto of small domestic markets, and entails less pollution.

2.5 Conclusions

The proliferation of statistical studies of the resource curse since the mid-1990s has failed to resolve the causes of the curse, and even whether a curse exists. A useful complement to the focus of the statistical studies on silver-bullet explanations is provided by a case study approach set within an historical context that synthesizes the literature into a nuanced theory to explain the resource curse. Rent cycling theory offers such an approach. It considers the resource curse as nondeterministic and rooted in policy failure arising from the incentives that rent confers on the elite. This approach explains the observed fluctuation of the global incidence of the resource curse with

[4] The three subsectors comprise: local processing of metals, food, plastics, and printing for regional markets (31% of manufacturing output); resource processing via petroleum refining, base metals, and pulp and paper processing (22% of manufacturing output); and labour-intensive manufacturing for export (8%).

[5] In contrast, agriculture had 56% of the workforce but only 18% of GDP, indicating low productivity, which Mellor (1995) also attributed to long-standing pro-industry policies.

changing post-war fashions in development policy. Moreover, it explains that the resource curse is part of a broader rent curse that can also be caused by geopolitical rent, regulatory rent, and remittances. In short, rent cycling theory reveals that the resource curse is a more complex and subtle phenomenon than the literature has hitherto assumed.

Basically, rent cycling theory posits that elite incentives determine the choice of development strategy that drives structural change, which moulds social capital accumulation and the rate of political maturation. Low rent motivates the elite to grow the economy by providing public goods and diffusing competitive markets. This aligns the development trajectory with the underlying comparative advantage of the economy, which in the presence of low rent lies initially in the export of labour-intensive manufactures. Early industrialization quickly exhausts surplus labour, which triggers pressure to raise wages by boosting productivity through diversification into capital-intensive and skill-intensive manufacturing. Elimination of surplus labour also puts a floor under the wages of the poor and caps the skill premium, which confers economic growth that is relatively egalitarian as well as rapid. Early industrialization also brings early urbanization that accelerates the onset of the demographic transition and the demographic dividend, which boost saving and accelerate economic growth. Finally, the singular structural change in the low-rent economy accumulates a self-reliant form of social capital. It also multiplies social groups ready and able to contest policy capture by any vested interests and to pressure governments into strengthening institutions, civic voice, and transparent public finances.

In contrast, high rent encourages elite contests to capture rent for immediate personal enrichment at the expense of long-term growth. This causes the overrapid domestic absorption of the rent, which is inflationary and triggers Dutch disease effects that abort competitive diversification and retard labour absorption. Concern for unemployment prompts governments to deploy rent to provide jobs that markets would not support. The subsidized urban activity has little incentive to boost productivity and its burgeoning appetite for rent eventually outstrips the supply of rent due to falling prices or the exhaustion of reserves, causing a growth collapse that is protracted in the absence of economic reform, which rent-seeking interests resist. This is the essence of the high-rent staple trap model: revenue is extracted from the primary sector to expand an uncompetitive urban sector at a rate that undermines the primary sector upon which the urban sector increasingly relies. In contrast to the low-rent model, structural change in high-rent economies creates a dependent social capital and muted civic voice, reflecting reliance on government subsidies. In addition, political maturation stalls because businesses find it more rewarding to lobby politicians for favours rather than invest to boost productivity or push for improved institutions, while rent-sourced public finances elicit little pressure for improved accountability.

In Chapters 3–5 we draw upon two case studies to demonstrate how the models work: Trinidad and Tobago broadly conforms to the high-rent staple trap model, whereas Mauritius conforms to the low-rent competitive diversification model. The two countries had comparable initial conditions at independence, aside from the mineral endowment. Although they are small economies, they share development trajectories with economies of varying sizes from differing cultures. However, initial conditions in Trinidad and Tobago intensified development challenges on account of a relatively high ratio of natural resource rent to GDP, which proved to be volatile and was concentrated on a handful of economic agents within a society where rent-seeking was long established.

The rent curse is not deterministic, however, so that astute policies to manage political pressures for overrapid rent absorption can avoid the staple trap and associated growth collapse. Malaysia and Soeharto's Indonesia provide examples of successful high-rent development (Auty 1990). More generally, however, the risk of rent mismanagement was heightened through the immediate post-war decades by the prioritization of industrialization, and the widespread espousal of industrialization by import substitution in particular. This policy closed the economy, which amplified scope for rent extraction. The strategy of import substitution was especially inappropriate for small economies, while the resource-based industry pursued by mineral economies like Trinidad and Tobago proved a minimal diversification away from rent dependence, since it failed to generate strong downstream linkages.

Yet manufacturing dominated economic diversification in the post-war decades, partly through a widely held conviction that industrialization was central to economic development. This led to the neglect of agriculture, despite its considerable development potential at low income levels. Services were also viewed as a residual sector, until perspectives began to change from the 1990s. It is now recognized that the service sector can both raise welfare on a sustainable basis and boost productivity and economic diversification, along with the associated sociopolitical benefits. Loungani et al. (2017) identified the potential of a service revolution that puts services at the heart of world trade. They argue that the increasing tradability of services can help both high-rent economies and low-income economies to diversify by leapfrogging manufacturing.

Section 2

Emergence of Rent-Dependent Development

3

The Rent-Seeking Legacy of the Plantation Economy in Trinidad and Tobago

3.1 Introduction

Plantation agriculture has played a pivotal role in shaping the political economy of modern-day Trinidad and Tobago. The plantation dominated the political economy from the late-eighteenth century until hydrocarbon extraction displaced it through the closing decades of the twentieth century. In this chapter we evaluate models of plantation society; explain the plantation's economic legacy, notably rent dependence; and trace the origin of the rent-seeking political system that led to the plantation's eventual collapse. We argue that the plantation not only established a rent-dependent economy in Trinidad and Tobago, but also supported a large workforce on low incomes for most of its existence; created an ethnically diverse society that hinders the emergence of class-based politics; and inadvertently engendered political parties that prioritized rent extraction over sustainable long-term economic development. Rent dependence is not inevitable in plantation society, however, as is shown by Mauritius, which had much in common with Trinidad and Tobago at independence, but managed to adapt its plantations to cope with changing global competition.

The chapter is structured as follows. Section 3.2 evaluates models of plantation society developed by dependency theory and the mainstream economic literature. Section 3.3 applies the models to explain the persistently low welfare generated by the plantations until the mid-twentieth century. Section 3.4 explains how colonial government reforms in the 1940s expanded geopolitical rent to spur investment in raising plantation productivity so as to boost worker incomes to match levels in the UK. Section 3.5 traces the rise of the political system, which inadvertently engendered rent-seeking contests that eroded the viability of the plantation in Trinidad and Tobago and intensified the economy's dependence on hydrocarbon rent. Section 3.6 summarizes.

3.2 Perspectives on the Plantation as a Development Agent

Dependency theorists rightly argue for the primacy of sociopolitical factors over economic ones in explaining why the colonial plantation failed to raise mean incomes through the nineteenth century (Walton 1975), but both they and mainstream critics like Baldwin (1956) underestimate the flexibility of the plantation. Consequently, the theorists neglect the capacity of the plantation for reform. We argue that both internal colonialism and rent cycling theory offer convincing explanations of the dynamics of plantation society because they correctly identify as the critical issue the incentive of the domestic elite to extract rents.

3.2.1 *Best's Model of the Plantation Economy*

The early association of the colonial plantation with slavery and cheap labour has ensured its controversy as an agent of economic development. Critics on the left, including dependency theorists, argue that the plantation builds an external dependence that confers the principal benefits from trade upon a metropolitan power while minimizing the economic stimulus to the plantation hinterland. This perspective strongly influenced young West Indian scholars through the 1960s and 1970s who employed it to criticize the plantation as a negative feature of contemporary political economy (Beckford 1972). Girvan (1971) focused upon multinational corporations as the successors to colonial governments as the external economic agents exploiting a dependent polity. Although Girvan studied Caribbean mining, analysing the product strategy and organizational structure of the four leading global aluminium producers (Alcoa, Alcan, Kaiser, and Reynolds), his work also carried implications for the vertically integrated multinational firms producing sugar within the Caribbean, notably Booker McConnell and Tate and Lyle. Lewis (personal communication, 1983), however, concludes that independence undermined dependency theory. Rather, the dependency theorist's concept of internal colonialism is more insightful (Walton 1975). Like rent cycling theory, internal colonialism argues that national elites distort and weaken the economy by extracting rents for personal enrichment and political influence.

Best (1968) criticized plantation society in a three-stage historical model, starting with the pure plantation under colonialism. This first stage ended with the abolition of slavery in 1838 (Sudama 1979). Best termed the second phase 'modified plantation economy', while his third stage was dubbed the post-independence 'further modified plantation economy'. According to Best, five basic conditions define relations between the metropolitan power and the hinterland that it dominates. First, the metropole controls all economic, political, and social aspects within the colonial hinterland. Second, within the vertically integrated chain of production, activity in the hinterland is confined to primary production, whereas processing occurs in the metropole region, which captures the bulk of higher value-added activity. Third, the metropole furnishes the currency and manages financial intermediation, which facilitates the acquisition of hinterland assets by economic agents in the metropole. Consequently, the latter dominate capital flows to, and investment in, the hinterland. Fourth, all hinterland trade is controlled by the metropole through tariff and nontariff interventions. Fifth, the metropole controls the revenue of the hinterland through a trading system that varies the rate of preferential duties. Overall, this relationship ensures that the hinterland enriches the metropole, which supplies all the key inputs except land. Since subsistence activity is discouraged, the self-contained plantation dominates all aspects of economic, social, and political life in the hinterland, with a focus on production for export. Any change in the system benefits solely the agents of the metropole.

In the pure plantation economy, land is granted to notables who might subcontract key functions to joint-stock companies, which supply capital and traded inputs and provisions to the planters in exchange for the export product, leaving the planters to oversee estate management. A key feature of the pure plantation is assumed to be a rigid response to changing economic fortunes, because the large investment sunk in processing equipment limits scope to change the product in the face of diminishing returns due to, say, soil exhaustion or glutted markets. This helps to explain the steady build-up of debt by many planters. From a more mainstream perspective, Baldwin (1956) also identified a rigid response as a prominent feature of the plantation, but he attributes it to the nature of the production function rather than to politics, as explained below.

Best ascribes the termination of the pure plantation economy to the rise of industrial interests in the metropole that favour free trade. This led to the abolition of slavery, which ushered in the second stage of the 'modified plantation'. The abolition of slavery threatened acute labour shortages and raised the expectation among ex-slaves that they would cheaply acquire former plantation land. But instead, planters, especially in frontier sugar colonies like Trinidad and Tobago, British Guiana, and Mauritius substituted indentured labour, usually transported from South Asia. Many indentured workers declined to return to their homeland upon completion of their work contract and remained to evolve into a 'semi-independent' peasantry. Although indentured labour ameliorated the labour shortage caused by the abolition of slavery, the switch still inflicted hardship on the planters, which accelerated the consolidation of plantation ownership on the joint-stock companies that supplied them with credit. The colonial advocates of free trade also pressured the planters to abandon their preferential trade agreements, or at least to phase them out.

The third phase of the plantation economy model, the 'further modified plantation economy', sees the dominant role of colonial governments replaced after independence by that of international capital in the form of the multinational enterprise. Newly independent governments are assumed to be subservient in this relationship. Crucially, the model continues to assume that economic linkages in the hinterland economy fail to proliferate, so that structural transformation remains minimal. The central insight in Best's theory is the persistence of a damaging external dependence through all three phases of his model. A second feature is the constraint on economic diversification: shifts into domestic food production, for example, or into simple manufactures, such as occurred in response to disruption of global trade during the Great Depression and World War II in much of Latin America, risked being snuffed out in the Caribbean because they competed with the dominant monocrop plantation for land and labour.

The third stage of the plantation economy model also holds that the global terms of trade remain unfavourable to the plantation economy after independence because multinational companies extract concessions/rents in exchange for investment (Sudama 1979: 59). For example, Girvan (1971) calculated that Jamaica captured barely 6% of the total value added by its bauxite in the entire aluminium production chain, with the rest accruing to companies engaged in downstream processing in the advanced economies. In addition, industrial diversification was stunted within the plantation economy because manufacturing was dependent on technology that served imported tastes, used imported intermediate goods and capital goods, and relied upon imported managerial personnel and organizational procedures.

3.2.2 Mainstream Evaluations of the Plantation

Best's model holds that the terms of trade discriminate against plantation exports, which further mutes the local economic stimulus. As already noted in Chapter 2, this view was championed by Prebisch (1950) in the post-war years and provided support for the widely adopted policy of industrialization by import substitution. However, Baldwin (1956) argued that the unsatisfactory local development multiplier is caused by the production function of the plantation commodity rather than unfavourable trade relations. His starting premise is that although agricultural exports may be associated with disappointing local economic growth in the tropics, they have proved more successful in temperate regions like the American Mid West, the Pacific Northwest, the Pampas, south-eastern Australia, and South Africa. Baldwin analyzed this climatic contrast with reference to nineteenth-century America.

He attributed the greater dynamism of the temperate Mid West compared with the subtropical South to differences in the production function (the ratio of capital to labour) of the export crop—grain in the Mid West and cotton in the South.

The production function of the subtropical crop of the South required much initial capital to establish processing facilities, so that barriers to entry were high and favoured plantations over family farms. Thereafter, the crop demanded mostly unskilled labour because technology offered little scope to substitute capital for labour, which rendered the production function of the South inflexible, as Best also assumed. In contrast, the grain crops of the temperate Mid West required a small initial capital investment, so that entry by small farmers was easy. Thereafter, production responded positively to small increments in investment. This combination led to temperate crops being produced on yeoman farms rather than on plantations. The two systems of production generated very different local economic linkages, which explain the superior economic performance of the Mid West compared with the South.

The South region offers no alternatives to subsistence for labourers, given the high barriers to entry in most tropical crops, so that labour is drawn onto the plantations from the subsistence sector at a low wage. In marked contrast, the wealthy elite supply the capital for the plantation sector. The social structure is therefore highly skewed, comprising a few rich and many poor. The income skew stunts both fiscal linkage (taxation) and final demand linkage (expenditure by owners and workers) for two reasons. First, fiscal linkage is stifled because the elite oppose taxation since it is levied almost exclusively on them, given the income distribution. Second, final demand linkage is low because the elite can afford to import foreign goods, whereas the workers who might buy simple locally produced goods have little surplus to spend, so neither group creates much demand for local firms to supply manufactured goods.

The spatial structure of the plantation economy adds a further constraint: it is designed to extract the staple for export rather than to promote local exchange. There are few centres for local trade, so that the settlement hierarchy of market towns is underdeveloped. The resulting limited domestic market is further fragmented among the largely self-sufficient plantations. This spatial structure together with its associated social system does not encourage the emergence of regional entrepreneurs who might diversify the economy. Rather, profits from the staple are either ploughed back into producing the staple or leak abroad into overseas investments or into the plantation owners' imported luxury goods. These characteristics of Baldwin's South model echo those of Best's modified plantation economy, but Baldwin identified technology as the key determinant of plantation inflexibility and discounted both unfavourable terms of trade and sociopolitical factors.

51

Baldwin (1956) characterized linkages from yeoman farms as conducive to the economic development of the producing region. He argued that low barriers to entry into temperate grain production encouraged production on small farms, as in the Mid West. Small increases in investment can steadily raise crop yields, productivity, and, most importantly, incomes. The rising incomes are, moreover, relatively evenly distributed across the entire population. Such a community supports taxation to improve the infrastructure, including local transport and education, because all contributors can expect to benefit from it. The settlement pattern also evolves a fully articulated central place hierarchy of nesting markets that facilitate trade and sustain an expanding domestic market, first for basic consumer goods and then for a widening range of increasingly sophisticated producer goods such as farm machinery. Mid West society also provides a stream of entrepreneurs, namely those farmers' sons who do not inherit land, to exploit new economic opportunities. It also supplies the capital with which to do so.

Baldwin's explanation for the divergent success of tropical and temperate regions is more sophisticated than that of Best, but he overstates the role of the production function. This oversimplifies his regional models for two reasons: Baldwin neglects the political economy and also the ease with which the export staple can be substituted. With respect to politics, Lewis (1978) argues rightly that the elite in tropical regions came to depend on cheap labour, first in the form of slave labour, mostly African, and when that was declared illegal, on the labour surplus of South Asia and East Asia. He posits that in order to attract Asian labour, the nineteenth-century plantation owners needed to provide an income just above that earned by the Asian farmer, which was basically a subsistence income. In contrast, the Mid West settlers from temperate Europe looked for an income greater than their alternative opportunity on the more productive farms of Europe, where scientific technology was applied earlier than in the tropics. Lewis estimates that European farms yielded almost 2 tons of grain per hectare in the nineteenth century, compared with less than half that on Asian farms, which remained near subsistence.

Lewis also notes that an important consequence of this dualistic labour supply in the nineteenth century was two global migration streams: one white that was increasingly expensive and flowed from Europe to the temperate colonies, and one coloured that was cheap and flowed within the tropics. Lewis wryly notes that white workers applied political pressure to ensure the two labour streams did not mix, because they were well aware of the threat to their higher wages from any mixing of the labour streams. A key implication of Lewis's insight is that, contrary to both Best and Baldwin, tropical crops do not inevitably imply low incomes for their workers: the diffusion of scientific agriculture can raise incomes if it is politically opportune to do so. This was the case in the British West Indies sugar industry from the early-1940s (Auty 1976). It was not the production function that had previously depressed wages in tropical crop production, nor was it an inevitable consequence of colonial settlement per se, but rather it reflected the labour surplus in the tropics, which diminished the incentive to substitute capital for labour.

The second omission from Baldwin's regional models is the flexibility of crop *substitution*, which is greater for temperate crops than for tropical crops. The Mid West staple of grain could be substituted more easily in the face of unfavourable prices than many tropical crops could be substituted. This is because leading temperate crops are annuals and also require little investment in processing for export. In contrast, the high fixed investment of the cotton gin, sugar cane mill, palm oil plant, or coffee bush planting creates inertia, which during difficult times encourages cost reduction rather than substitution of a more profitable crop. Adamson (1972) reported that nineteenth-century West Indian planters repressed peasant agriculture for fear of competition for land, labour, and government aid. Basically, lower crop prices elicited cost cutting instead of crop diversification. This increased the risk of tropical regions becoming locked into a staple trap of monocrop production, which was vulnerable to slow economic growth or even collapse.

Finally, Graham and Floering (1984) drew upon the nucleus plantation in modern Malaysia to confirm the flexibility of the plantation. The nucleus plantation recognizes that whereas there are often economies of scale in crop processing, this is less true of most crop growing, which is more efficiently undertaken on family farms. The nucleus plantation therefore splits the plantation functions, so that activities that benefit from the economies of scale like plant breeding, crop processing, and crop export are handled by the nucleus plantation. Small farmers grow the bulk of the crop, which they send for processing at the nucleus site. The nucleus plantation farms a relatively small area of land itself, which furnishes a model of best practice for surrounding small farmers to follow. In this way, modern skills diffuse through the economy without alienating large tracts of land to 'outsiders', whether from overseas or elsewhere in the country.

Summarizing, explanations for persistently low plantation incomes that are rooted in dependency theory rightly stress the key role of sociopolitical conditions, which prior to the mid-twentieth century, mobilized cheap labour in the tropics that depressed the local multiplier and minimized the local development linkages. But dependency theorists are mistaken in casting multinational firms as the agents of exploitation since independence. Rather, as demonstrated in later sections, such companies were acutely sensitive to adverse changes in production costs, including the long-term costs of social discontent, which they sought to ameliorate. In fact, internal colonialism and rent cycling theory offer more convincing explanations than dependency

53

theory for the often disappointing economic performance of the plantation, which is rooted in contests among the elite for rent.

3.3 Rents and the Low-Income Plantation Economy 1783–1935

This section establishes the legacy of Trinidad and Tobago's plantation economy. For one-and-a-half centuries, the plantation provided a basic minimum standard of living for the majority of workers. This was not the inevitable outcome predicted by dependency theory or the mainstream concept of a rigid production function. Rather it reflected the availability of cheap Asian labour, along with the lagged diffusion of scientific agriculture and the mores of colonial society. When socioeconomic pressures demanded higher welfare for workers, the plantation proved remarkably adaptive, especially when functioning within a developmental political state like Mauritius.

3.3.1 *Securing Labour for Colonization by Plantations and Peasant Farms*

European colonial settlement within much of the Caribbean region took off in the seventeenth century, but lagged in Trinidad and Tobago until the close of the eighteenth century. The two islands had become a Spanish colony in the sixteenth century, but remained neglected until the 1780s, when the population numbered just 2,763, three-quarters of them Amerindian (Blouet and Blouet 1982: 318). The UK annexed Trinidad in 1797 during the French wars, and encouraged plantations. Through the nineteenth century, Trinidad and Tobago, along with British Guiana, functioned as the frontier of Caribbean colonial settlement. The abolition of the slave trade in the British Empire in 1807 threatened the viability of the plantations, however. The colonial government responded by making crown lands available at low prices to settlers, including European planters fleeing Haiti. It also offered land grants to former slaves from more densely settled British islands to establish small farms alongside the white settlers (Johnson 1972: 8).

Planters in the frontier territories replaced slave labour with indentured labour, importing workers mostly from South Asia on contracts that when they expired carried the right to repatriation. Many South Asian workers eschewed the option to return home, so that indenture radically altered the ethnic mix of the population. Indenture lasted over seventy years, from 1845 to 1917, and solved the labour shortage. In doing so, it introduced 143,900 South Asian workers into Trinidad and Tobago (Niddrie 1983: 95) and helped boost the total population to 342,500 by 1921. When indenture ended, the population of Trinidad and Tobago remained evenly split between Afro-

Caribbean and South Asian.[1] Despite this major demographic change, the heyday of the plantation sustained a stratified society that concentrated political influence on a small elite, comprising leading estate owners and the more prosperous urban residents.

The vast majority of the population comprised plantation workers and small farmers on modest incomes. Sugar cane dominated the economy of Trinidad and Tobago, apart from the half century between the 1870s and 1920s when cacao became the leading crop. The prosperity of the sugar industry was threatened by the UK's steady shift towards free trade, however, which conferred: the abolition of slavery in 1834; the phased reduction in the imperial import preference on sugar through 1852–74; and competition from the vigorous expansion of sugar beet in Europe. Sugar beet increased its share of total world production from one-tenth in the early 1850s to more than half by the 1880s (Shepherd 1929: 151).

The sugar plantations developed synergies with neighbouring peasant farmers who supplemented their incomes from plantation work. Small farms steadily increased their cane production, although plantations still dominated. The share of small farmers in cane production increased from one-third during 1900–20 to around 45% by the late-1930s. Many freed slaves had saved money and they bought land. Their ranks were swelled by both immigrant freed slaves from more crowded islands and indentured workers. The latter became eligible to purchase crown land from 1869 and many did, so that a sizeable peasant class of South Indians emerged through the 1870s and 1880s. Although South Indians comprised 87% of the sugar workers by 1895, no more than one-third of them worked as indentured labour by then (Dhanda 2004).

3.3.2 Technology Initially Improves Competitiveness and then Welfare

Prices for West Indian sugar halved through 1881–96 to £11/ton, yet global competition intensified still further as the US encouraged a rapid expansion of cane production by newly independent Cuba from 345,000 tons in 1899–1900 to 5,126,000 tons by 1930. Colonial governments began accumulating losses, prompting the British Colonial Office to furnish subsidies that ultimately led to the reform of trade preferences within the UK sugar market in the late-1930s so as to encourage investment in productivity and improve competitiveness. Critically, the higher geopolitical rent was intended not only to boost profitability but also to raise the welfare of sugar workers.

---

[1] In contrast, Afro-Caribbean citizens overwhelmingly dominate in Jamaica and Barbados, which imported 748,000 slaves and 387,000 slaves, respectively (Niddrie 1983: 92).

The squeeze on sugar prices through the nineteenth century elicited changes in technology, most notably the construction of large sugar factories to capture the economies of scale, which could halve processing costs. Scientific improvements in cane growing lagged those in the factories, so that regional cane yields were below global best practice, averaging 47 tons per hectare. The British government began to subsidize research through the Imperial Department of Agriculture, which helped stabilize British West Indies sugar production at 230,000 tons annually through 1900–25. Improved technical efficiency along with the expansion of peasant cane production helped the sugar industry survive the intensified international competition in the late-nineteenth and early-twentieth century. The plantation sustained a basic existence for workers and small farmers, but without raising incomes. Social improvement was eventually triggered in response to the economic hardship of the inter-war years, however. This suggests that the low-wage, employment-maximizing plantation that dominated Trinidad and Tobago for 150 years reflected sociopolitical conditions rather than Baldwin's rigid crop production function.

Low as they were, incomes were squeezed further through the second half of the nineteenth century as the UK embraced free trade, which cut sugar prices and the associated rents. Yet sugar production proved resilient and the West Indies remained the most competitive producer within the British Empire/Commonwealth until the 1960s, more so than larger imperial producers like Australia and South Africa. The production cost in the British West Indies was 2 cents/lb in 1945, slightly above Cuba at 1.5 cents but below that of Australia (2.7 cents) and Louisiana (3.1 cents), and below sugar beet in the US and UK (over 4 cents). Nevertheless, although it was competitive, the West Indies remained among the least prosperous of sugar-growing regions. Daily wages in Trinidad in the mid-1920s ranked with those of the Philippines. The Trinidad wage of 35 cents per day compared with 85 cents in Mauritius, US$1.20 in Cuba, US$1.50 in Hawaii, and US$4.08 in Queensland.

The sustained price squeeze eventually revealed the flexibility of the plantation production function: new technology in the factories and to a lesser extent in cane farming helped boost productivity and contain costs. Estimates for the 1930s suggest that the minimum viable size of a factory was by then 5,000–10,000 tons, although many smaller factories survived by skimping on maintenance and investment, cannibalizing fossil plants, or selling specialized branded by-products, notably rum. An executive of the progressive multinational Tate and Lyle, which owned two large new factories in southern Jamaica (Monymusk and Frome), estimated that a factory capacity of 30,000 tons of sugar per year would not only earn an adequate return on capital but also raise worker welfare to match that of UK farm workers (Auty

1973: 76). The catalyst that unlocked this change was provided by civil unrest during the Great Depression of the 1930s.

3.4 Plantation Reform Inadvertently Entrenches Rent-Seeking 1935–75

For three centuries throughout the Caribbean, the plantation economy provided a minimum standard of living for the disenfranchized many. But in 1938 a British Royal Commission reported that working conditions across the West Indies had become unacceptable and proposed reform. The reform adjusted trade preferences so the geopolitical rent was high enough to attract investment that would boost worker productivity and wages. The economic reform was accompanied by a shift towards parliamentary democracy, but full implementation of the reform was delayed by World War II and formalized in the 1951 Commonwealth Sugar Agreement (CSA) (Auty 1973: 55). The initial success of the reform confirms the potential flexibility of the plantation production function and also the role of sociopolitical factors in driving change, contrary to both Baldwin and Best.

The eventual collapse of the sugar industry in Trinidad and Tobago was an unintended consequence of plantation reform. One key assumption of reform was that higher productivity would shrink the workforce and thereby render it easier to improve the welfare of the remaining workers. A second key assumption was that surplus sugar workers would be absorbed within a diversifying economy. In the event, whereas higher geopolitical rent did initially raise incomes, which continued to rise after independence, economic diversification and the growth in nonsugar employment lagged. Consequently, the labour market of Trinidad and Tobago trailed that of Mauritius in reaching its turning point, which Mauritius achieved by the early-1990s (see Chapter 5). Moreover, the welfare gains of Trinidad and Tobago proved fragile because they relied heavily on rent that was volatile. Meanwhile, the shift to parliamentary democracy was associated with rent-seeking on a scale that in Trinidad and Tobago outstripped the capacity of the sugar industry to sustain it. In fact, the economy-wide demands for rent subsequently also outstripped the much higher rent generated by the hydrocarbon-driven economy.

3.4.1 *Higher Sugar Prices Initially Boosted Both Welfare and Rent Dependence*

Colonial trade policy reform boosted worker welfare in Trinidad and Tobago prior to independence in 1962. The reforms reduced import duties on imperial/commonwealth sugar production, conferring higher prices on producers.

57

In the 1930s, most global sugar was sold within regulated markets controlled by import duties, so that only 10–15% was sold on the free market. Leading sugar importers, most notably the US and the UK, offered varying degrees of import concession to support prices, along with guarantees of market access to suppliers, depending on their political ties. One important consequence of this trade regime was to support a wider range in production costs that extended global sugar production over a wider area than a less-regulated market would allow. A second consequence was that changes in import tariffs and market access could boost revenues to producers, and also inflict sizeable revenue loss if trade privileges were withdrawn.

The CSA provided producers with security by allocating a production quota to each participating country or colony at a guaranteed price. In order to maintain efficiency incentives, however, the price was linked to the average annual costs of participating producers, which changed over time. In addition, one-third of the output was excluded from the preference and meant to be sold on the free market. In fact, Commonwealth sugar producers could sell most of their residual sugar at higher prices to Canada, and later to the US after that country broke ties with Castro's Cuba. Taking the 1930s as the base level of 100, by 1945 the sugar price had risen to 170, and then to 400 by 1956 and 450 by 1965 (Auty 1973: 142). The guaranteed sugar price triggered a surge in investment. It also prompted Caribbean governments, trade unions, and cane farmers to compete to increase their share of the expanded rent. As price rises slowed, continued rent-seeking shrank the sugar companies' flow of cash for reinvestment, including investment to boost productivity.

The CSA triggered a marked expansion of production as well as improvements in living standards. The boom boosted Jamaican annual production to regional dominance, with around 500,000 tons in 1965, more than five times the level a generation earlier and almost double the production of Trinidad and Tobago, which peaked at 255,000 tons in 1965. Total annual sugar production in the Commonwealth Caribbean increased from 400,000 tons in the early 1930s to 1.3 million tons in the mid-1960s. But output then declined to 1.1 million tons in 1974 (Smith 1976) and 800,000 tons by 2000. Trends in profitability reflected this rise and fall. Rates of return within the industry more than doubled into the mid-1950s, averaging 13.7% in Trinidad and Tobago 1955–59 and slightly less in Jamaica (Auty 1973), but the return on capital halved through the mid-1960s and turned negative thereafter.

The rent-seeking interests invariably overestimated the scale of the geopolitical rent, thereby squeezing sugar company margins. Ironically, even as dependency theorists like Beckford (1972) and Girvan (1971) castigated multinational companies for stunting domestic economic linkages in sugar and mining, the British sugar multinationals Tate and Lyle and Booker McConnell struggled to justify investment in maintaining the higher living standards of their workers. Meanwhile, many domestically owned sugar estates, notably in Jamaica, paid lower wages than the multinationals, as well as lower prices for cane, citing their uneconomic size as the reason for paying less. The net outcome was that the locally owned factories of suboptimum size made more profit per ton of sugar than the state-of-the-art multinational factories, and remained in production longer than they otherwise would have done (Auty 1973). Critically, neither set of companies earned a sufficient return to justify investment to remain competitive: they reacted to falling margins by skimping on maintenance and running their factories into the ground.

The sugar industry of Trinidad and Tobago became highly rent dependent under the CSA. The share of the rents captured by sugar workers and cane farmers inflated production costs, to the extent that the companies ceased to be viable. The CSA was not renewed in 1967, which, given the lags built into the agreement, meant it automatically lapsed in 1974, by which time the UK had joined the European Common Market. Thereafter, Commonwealth Caribbean sugar production declined through much of the region, contributing to the worsening of the economic problems that many countries experienced in the 1970s and 1980s. Unfortunately, the political economy of rent-seeking in Trinidad and Tobago survived the demise of the plantation economy thanks to windfalls from the hydrocarbon sector, which intensified the rent dependence of the economy.

3.4.2 *Investments to Boost Productivity and Welfare*

During the post-war sugar boom, the planters initially made sizeable investments to expand output and boost competitiveness. The pursuit of economies of scale remained critical as the maximum viable size of the sugar factory and also the minimum viable size both continued to increase. The rising minimum size threshold forced smaller island producers like Nevis and Antigua to abandon production entirely due to insufficient cane land. In the Commonwealth Caribbean overall, the number of sugar factories halved during the post-war boom to around fifty, and the average size of the surviving factories increased sixfold in 1930–65, rising to 25,000 tons (Auty 1976).

Smith (1976) estimated the upper size limit for sugar production at 100,000 tons by 1970, which matched the capacity of Tate and Lyle's Monymusk factory in Jamaica. In Trinidad, Tate and Lyle expanded in 1960 when it bought Caroni and acquired the Ste Madeleine factory. The company consolidated sugar production on four factories in place of eleven that had served the same cane area three decades earlier. In 1968, the Tate and Lyle factories produced 92% of the total sugar output of Trinidad and Tobago (around 220,000 tons), with Ste Madeleine and Brechin Castle each having a capacity of over 60,000 tons (Beckford 1972: 129; Smith 1976: 133).

In addition to increasing factory size, the plantations intensified cane yields and mechanized field operations. The application of scientific research to tropical farming steadily improved cane yields, which diffused out from the largest plantations that could afford to run testing laboratories. But the sugar companies faced increasing pressure to abandon their domination of cane land in favour of local farmers as democracy fed nationalism (Beckford 1972). The factories preferred, however, to grow at least half their cane so as to ensure a basic supply through price downswings, and also to control quality and yield.

The plantations were unable to take full advantage of field mechanization because trade unions exploited their links to the main political parties to oppose the import of productivity-boosting machinery. The government of Trinidad and Tobago banned imports of mechanical harvesters, for example, which could boost labour productivity sixfold. The restriction pushed field costs above those of Australia. As a result, geopolitical rents were captured to both maintain employment and boost wages at the expense of the return on capital. Smith (1976: 135) reported that wages within the Trinidad and Tobago sugar industry increased by 130% in real terms between 1963 and 1973 (the eve of the first oil price shock), while productivity measured in man-hours per ton of sugar contracted by 14% over the same period, causing a sharp escalation in real costs. The total cost of sugar production in Trinidad and Tobago more than tripled from 1965 to 1975 to reach £150 per ton (Smith 1976: 136). Jamaican costs were similar by 1975, but the Guyanese industry held the average cost to £110 per ton.

The loss of competitiveness through the late-1960s occurred despite increased factory size and field improvements and reflected pressure on governments to maintain employment. The smaller factories were run into the ground and then cannibalized for parts by surviving rivals, but even the largest factories struggled to raise productivity due to pressure for overmanning (Auty 1976). When the termination of the CSA shrank the geopolitical rent, Tate and Lyle and Booker McConnell withdrew from the Caribbean sugar industry. This forced Caribbean governments to internalize the costs of rent-seeking. In Trinidad and Tobago, the government took a 51% share of Caroni in 1970 and then outright control in 1975 (Sookraj 2011), but nationalization failed to curb rent-seeking, which came to rely upon sizeable transfers from the government's hydrocarbon rent.

3.4.3 *Political Pluralism and Rent Extraction*

Political change precipitated by the hardship of the Great Depression witnessed the rapid evolution of the plantation from employment maximizer to productivity maximizer and then rent extractor. Radical change in the politics of Trinidad and Tobago was set in motion by World War I. The origin of political parties lay in the return of local soldiers from fighting, which led to the emergence of trade unions to lobby for improved working conditions (US Library of Congress 2011). Led by a moderate, a Captain Cipriani, the initial demands included a minimum wage, an eight-hour day, limitation on the use of child labour, compulsory education, heavier taxation of international oil companies, and broad-based social reform. In 1925 Cipriani became one of the six elected members of the twenty-five-man state legislature (only 6% of the adult population had the vote) and served as mayor of the second city, San Fernando, on several occasions. In 1934 he converted the Trinidad Working Man's Association into the Trinidad Labour Party, which boasted 125,000 members by 1936.

Deteriorating economic conditions through the Great Depression intensified poverty, sparking civil disturbances that turned into rioting in 1937. Political change accelerated: in 1941 the constitution was reformed to make the elected members in the legislature into the majority. The first election under universal suffrage was held in 1946, although barely half the electorate took part (Trinidad and Tobago News 2003). Universal suffrage consolidated the political parties' links to either rural (plantation) or urban (civil service) trade unions, which vied to boost their members' welfare. The cost pressures exerted by urban unions, which were mostly in the service sector and especially the civil service, could ostensibly be passed on more easily through the domestic economy than those from rural workers, who faced international competition. The sugar companies sought to maximize the industry's return from the British government commitment to improving welfare within the region. They citied union pressure when initially bargaining for higher prices and therefore for higher rent at CSA price reviews.

The two leading political parties in Trinidad and Tobago became ethnically aligned in the 1950s: the Afro-oriented People's National Movement (PNM) and an Indian-oriented party, most recently the United National Congress (UNC). Neither ethnic group was in a majority, a condition that spurred them to bid for support from opposite ethnic groups and from minority groups in order to build viable coalitions. The political debate therefore sought to maximize votes by favouring special interests and downplaying ideological and class values. In 1956 the PNM secured sufficient support to form the first party-based government. The PNM represented urban society and had strong links with unions in the public sector and manufacturing. At independence in 1962 the PNM prioritized urban development and industrialization by import substitution. In contrast, the party in parliamentary opposition favoured rural development, which reflected its reliance on Indian groups and the agricultural unions. As the two main parties vied to form a majority government, splinter parties formed around charismatic leaders to secure patronage for particular social groups.

Nevertheless, the PNM won six consecutive elections and governed the country from 1956 to 1986, led by an academic, Eric Williams, until his death in 1981. The PNM oversaw independence from the UK in 1962 and the establishment of a republic within the Commonwealth in 1976. Trinidad and Tobago gained independence as an ethnically mixed parliamentary democracy. Around 39.5% of the population comprised Afro-Caribbean people, mostly descendants of freed slave *immigrants* from other UK territories. They resided mainly in the urban north-west, extending east from Port of Spain. Some 40% of the population was descended from Indian indentured workers, who mainly resided in the former sugar belt of western Trinidad and worked in agriculture and business. Barely 19% of the Indian population was urbanized at independence compared with 50% of Afro-Caribbean people (Owolabe 2007: 15). Finally, some 17% of the population was mixed, leaving 3% Syrians, Europeans (dominating finance), and Chinese (World Bank 1999).

Closer inspection reveals subgroups in each of the two main ethnic groups. For example, the Indians are roughly divided by religion into Hindu plantation workers and more urban-oriented Muslim and Presbyterian groups. Among the Afro-Trinidadians, Meighoo (2008) identified four geographical subgroups, namely 'Afro-Saxons' (dominating the east–west urban axis from Port of Spain), Grenadians (mainly oil-sector workers), Afro-Tobagon small farmers, and Garveyites (Black Power activists). The remaining 'mixed' and smaller groups add further possible permutations to the process of political coalition building. Meighoo (2008: 122) noted that one important consequence of ethnic diversity is that ideology plays little part in elections. After the demise of the PNM in the mid-1980s, contests to access patronage grew increasingly corrupting. Table 3.1 shows that control of corruption deteriorated through 1996–2015, although the rise in income might be expected to see control strengthen.

The majoritarian nature of democracy in Trinidad and Tobago encouraged ethnic voting (Owolabe 2007), unlike in Mauritius where the elite embraced inclusive government through proportional representation and grand coalitions (Auty 2010). The PNM sustained its dominance throughout 1956–86 by co-opting elements of the urbanized East Indian community, notably Presbyterian Indians (Owolabe 2007). Politicians in Trinidad and Tobago arguably showed little concern for allocating cabinet posts to achieve ethnic balance, which became a source of friction. Yet despite the contrasting urban/rural focus of the two basic parties, a statist consensus prevailed until the 1980s.

Table 3.1 Institutional quality, 2015, comparative case study countries

Country	Per capita GDP (US PPP)	Voice and account-ability	Political stability	Effective governance	Regulation quality	Rule of law	Control of corruption	Aggregate index
Uganda	1,777	-0.6	-0.8	-0.5	-0.3	-0.4	-1.1	-3.7
India	6,139	0.4	-0.9	0.1	-0.4	0.0	-0.4	-1.2
Brazil	15,647	0.5	-0.3	-0.2	-0.2	-0.1	-0.4	-0.7
Mauritius	20,126	0.8	1.0	1.0	1.1	0.9	0.3	5.1
Chile	23,579	1.0	0.4	1.1	1.3	1.3	1.3	6.4
Trinidad and Tobago	33,377	0.5	0.3	0.2	0.2	-0.1	-0.3	0.8
South Korea	34,421	0.6	0.2	1.0	1.1	0.9	0.4	4.2
Saudi Arabia	54,118	-1.8	-0.6	0.2	0.0	0.1	0.1	-2.0
Memo item								
Mauritius 1996	6,868	0.9	1.1	0.2	-0.1	0.9	0.0	3.0
Trinidad and Tobago 1996	10,210	0.7	0.3	-0.1	0.6	0.5	0.9	2.0

PPP, purchasing power parity.

Source: World Bank (2017a). Each index ranges from 2.5 to –2.5 and is based on several surveys in each country.

3.5 Post-1975 Collapse of Plantation Agriculture

3.5.1 *Oil Windfalls Exacerbated Dutch Disease Effects*

The 1974–78 and 1979–81 oil price hikes sharply boosted hydrocarbon rent and consolidated the dominance of the hydrocarbon sector in the economy of Trinidad and Tobago. The positive oil shocks each expanded hydrocarbon rent by one-third of nonmining GDP annually and intensified the Dutch disease effects (Auty and Gelb 1986). Unlike plantation agriculture, the oil sector generated relatively few jobs directly, despite its sizeable revenues. On the eve of the oil shocks, with sugar in decline, hydrocarbon extraction and refining accounted for almost three-quarters of exports, one-fifth of government revenue, and one-fifth of GDP, but barely 1% of employment (Gelb and Associates 1988). Within the nonoil sector, agriculture (mostly sugar) contributed just 6% of GDP and manufacturing 22%, but half of manufacturing output comprised petroleum refining and the rest was manufacturing that was protected. The expected size of the tradeable sector for a small economy at the income level of Trinidad and Tobago was 42% of GDP, so the actual size (28% of GDP) was two-thirds of the norm. But even that low ratio is flattering because by then more than half of the tradeable actively was, like sugar, uncompetitive at world prices. Trinidad and Tobago therefore exhibited strong Dutch disease effects.

The government used the windfall oil revenues of the 1970s to accelerate its economic diversification strategy of state-led resource-based industrialization. It also deployed oil rent to complete the nationalization of the sugar industry in 1976. It planned to use Caroni to diversify agriculture and maximize rural employment until resource-based industry attracted sufficient downstream manufacturing to absorb surplus labour. As Chapter 4 explains, the resource-based industry included a state-owned steel mill based on directly reduced iron ore and joint-venture petrochemical plants producing ammonia fertilizer and methanol. These were capital-intensive activities although steel was expected to attract private investment in manufacturing more labour-intensive steel-based products further downstream (Auty and Gelb 1986). Unfortunately, the industrialization drive was associated with the overrapid absorption of the oil windfall, which triggered inflation, undermined investment efficiency, and established unsustainable subsidies and social entitlements. The windfall expenditure therefore further heightened Dutch disease effects and triggered a growth collapse from 1981 to 1993 (Table 3.2).

The growth collapse unseated the long-serving PNM government in 1986 and ushered in a period of political instability and constitutional crisis. The PNM won just three seats in the thirty-six-seat parliament of 1986. Owolabe (2007) argued that the end of PNM dominance rekindled competitive politics and ethnic voting. Yet the incoming government in 1986 comprised a loose

Table 3.2 Selected economic indicators, Trinidad and Tobago, 1960–2014

	1960–64	1965–69	1970–74	1975–79	1980–84	1985–89	1990–94	1995–99	2000–04	2005–09	2010–14
Rent proxies											
Total natural resource rent (% GNI)	n.a.	n.a.	3.4	17.5	15.6	10.7	10.9	8.3	11.4	18.9	16.4
Oil rent (% GNI)	n.a.	n.a.	3.3	17.2	14.9	9.7	9.6	6.9	7.5	9.1	6.9
Natural gas rent (% GNI)	n.a.	n.a.	0.0	0.3	0.7	1.0	1.2	1.4	3.8	9.9	9.5
Regulatory rent (% GNI)	n.a.	n.a	n.a.	n.a.	n.a.	n.a.	n.a	n.a.	n.a.	n.a.	n.a.
Remittances (% GNI)	n.a.	n.a	0.0	0.0	0.1	0.0	0.2	0.6	0.7	0.5	0.5
Net ODA received (% GNI)	1.0	1.2	0.5	0.2	0.1	0.3	0.2	0.4	0.0	0.0	0.0
Arable land per head (ha)[1]	0.1	0.1	0.1	0.1	0.0	0.0	0.0	0.0	0.0	0.0	0.0
Economy openness											
Exports (% GDP)	65.3	46.7	45.2	49.5	38.2	36.4	41.6	50.5	54.2	65.9	65.8
FDI (% GDP)	n.a.	n.a.	8.1	3.5	2.4	1.0	5.4	10.1	8.7	5.6	-1.3
Terms of trade[2]	n.a.	n.a.	n.a.	n.a.	155.6	97.4	n.a.	n.a.	100.9	135.1	142.0
REER[3]	n.a.	81.0	74.8	75.6	98.7	92.3	76.5	67.8	74.9	83.4	106.7
Absorption (% GNP)											
Fixed capital	25.8	20.0	24.3	24.1	26.6	18.2	15.4	25.5	22.2	17.5	12.2
Final government consumption	11.1	12.0	14.1	12.9	17.0	19.7	16.6	15.2	12.8	11.4	12.8
Household consumption	60.5	62.7	54.2	48.3	55.9	59.0	56.4	55.1	53.1	43.0	50.6
Structural change (% GDP)											
Agriculture	n.a.	n.a	n.a.	n.a	2.6	2.9	2.6	2.2	2.0	0.5	0.5
Industry	n.a.	n.a	n.a.	n.a	45.3	41.7	46.9	44.4	50.4	61.1	54.2
Manufacturing	n.a.	n.a	n.a.	n.a	9.2	10.8	10.3	8.4	7.7	5.4	5.9
Services	n.a.	n.a	n.a.	n.a	52.0	55.4	50.6	53.4	48.4	38.4	45.3
Growth											
Per capita GDP (US$, 2000)	5,719	6,647	7,431	8,721	9,138	6,989	6,543	7,953	11,323	15,969	16,763
GDP growth (%/year)	7.5	2.9	3.2	6.1	-1.5	-3.3	0.9	7.1	8.3	4.6	1.3
Per capita GDP growth (%/year)	5.8	2.2	1.9	4.6	-3.3	-4.3	0.1	6.8	7.8	4.2	0.8
Population growth (%/year)	1.7	0.8	1.2	1.4	1.6	1.0	0.6	0.2	0.4	0.5	0.5
Crop output index[4]	213.1	225.0	218.2	189.2	134.3	120.2	138.5	131.0	115.2	89.2	60.8

n.a., Not applicable; GNI, Gross national income; ODA, official development assistance; FDI, foreign direct investment; REER, real effective exchange rate; GNP, gross national product.
[1] Cropland rent 2014 (% GDP) = 0.1 (Lange et al. 2018).
[2] 2000 = 100.
[3] 2010 = 100.
[4] 2004–06 = 100.

Source: World Bank (2017a).

coalition of four opposition parties in the multiethnic National Alliance for Reconstruction (NAR) under a Tobagonian named A.N.R. Robinson. It launched a stabilization and structural adjustment programme that through 1988–94 required reform of both trade policy and fiscal policy, including a cut in public expenditure from 56% of nonenergy GDP to 36%. However, the reforms lagged due to the inertia of rent-seeking and labour market rigidity. The state directly employed one-quarter of the workforce, while subsidized agriculture and industry employed a further one-fifth. This shielded almost half the total workforce from competitive pressures to boost productivity (World Bank 1999). The reluctance of successive governments to withdraw protection and reduce subsidies, notably in agriculture, reflected fears of unemployment (Rajapatirana 2001). Meanwhile, the slow pace of reform shrank foreign exchange reserves to US$0.2 billion by 1992 compared with US$3.4 billion a decade earlier (Artana et al. 2006).

The economic retrenchment that did occur strained the NAR coalition. In 1988, the Indian faction led by Basdeo Panday withdrew its support after a cabinet reshuffle reduced its share of ministries (Owolabe 2007). The NAR government was weakened and virtually eliminated in elections in 1991, which returned the PNM to power until 1995. The economic recovery finally commenced (see Table 3.2) after a 25% real exchange rate depreciation in 1993 but mainly through a sustained expansion of foreign investment in natural gas. In 1995, Panday became the first Indo-Trinidadian prime minister as leader of the Hindu-dominated UNC government, but he also relied on the support of the rump NAR and subsequently two defectors from the PNM. Panday wooed Afro-Trinidadian and Chinese businessmen who had previously mistrusted his statist attitude. Such manoeuvring for political support to retain power fed suspicions of corruption (Economist 2000), which is not unexpected in the presence of a rent-fuelled state sector.

3.5.2 Rent-Seeking Inertia

Notwithstanding the political dynamics, flaws in rent deployment lay at the root of failure to competitively diversify the economy of Trinidad and Tobago. Both governments and unions underestimated the extent to which firms were constrained by international competition. They pursued higher tax revenues and wages, respectively, which squeezed company returns and threatened their survival. As in other rent-driven economies, private firms responded by minimizing investment outside the hydrocarbon sector (Warner 2015). The sugar industry was deemed too large an employer to shut down, so the government nationalized it. However, the sugar industry unions knew that the size of the workforce conferred political clout and continued to resist the productivity-enhancing change that was required to achieve viability in order to limit redundancy.

The accelerating costs of the sugar industry collided with softening real prices on global markets, which fell by one-third during 1975–2003. By the early-2000s only three global producers sold sugar at unsubsidized prices, namely Cuba, Brazil, and Australia, which were responsible for one-fifth of world output and 40% of exports. Following the expiry of the CSA, sugar producers in the Commonwealth Caribbean were initially insulated by the Lome Convention of 1975, which conferred preferential access to the European Union (EU) market for 1.3 million tons of sugar, allocating a share to each producer with previous colonial links to EU members. During 1970–2005 the world price fluctuated around 5–15 cents/lb (apart from brief spikes to 30 cents in 1974 and 1981) compared with the EU price range between 16 and 30 cents/lb, usually above 25 cents after 1990. Quota allocations were adjusted downwards where countries failed to meet their commitments (Mitchell 2005).

Sugar unions and cane farmers in Trinidad and Tobago pushed wages and prices above what the geopolitical rent could sustain. This was not inevitable and depended on the dynamics of the political economy, as Mauritius shows (see Chapter 5). The state-owned sugar industry of Trinidad and Tobago continued to face damaging strikes and high absenteeism. Labour became difficult to secure for onerous tasks like cane cutting, entailing increased reliance on temporary migrant labour. Yet governments throughout the region resisted closing their sugar industries because of the contribution to exports and above all employment. Under the 1978–83 Caroni rationalization plan, the government of Trinidad and Tobago consolidated sugar on one large state-owned mill, while also diversifying some plantation land into prawns, large and small ruminants, and rice. The unions were concerned that diversification would reduce the significance of sugar, and hence dilute their bargaining power.

Further problems arose because sugar company staff lacked expertise in the new crops. Trinidad and Tobago's state-owned agricultural firm failed to generate profits during its entire three decades of operation and underwent further restructuring in the mid-2000s. Mitchell (2005) calculated that importer preferences conferred sugar prices 60% above the world price, yet within the Commonwealth Caribbean only Guyana and Belize were capable of competing without extra subsidies. In Trinidad and Tobago the restructured state-owned business operated like a nucleus plantation: it undertook to purchase cane from around 6,000 private cane farmers. The farmers produced sugar cane under contract on land that they owned or else leased back from the sugar company. However, Palmer and Pemberton (2007) estimated that the disappointing average cane yield of 52.5 tons per hectare reflected the fact that 99% of farms were below the minimum efficient size (13 hectares). The sugar factory had 80,000 tons capacity, sufficient to capture the economies of scale, but restructuring cost US$240 million (Mitchell 2005) and the accumulated debt of Caroni was around US$540 million.

In 2005, the sugar support systems came under pressure from WTO rulings for being in breach of earlier trade agreements. This prompted the EU to cut the support price by 39% over two years, a move that finally terminated sugar production in Trinidad and Tobago. The bold post-war strategy of setting sugar prices to attract the investment required in order to sustain rising productivity and incomes had failed. In 1945, the sugar industry of Trinidad and Tobago had ranked among the most competitive global producers. Sixty years later, rent-seeking had inflated its costs to some 250% above the most competitive world producers. The closure of the sugar industry of Trinidad and Tobago in 2007 retrenched 9,000 workers, while a further 35,000 were believed to be indirectly dependent on the industry. The closure released over 30,350 hectares of land, often for urban development (Palmer and Pemberton 2007).

3.6 Incomplete Transition to Productivity-Driven Development

The plantation spearheaded the rapid expansion of settlement in the frontier economy of nineteenth-century Trinidad and Tobago. It also spawned ethnic diversity when the predicted collapse of the plantation after the abolition of slavery was averted by tapping the Asian labour surplus through the indenture system. In switching from an initial reliance on slave labour to the indenture system, the plantation established a multiethnic society without damaging social cohesion. The nineteenth-century plantation was paternalistic and rested on an unstated social bargain whereby it provided a basic living for the majority of the islands' workers.

The plantation economy is more complex than Best (1968) allows for three main reasons. First, small farming introduced a cheap and flexible labour supply that facilitated adjustment to changing markets. Second, the plantation production function proved more pliable than either Best or Baldwin assumed, capturing the economies of scale in the sugar factories from the nineteenth century and subsequently boosting cane yields. Third, Best accuses multinational corporations of perpetuating dependency, whereas they aspired to be agents of socioeconomic improvement within the sugar industry. Rather, a more convincing explanation for the reformed plantation's eventual inability to sustain rising welfare than either external dependence or an inflexible production function is provided by political drivers, namely competition for rent.

The social bargain of nineteenth-century plantation society unravelled in the inter-war years when depressed commodity prices exacerbated poverty and triggered social unrest. Riots prompted the UK to raise sugar prices through the 1940s in order to replace the managed poverty of the paternalistic plantation with improved welfare for a smaller workforce based on rising productivity in globally competitive agribusinesses. The welfare reforms were funded by higher and more stable geopolitical rent, enshrined in the CSA, which initially encouraged investment in productivity that boosted labour welfare as the colonial administration intended. The multinational companies espoused more socially progressive policies than most locally owned plantations.

However, the political reform that accompanied economic reform generated unintended consequences in Trinidad and Tobago. The need for governments to build coalitions encouraged rent-seeking that motivated parliamentarians to prioritize immediate electoral success at the expense of long-term economic growth. The political and trade policy reforms spurred by the Great Depression intensified rent-seeking, which was supported by the unions, whether in the sugar estates, cane farms, government bureaucracy, or protected manufacturing sector. One important consequence of rent-seeking was to insulate a high fraction of the workforce from immediate pressure to boost productivity that an effectively functioning market economy would not sustain.

The failure of the plantation to maintain productivity-driven development in Trinidad and Tobago was not inevitable, however, as the rest of Section 2 illustrates. Chapter 4 shows how Trinidad and Tobago's hydrocarbon rent deployment served to heighten rent dependence rather than reduce it. Chapter 5 explains the more successful development trajectory of low-rent Mauritius, which diversified into productivity-driven economic growth and maintained a large and robust sugar industry. Mauritius also made steady but sustained gains in welfare that partially closed the income gap with Trinidad and Tobago and proved more stable. Finally, Mauritius suggests how policy reform in Trinidad and Tobago might build a political consensus to reduce rent dependence.

4

The Staple Trap in High-Rent Trinidad and Tobago

4.1 Gas-Based Industrialization as a Development Strategy

Like most developing country governments, the first independent government of Trinidad and Tobago prioritized industrialization by import substitution rather than by exporting manufactured goods. However, it soon switched to gas-based industry exports in line with the economy's emerging comparative advantage. Gas-based industry is capital-intensive, but investment in the downstream processing of basic metals and petrochemicals is more labour-intensive. The government of Trinidad and Tobago deployed some of the windfall revenue from the 1973–78 oil shock to increase the scale of gas-based industry. However, the fact that numerous other energy-exporting countries did the same led to global overcapacity and outcomes were invariably disappointing (Auty 1990). This chapter explains why Trinidad and Tobago's industrial strategy also disappointed, and in doing so it provides a detailed case study of the staple trap trajectory, which the majority of high-rent developing countries traced, whether energy-rich or not.

Although the *economic* policies required to deploy commodity windfall rents have long been understood, governments have struggled to manage political pressure for overrapid domestic rent absorption (Gelb and Associates 1988). Fundamentally, the rent should be deployed to diversify the economy away from dependence upon the rent-generating assets, so that welfare gains are driven by rising productivity, rather than by increases in the rent stream, which are likely to prove ephemeral. More recently, the emergence of environmental accounting (World Bank 2011) has reinforced this basic rationale for rent deployment. The rent should be deployed to accumulate the economic infrastructure, human capital, and institutional capital that a modern economy requires. Investment in these assets will facilitate economic diversification and drive productivity growth through the long term, both of which are required to sustain rising living standards as the rent, whatever its source, eventually declines (Clarke 2011).

There are four critical policy requirements to incentivize investment in the diversification of a high-rent economy. First, as noted above, sufficient rent should be invested to help build the stocks of economic infrastructure and human capital through the long term. Second, part of the rent should be sterilized in an offshore account to help insulate macroeconomic policy from revenue volatility. The rate of accumulation of offshore revenue during booms is governed by rules to provide a buffer that can be drawn down to smooth adjustment to revenue shortfalls. Third, the rate of domestic rent absorption should not exceed the absorptive capacity of the economy, so as to minimize Dutch disease effects. Fourth, investment in competitive activity of increasing sophistication should be encouraged in order to steadily reduce rent dependence.

The permanent income hypothesis provides guidelines for the sustainable management of public finances in a rent-driven economy (Segura 2006). In the case of mineral rent, the approach converts the projected revenue into a stock of capital and estimates the annual income stream that the natural capital stock can generate. The annual return determines the upper limit of the fiscal deficit that the nonmining economy can sustain indefinitely. Unfortunately, the policy is easier to identify than it is to pursue, given the political pressures on governments to spend more. Most resource-rich governments struggle to manage political contests for rent, which exert pressure for over-rapid domestic absorption of the rent (Gelb and Associates 1988). Political goals may therefore override economic ones, even for a government with strong development priorities.

To promote economic diversification, governments need to provide an enabling environment for investors not only by expanding infrastructure and human capital but also by identifying and correcting market failure. These measures also reduce scope for rent-seeking and strengthen the lobby for prudent macroeconomic policy that avoids overrapid rent absorption and associated inflation, and thereby sustains a competitive exchange rate. All too often in high-rent economies, private investment flows overseas or into non-tradeable domestic activity that is protected from external competition. Warner (2015) confirmed that mineral booms tend to be associated with weak private investment in nonstaple tradeable activity.

In this context, Trinidad and Tobago illustrates since independence in 1962 the challenges to effective rent deployment; the mechanism of the staple trap trajectory; and the inertia of rent-seeking activity. The rest of this chapter follows the development trajectory and is structured as follows. Section 4.2 estimates the scale of the rent, which exhibited sizeable fluctuations and governed economic performance. It also assesses the initial conditions for economic development in Trinidad and Tobago on the eve of the oil shocks. Section 4.3 describes and evaluates the overrapid deployment of the two oil rent windfalls of 1974–78 and 1979–81. The subsequent protracted growth collapse of 1981–93 is examined in Section 4.4. Section 4.5 explains the eventual economic recovery and liquefied natural gas (LNG) boom of 2004–08, and assesses the extent to which policy lessons were learned. Section 4.6 concludes: we argue that a strategy of gas-based industrialization provides a minimal diversification from rent dependence and exerts strong inertia that impedes reform.

4.2 Inauspicious Initial Conditions for Effective Rent Deployment

This section applies rent cycling theory to demonstrate that Trinidad and Tobago was highly vulnerable to rent curse effects. This was partly because the scale of the hydrocarbon reserves conferred a relatively high ratio of rent/GDP, which moreover, being mineral rent, was strongly concentrated on a handful of economic agents, notably the government, and potentially volatile. This jeopardized macroeconomic stability by increasing the likelihood of inefficient rent deployment compared with modest rents and a more dispersed distribution. Further vulnerability arose from an ethnically diverse society, youthful democracy, and interventionist economy policies.

4.2.1 *Scale of the Hydrocarbon Rent*

Commercial hydrocarbon production commenced in Trinidad and Tobago in 1908 based initially on onshore oil fields. A small refinery was completed in 1912, which helped to fuel the British Navy during World War I. Exploration steadily increased the hydrocarbon reserves, revealing that Trinidad and Tobago lies at the edge of hydrocarbon fields that extend eastwards from northern Venezuela. Most of the fields lie offshore and require elaborate technology to extract the resources. By 2004 exploration had boosted the total proven reserves of hydrocarbons to an estimated 4.5 billion barrels of oil equivalent. Of this, oil comprised just 17% and natural gas most of the rest. The total reserves double in size if probable and possible reserves are included (IMF 2005a: 3).

Oil production initially dominated and output peaked in 1978 at 230,000 bl/d (barrels per day), when it generated 30% of GDP. By 2003 oil output had declined to 134,000 bl/d, however, as fields matured and new oil discoveries initially disappointed (IMF 2005a). The International Monetary Fund (IMF) (2007) projects that oil production will stabilize at around 125,000 bl/d and then abruptly cease around 2042. The reserves of natural gas are much larger, but their accelerated exploitation implies that annual gas production peaked in 2010 at around 44.8 billion m^3/d and on current trends is likely to cease, possibly abruptly around 2025 (BP 2014) based on proved reserves only. The reserve and production projections could be underestimated, however, because barely half the potential geological reservoirs have been explored. On the other hand, costly investment in exploration may be discouraged by technological innovation like fracking, which exerts downward pressure on global natural gas prices.

Each of the three hydrocarbon booms that Trinidad and Tobago experienced (1974–78, 1979–81, and 2004–08) generated rent that was substantial relative to the size of the economy. The revenue/GDP ratio was significantly higher than that of most oil exporters, excluding those in the Gulf. The 1973–74 price shock coincided with a two-thirds expansion in hydrocarbon production in Trinidad and Tobago. It conferred windfall revenues during 1974–78 that, relative to nonenergy GDP,[1] were larger than those of the five comparator countries studied by Gelb and Associates (1988), which comprise Algeria, Ecuador, Indonesia, Nigeria, and Venezuela. Through 1974–78 the hydrocarbon windfall conferred an extra 39% of nonenergy GDP annually on Trinidad and Tobago. The 1979–81 boom reflected a doubling of the oil price, but was shorter than the first boom. It conferred windfall revenue equivalent to an extra 35% of nonenergy GDP annually on top of the previous rise. The two shocks combined reflected an eightfold gain in the oil price through 1973–79.

Data from the IMF (2009) indicate the third hydrocarbon boom of 2004–08 owed more to price effects (three-fifths) than volume effects (two-fifths) and exceeded the two earlier booms in relative size. A massive expansion of natural gas production quadrupled annual output through 1998–2008 to reach 42 billion m^3/d. In addition, oil production briefly reversed its long-term decline to average 166,000 bl/d during 2005–07 compared with 134,000 bl/d in 1998 (BP 2017), while the average price of oil increased almost 2.5-fold comparing 2004–08 with 1999–2003 and spiked at US$98/bl in 2008. The combined effect of the expansion in hydrocarbon production and the sharp rise in energy prices almost doubled the share of energy rent in GDP in 2004–08 compared with 1999–2003, and trebled it compared with the cyclical

---

[1] Nonenergy GDP is used to measure changes in the relative size of rent and its impacts because the nonenergy economy is assumed to be the 'normal' or 'long-term' economy and the finite mineral sector is viewed as a temporary phenomenon. The critical index is therefore the response of nonenergy GDP to fluctuations in energy sector revenue. In addition, nonenergy GDP gives a constant reference against which to measure fluctuations in energy rents and their impacts, whereas if GDP is used as the benchmark it too balloons along with the windfall rent, so both the baseline and the rent would be fluid.

low point of 1995–99. The windfall revenue amounted to an extra US$6.1 billion (TT$38.2 billion) annually, which conferred additional revenue equivalent to 59.3% of nonenergy GDP annually, or an extra 32.1% of total GDP per annum (Table 4.1).

4.2.2 Prospects for Effective Rent Deployment

Rent-cycling theory suggests that initial conditions at independence posed significant risks of rent mismanagement for Trinidad and Tobago. To recap briefly, the theory suggests that the risks of rent curse effects are heightened: (i) the higher the share of rent in GDP, which feeds elite contests for rent extraction (Auty 2001); (ii) the more concentrated the rent is on a few economic agents, which facilitates elite rent-seeking (Isham et al. 2005); (iii) the greater the reliance on statist economic policies, which amplifies scope for rent extraction and revenue misallocation (Krueger 1992); (iv) the higher the level of ethnic diversity, which boosts the share of rent deployed for patronage (Montalvo and Reynal-Querol 2005: 294); (v) the smaller the size of the domestic economy, which constrains economic diversification options (Alesina et al. 2005; Jorgensen 2013); and (vi) the less mature the democracy, which boosts the share of rent deployed to secure election votes (Collier and Hoeffler 2009).

Montalvo and Reynal-Querol (2005: 294) found ethnicity to be negatively associated with the rate of investment, the rate of economic growth, and the quality of government. Ethnic diversity within a democracy heightens the likelihood that promises made to secure votes in electoral contests will skew investment and expenditure away from an allocation that optimizes economic growth. Universal goods and services, like education and health expenditure that confer economy-wide benefits, tend to be undersupplied in favour of expenditure on projects that can be targeted at electoral groups in specific locations solely in order to win political support.

In addition, increased state intervention through public ownership and higher public expenditure is likely to lower investment efficiency and increase scope for corruption compared with allocation by the private sector within well-regulated competitive markets. Finally, Gaddy and Ickes (2010) argued that countries like Trinidad and Tobago risk a particularly intense form of the rent curse since the challenging initial conditions are compounded by what they define as rent addiction. The adverse outcomes are not inevitable, however. Assessments of how successfully Trinidad and Tobago has managed to expand its hydrocarbon rents (Furlonge and Kaiser 2010) and deploy them to raise welfare range from a model of development to yet another victim of the resource curse (Gelb and Associates 1988).

Table 4.1 Impact of the LNG boom, Trinidad and Tobago, 1999–2008

	Pre-boom						Boom			
	1999	2000	2001	2002	2003	2004	2005	2006	2007	2008
Hydrocarbon output										
Oil price (US$/bl)	18.0	28.2	24.3	25.0	28.9	37.8	53.4	64.3	71.1	97.5
Oil output (million bl/d)	141	138	135	155	164	152	171	174	154	139
Gas output (bcf/d)	1.1	1.5	1.6	1.9	2.6	2.9	3.2	3.9	4.1	4.0
Revenue (TT$ billion)										
Total revenue	10.14	12.16	14.20	13.86	17.35	20.63	29.65	38.91	40.06	55.58
Nonenergy	8.85	8.84	9.21	10.55	10.63	12.14	14.03	14.84	17.34	23.43
Energy	1.17	3.30	4.95	3.27	6.72	8.48	15.61	24.07	22.69	32.11
Royalties	0.52	0.58	0.75	0.61	1.01	1.09	1.23	1.68	1.68	1.85
Corporation tax	0.48	2.46	3.77	2.18	5.03	6.52	12.64	19.98	18.52	27.57
Other	0.17	0.26	0.43	0.48	0.68	0.77	1.74	2.41	2.49	2.69
Memo items (TT$ billion)										
GDP	42.89	51.37	55.00	56.29	71.17	82.65	100.39	122.11	137.43	151.36
Nonenergy GDP	32.98	35.49	39.39	41.31	45.69	51.16	54.16	61.75	73.75	79.85
Energy GDP	9.64	16.07	15.56	14.77	25.61	32.34	46.19	60.05	62.90	70.45

Source: BP (2017); IMF (2009).

4.3 Overrapid Domestic Rent Absorption 1974–81

The abrupt onset of the 1974–81 boom in hydrocarbon rent prompted most oil-exporting governments to make overoptimistic assumptions about both the duration of the windfall and their capacity to deploy it effectively (Gelb Associates 1988). Consistent with the staple trap model (Table 2.2), most governments absorbed their rent too rapidly, albeit with rare exceptions like Indonesia and Malaysia (Auty 1990), which fearful of destabilization by large rural populations diffused the rent more widely through their economies. More usually, government policies triggered Dutch disease effects that weakened the nonenergy tradeables sector and established social entitlements that were politically difficult to scale back. When the rent stream shrank in the 1980s, governments struggled to close their fiscal deficits and to tame inflation. Most economies experienced protracted growth collapses that slashed real incomes and invariably required international financial institution (IFI) assistance with economic stabilization. Trinidad and Tobago was no exception.

4.3.1 Domestic Rent Absorption 1974–81

Trinidad and Tobago initially diverged from the high-rent staple trap model in terms of elite incentives, having more in common at that stage with the competitive diversification model (Table 2.2). This is because the modest oil reserves encouraged caution, so that the government under Eric Williams functioned initially as a developmental political state, having both the aim of raising welfare and the autonomy to achieve it. The government reduced the production risks by relying on international oil companies (IOCs) to develop the offshore hydrocarbon reserves. Both exploration and exploitation required sophisticated technology, which together with remoteness from major markets demanded expertise and capital on a scale that was too much for a small country. Recourse to IOCs almost certainly lifted the efficiency of physical production compared with reliance on a national oil company.

The government made a propitious start with rent deployment. It built a pro-growth political consensus around gas-based industrialization and provided annual reports on public expenditure to boost transparency (Ministry of Finance 1980). However, development policy became more nationalist and interventionist in response to an extra-parliamentary challenge to the government in 1970 by black youths protesting at unemployment. The government responded quickly to the 1974–78 oil windfall by expanding its state-led strategy of gas-based industrialization to accelerate economic growth, speed diversification, and increase domestic employment (Mottley 2008).Thereafter, the economic trajectory increasingly conformed to the staple trap model

(Table 2.2). Although the polity remained pluralistic despite another extra-parliamentary challenge, corruption increased as per capita income rose, whereas it would be expected to fall (Table 2.2).

Gelb and Associates (1988) estimated that some 70% of the 1974–78 wind-fall was saved abroad by the Williams government. This pushed international reserves to US$1.8 billion and subsequently to a peak of US$3.4 billion around 1981. But the scale of domestic rent absorption then increased through the second (1979–81) windfall, when barely half of it was saved abroad. Dutch disease effects intensified and the industrialization strategy encountered implementation problems, but the government failed to slow the rate of rent absorption. Instead, as in many oil-exporting countries, the second rent windfall was deployed to accelerate struggling investment projects and boost consumer subsidies to maintain electoral support. The 1979–81 windfall proved unexpectedly short-lived, however, and the subsequent price down-swing triggered growth collapses in most oil-exporting countries.

4.3.2 Composition of Rent Deployment

Of the 30% of the 1974–78 windfall that was absorbed into the domestic economy of Trinidad and Tobago, some 12% was allocated to investment and 18% to consumption (Gelb and Associates 1988). Approximately half the domestic investment went into infrastructure and just under one-third into gas-based industry. Much of the rest went to expand state ownership, which included the nationalization of some existing hydrocarbon operations like the Shell oil refinery. Instead of restructuring the sugar industry to restore competitiveness, the government nationalized it and subsidized it from hydrocarbon rent to maintain rural employment. The rate of domestic rent absorption had already been too high towards the close of the 1974–78 boom and expanded through the second boom, accelerating inflation, which further reduced investment efficiency.

The selection of gas-based industry prioritized domestic value added rather than the efficient use of resources, aiming to limit the scale of 'unprocessed' commodity exports. Stauffer (1975) criticized gas-based industrialization into metals and petrochemicals as counter-productive. He estimated that the rent from gas, when expressed per unit of heat value is far less than the rent from oil because gas incurs far higher transport costs per unit of heat value than oil. Transporting gas is more expensive whether the gas is shipped by pipeline, LNG tanker, or as metals and petrochemicals. The rent component is a residual within the price, so a higher transport cost for gas per unit of heat value shrinks the rent component, compared with oil exports which are far cheaper to ship. Moreover, by displacing metal and petrochemical production in industrial countries, which often used imported oil to fuel their factories, the gas-based exports effectively substituted sales of low-rent gas in industrial country markets for sales of high-rent oil, which industrial countries would have imported had they retained their own domestic metals and petrochemical manufacturing industry.

In the case of Trinidad and Tobago, the government strategy selected gas-fuelled projects that generated the lowest rent per unit of heat value, but relatively more employment than other gas-fuelled options. Feasibility studies indicate that direct-reduced iron (DRI) steel, the largest investment made by the government of Trinidad and Tobago in the 1970s, yielded considerably less rent per unit of gas than petrochemicals, which in turn generated less rent than LNG (Table 4.2). The fact that the scale of LNG investment would dictate a dominant foreign investor was seen as a further drawback, but, with hindsight, it would have conferred the advantage of limiting government losses due to cost overruns or negative price shocks. In any event, the government opted to ignore LNG and prioritize a wholly state-owned steel plant, along with joint-venture petrochemicals plants.

With respect to strategy implementation, the wholly state-owned Iron and Steel Company of Trinidad and Tobago (ISCOTT) experienced severe construction and operating difficulties (Auty 1990). The US$0.5 billion plant incurred a 30% cost overrun and then lost US$108 million annually through 1982–85 before management was contracted to private European firms. The plant was eventually sold in 1988 to Mittal as a viable concern, but for a nominal sum. The methanol and fertilizer plants, which were constructed as joint ventures with multinational firms, proved more profitable, however.

The ISCOTT cost overrun was symptomatic of the government's gradual loss of control of public expenditure towards the end of the 1974–78 boom and into the 1979–81 boom. Although the economy was overheating, half the extra rent from the 1979–81 windfall was absorbed domestically, compared

Table 4.2 Potential netbacks for the gas-based industry, Trinidad and Tobago, 1980s

Gas-based industry	Gas input (million ft^3/ton)	Investment (US$/ million ft^3/year)	Gas netback (1982, US$/million ft^3)	Product price (US$/ton)
Metals				
DRI	12.5	12.68	0.07	130
Steel	19.9	26.98	0.85	330
Aluminium	128.0	16.24	1.30	1989
Chemicals				
Ammonia	33.0	13.37	1.76	231
Urea	23.8	1.47	2.76	231
Methanol	29.3	14.09	0.85	240
Gas export				
LNG	59.0	8.69	3.51	5.9[1]

[1] US$/million ft^3.

Source: Gelb and Associates (1988: 284).

with 30% in the first boom, and split evenly between investment and consumption. The acceleration of domestic absorption exacerbated Dutch disease effects. The real exchange rate appreciated by almost one-third comparing 1980–84 with 1976–79, and subsequently depreciated only slowly (Table 3.2) as the financial reserves were drawn down to cushion the economic adjustment.

With respect to economic diversification, gas-based industrialization failed to expand the relative size of the nonenergy tradeable sector and instead was associated with a relative decline. Rather than combating Dutch disease effects by boosting productivity in the nonenergy tradeables sectors, the government protected agriculture and manufacturing, which blunted their incentives to be efficient. Whereas on the eve of the oil boom in 1972, the share of the nonenergy tradeables in nonenergy GDP had been two-thirds of the size expected for an economy of Trinidad and Tobago's size and per capita income (Table 3.2), by 1981 the ratio had shrunk by a further 10% of nonenergy GDP. Moreover, much of the nonenergy tradeables activity was protected and not globally competitive. Services bridged the employment gap (Gelb and Associates 1988: 88).

As Seers (1964) warned, high wages in the oil sector stimulated economy-wide wage inflation, which diminished the efficiency of public investment. The cost of projects such as new schools and hospitals quadrupled, indicating leakage of rent into the overstretched domestic construction industry. The subsidies for protected economic activity along with the cost overruns on the gas-based industry accelerated the drain on the financial reserves. The inflated capital costs during construction combined with low global steel prices due to oversupply to intensify losses on steel. The steel sector of Trinidad and Tobago became a net drain on public finances rather than the positive contributor of revenue that was planned. The petrochemical plants were viable, but, as explained below, represent a minimum diversification from rent dependence.

Turning from rent investment to rent consumption, the rent deployed for domestic consumption through the 1974–81 windfalls fed inflation and benefited mainly the urban middle class. The government lowered nonenergy taxation by substituting rent for both income tax and value added tax. It also increased subsidies on items like energy (electricity and transportation), which on a per capita basis the middle class consumed more of. Through 1981–83 consumer subsidies absorbed one-quarter of the hydrocarbon revenue. In addition, the rent subsidies created a burgeoning protected sector, consistent with the staple trap model (Table 2.2), as the government expanded public sector employment to offset the disappointing employment multiplier from gas-based industry. The public sector became the largest single source of jobs, although many of the jobs were deemed to be uneconomic (Central Bank of Trinidad & Tobago 2009). The jobs also insulated workers from the incentive to boost productivity, the reverse of the required incentive for competitive diversification. The subsidies to consumers, public sector workers, and state-owned projects proved difficult to trim during the economic downswing. The rent cycling displayed strong inertia that all but eliminated the accumulated financial reserves, even as incomes contracted. When subsidies to the rent-seeking sectors outstripped the faltering supply, the economy entered a protracted growth collapse during 1981–93 (Table 3.2).

4.4 Protracted Growth Collapse 1981–93

The high-rent staple trap model (Table 2.2) predicts that excessive rent demands will lead to a growth collapse that will be protracted because the beneficiaries of rent-seeking resist economic reform. It also predicts that a growth collapse will eventually be self-correcting, however, because continued population growth will shrink the per capita rent endowment, which will incentivize the elite to grow the economy. But this self-correcting outcome assumes no revival of resource rent or substitution of rent from other sources such as foreign aid.

4.4.1 *Political Constraints on Economic Reform*

The growth collapse destabilized domestic politics in Trinidad and Tobago. It terminated the country's long-serving first independent government. Three successive governments struggled through 1986–93 to cut public expenditure and ration the reduced rent in order to reach fiscal balance. Owolabe (2007) argues that the termination of single party dominance in 1986 intensified political competition and rekindled ethnic voting. Certainly, the ethnic roots of the two main political parties prevented either one of them from achieving a majority based on its core ethnic support. Both the main parties had to bid for the support of additional political factions in order to secure enough parliamentary seats to govern. For their part, the minority factions pursued their own rent-seeking agendas, rather than more long-term ethnic or class interests (Meighoo 2008).[2]

The 1986 election ushered in a period of political weakness that retarded economic reform, which required cuts in social entitlements and real incomes. During the final years of the long-serving first independent government,

---

[2] In Guyana, the mainly urban black minority, at around 37% of the population, maintained power after independence in 1966 by manipulating elections and extracting rent by nationalizing the bauxite industry in 1970 (which subsequently collapsed), nationalizing the erstwhile efficient sugar industry in 1976, and controlling the price of rice paid to the farmers, who were predominantly Indian and formed over half the population.

public sector unions had secured a 60% rise in real wages, which prompted other unions to pursue similar rises, transmitting inflationary pressures throughout the economy (Braumann 1997: 5). The wage gains were not matched by productivity increases, however, so they postponed the necessary adjustment of real wages to the competitive pressures arising from the negative oil shock. As real labour costs rose, the rate of domestic investment declined by two-thirds, which retarded new job creation and limited gains from higher productivity.

The resistance of rent-seeking groups to the realignment of costs perpetuated fiscal deficits, which delayed stabilization and postponed economic recovery. Belatedly, the new government elected in 1986, which was a loose coalition of four erstwhile opposition parties in the multiethnic National Alliance for Reconstruction (NAR), turned to the IMF for assistance, and launched a stabilization and structural adjustment programme over 1988–94. The IMF-backed programme required reform of both fiscal policy and trade policy, but the pace of reform remained slow due to political weakness and labour market rigidity. The government directly employed one-quarter of the workforce, compared with only one-fifth in private sector tradeables, and was reluctant to create redundancies (World Bank 1999). Trade policy reform also proved challenging as successive governments struggled to dismantle the protected economy. Nontariff assistance persisted, notably for agriculture (Rajapatirana 2001).

By 1992 the foreign exchange reserves had fallen to US$0.2 billion compared with around US$3.4 billion a decade earlier (Artana et al. 2006). The fiscal reform sought to cut public expenditure from 56% of nonenergy GDP to 36% and eventually reduced real wages by 60% through the late-1980s, returning them to their level of 1978. Real income per capita declined by more than one-third, while unemployment doubled to 22% in 1989, leaving one-fifth of the workforce in poverty (IMF 2007: 3). Both the capital stock and total employment were lower than before the early-1980s wage boom. Having grown at 4.9% per annum during 1975–79, the per capita GDP of Trinidad and Tobago contracted by 1.7% annually through 1980–94. By the early-1990s the mean income per capita was back to its level in the late-1960s (Table 3.2).

The tensions over economic retrenchment strained the NAR coalition, which in 1988 lost the support of its Indian coalition partners after a cabinet reshuffle reduced that faction's share of ministries (Owolabe 2007). In 1990 the NAR government faced an extra-parliamentary challenge from an Imam-led coup of around one hundred Muslims. The coup collapsed after holding MPs hostage within the parliament building for five days. The coup failed to unseat the NAR coalition, but the party was virtually eliminated in elections in 1991, which returned the People's National Movement (PNM) (the first independent government) to power until 1995.

4.4.2 *Retarded Economic Recovery*

Economic recovery finally commenced in 1993 (Table 3.2), but not as a consequence of the expansion of diversified employment-intensive exports. Instead, it accompanied a 25% depreciation of the real exchange rate and a sustained expansion of investment in natural gas. The recovery was not triggered by the nonenergy sector. Rather, recovery was driven by expanded natural gas extraction, which increased rent dependence. The oil price dipped briefly in 1998, which cut government revenue from hydrocarbons by a further 6% of GDP compared with 1996, underlining the dependence of the economy upon the energy sector. Energy and petrochemicals generated 46% of exports, 21% of GDP, but only 7% of government revenue at that time.

The IMF (1999: 22) estimated that at the prevailing historically low real energy prices, the hydrocarbon sector conferred annual revenue of US\$6.4 billion from oil (assuming a price of US\$12/bl) and some US\$12.3 billion from natural gas (assuming a price of US\$6.9/thousand ftft^3) for a combined sum of US\$18.6 billion. Although the IMF encouraged the government to focus on nonoil diversification, it had little effect. The IMF projected the government's share of the total revenue from the LNG expansion would be 21%. It projected the 1998 public sector deficit of 4% of nonenergy GDP (2% of total GDP) lay at the upper bound of the amount drawn for public expenditure that would keep the stock of hydrocarbon wealth constant, as the permanent income hypothesis required (Velculescu and Rizavi 2005: 11).

The IMF calculation was based on two cautious assumptions, namely persistent 'low' hydrocarbon prices and the ability to earn a 4% real rate of return on the sterilized hydrocarbon revenue. Higher deficits would merely shorten the longevity of the energy revenue stream. This in turn would compress the period available within which to reform the public finances to cope with the revenue lost since the early-1980s. In the event, IMF caution proved overdone due to the unexpected LNG boom of 2004–08. The boom tested the extent to which rent-rich governments like that of Trinidad and Tobago had learned the lessons from the 1974–81 windfalls. The answer proved to be: not nearly enough.

4.5 Rent-Seeking Inertia: LNG Intensifies Rent Dependence

4.5.1 *Deployment of the 2004–08 LNG Windfall*

The government of Trinidad and Tobago sensibly moderated resource nationalism and relied on both upstream and downstream international oil corporations to implement the LNG investments, which, by reducing state participation, spread the risk. In the event, the government share of revenue was sharply reduced by the assumptions made about markets when the LNG investment contracts were negotiated in the 1990s. The negotiations coincided with a period of low global gas prices that were expected to persist.[3] The government conceded tax breaks to the IOCs that were generous in light of the higher global energy prices of 2004–08. For example, the LNG contracts excluded provision for windfall taxation and granted a decade-long tax holiday for the first LNG plant, which coincided with the boom. Revenue therefore leaked abroad through accelerated capital recovery by the IOCs.[4] Nevertheless, the IMF (2007) estimated that net taxation from the hydrocarbon sector of Trinidad and Tobago, including taxes from oil as well as natural gas, secured one-fifth of the total hydrocarbon revenue, which is near the global average for hydrocarbon-exporting economies.

The government was also initially more cautious in deploying the 2004–08 rent windfall than with the earlier windfalls (Table 4.3). The 2004–08 windfall was larger than the previous (oil) windfalls and conferred an extra 59% of nonenergy GDP annually, of which two-thirds appears to have been saved, partly by the private sector and partly by the public sector (through additions to the Heritage Saving Fund and to the official reserves). The public debt/GDP ratio fell, albeit largely because debt held steady in absolute terms rather than

Table 4.3 Government revenue and expenditure, Trinidad and Tobago, 2000–08 (% GDP)

	Pre-boom				Boom				
	2000	2001	2002	2003	2004	2005	2006	2007	2008
Government revenue	23.7	25.8	24.6	24.4	25.0	29.5	31.9	29.1	36.7
Of which:									
Nonenergy	17.2	16.7	18.7	14.9	14.7	14.0	12.2	12.6	15.5
Energy	6.4	9.0	5.8	9.4	10.3	15.5	19.7	16.5	21.2
Government expenditure	23.5	25.2	24.8	22.6	22.8	24.1	25.5	27.5	30.2
Current	21.1	23.8	23.5	21.1	20.9	21.3	21.8	21.8	23.6
Transfers and subsidies[1]	7.7	8.5	8.9	8.3	7.0	10.3	12.2	12.2	13.6
Capital expenditure	2.8	1.9	1.7	1.4	2.2	3.1	4.0	5.7	6.6
Overall balance	0.2	0.6	−0.2	1.8	2.4	5.4	6.4	1.6	6.5
Overall nonenergy balance[2]	−6.3	−8.5	−6.1	−7.7	−8.1	−10.1	−13.3	−14.9	−14.7
Memo items									
GDP (TT$ billion)	51.47	55.00	56.3	71.2	82.7	100.4	122.1	137.4	151.4
Oil price (US$/bl)	28.2	24.3	25.0	28.9	34.4	49.9	63.7	64.0	97.3

[1] Public sector debt 2004 = 45.5% GDP and 2008 = 27.2% GDP (IMF 2009a: 9, 23).
[2] The nonenergy fiscal deficit averaged almost 90% of nonenergy GDP 2009–11 (IMF 2012a), three to four times a sustainable level.
Source: IMF (2009).

[3] Peter Thomson, World Bank, personal communication.
[4] 'On the upstream side, BP produces 70 percent of the gas yet they pay approximately 1.5–2.0 cents/thousand ft[3] and there is no supplemental tax on gas production. On the downstream side the petrochemical companies pay very little corporation tax' (Racha 2001: 17).

falling (Table 4.3). Much of the saving during the windfall was, however, made by the private sector as the oil companies recouped their investment.

The LNG revenues were boosted through the mid-2000s by the rise in real energy prices associated with the commodity super-cycle. The LNG boom deflected economic policy in Trinidad and Tobago away from stimulating long-term growth and economic diversification favoured by the IMF, and towards cycling rent for electoral gain. Once again, domestic rent absorption became overrapid. Around one-third of the windfall (one-fifth of nonenergy GDP) was absorbed domestically, which the IMF judged to be both unsustainable and inconsistent with intergenerational equity. Rather, the IMF estimated that in 2007 the hydrocarbon resource could sustain indefinitely a *constant* public sector deficit of 4% of nonenergy GDP. It later raised the ratio to 7.5% to reflect energy prices that were higher than initially projected (IMF 2012a). However, the post-2008 global financial crisis, during which energy prices dipped, saw the nonenergy fiscal deficit balloon to almost double the IMF's higher estimate of a sustainable ratio. Yet increased competition among LNG producers and softening global energy prices required a downward adjustment of the IMF's 7.5% estimate.

The domestic windfall absorption through 2004–08 was evenly split between consumption and investment. Prior to the boom, public expenditure had been sensibly targeted at reducing poverty and improving health and education rather than, as in the 1970s, on expanding subsidies for rent-seeking consumers and loss-making state enterprises. Although further state ownership of production was largely avoided, the share of public expenditure in GDP remained significantly higher than in comparator economies. Public consumption then increased by slightly more than private consumption, and as the boom persisted, the government unwisely began to boost subsidies and transfers. Section 4.5.3 provides a detailed evaluation of revenue allocation. The present section focuses on the overall scale and impact.

A major change was the tripling of public investment through the 2004–08 boom compared with the 1999–2003 pre-boom base period. This threatened to lower the economy-wide efficiency of investment because public investment in Trinidad and Tobago had a poor track record (IADB 2009). Expenditure on human capital included tertiary education through the Government Assistance for Tuition Expenses (GATE) programme, school construction, and university infrastructure expansion. Other new measures included an environmental initiative such as the Community-based Environmental Protection and Enhancement Programme (CEPEP), which took over a previous unemployment relief programme of low-skilled jobs. The construction sector was boosted through roads and housing construction. Overall, the surge in public investment almost exactly offset the sharp fall in private investment caused when the expansion of natural gas production tapered off (Table 4.4).

Table 4.4 Public/private investment, Trinidad and Tobago, 2000–08 (% GDP)

	Pre-boom				Boom				
	2000	2001	2002	2003	2004	2005	2006	2007	2008
Gross domestic investment	17.1	19.5	19.2	25.2	16.8	14.6	21.1	23.6	24.2
Of which:									
Public	5.8	6.0	4.6	4.3	6.3	8.1	10.5	11.8	12.0
Private	11.3	13.5	14.6	20.9	10.3	6.5	10.5	12.2	12.2

Source: IMF (2009: 21).

Critically, deployment of the 2004–08 windfall failed to boost the level of private investment in competitive diversification. Ominously, the rate of private *saving* increased, so that Trinidad and Tobago's low rate of private investment relative to nonenergy GDP persisted for yet a third decade.

Nor did the 2004–08 revenue expenditure accelerate GDP growth, which slowed slightly to around 6.9% annually through the mid-2000s from 7.6% during 1999–2003 (Table 3.2). This partly reflects the fact that the extra windfall expenditure failed to offset the decelerating multiplier from natural gas expansion. Nevertheless, the rate of domestic rent absorption was sufficient to increase the rate of inflation. The real exchange rate strengthened by two-fifths comparing 2010–14 with 2000–04 (Table 3.2), further discouraging private sector investment in nonenergy activity. Meanwhile, although the windfall expenditure was associated with a halving of unemployment to below 5%, this largely reflected a one-off doubling of workers in construction and make-work social programmes (Central Bank of Trinidad & Tobago 2009), which were both highly cyclical.

Consequently, forty-five years after the launch of the gas-based industrialization strategy, the economy of Trinidad and Tobago had still not reached its labour market turning point. In contrast, the turning points in South Korea and Taiwan occurred a decade after they launched export industrialization, while Mauritius took twenty years. Yet the competitive diversification model identifies the labour market turning point as the trigger for self-sustaining structural change that drives rapid economic and political maturation (Table 2.2). Sections 4.5.2 and 4.5.3 evaluate the processes of gas monetization and economic diversification.

4.5.2 Gas Monetization Limits Economic Diversification

Economic growth continued to depend on the hydrocarbon sector through the post-1993 recovery, responding mainly to fiscal linkage arising from government expenditure of energy revenue rather than the multiplier arising from hydrocarbon *productive* linkages. Upstream petrochemicals dominated diversification, but that sector relied on attractively priced gas and reflected a minimal reduction in rent dependence. In addition, the small size of regional demand imposes diseconomies of scale that reduce productive forward linkage in Trinidad and Tobago.

More specifically, natural gas production accelerated rapidly to dominate the economy. It expanded at 3% per annum through 1985–90, then 6% per annum 1991–96, and finally 18% per annum 1997–2002 as LNG took off (Sergeant et al. 2002: 13). In absolute terms, gas production jumped from 5.5 bcm^3/year in 1992, to 9.3 bcm^3 in 1998, to 27 bcm^3 in 2003, and to 39.6 bcm^3 by 2015 (BP 2017). In 2012 the LNG plants absorbed 58% of the total Trinidad and Tobago gas output, while a further 15.5% went to eleven fertilizer plants, 14.1% to seven methanol plants, 7.4% to power generation, 2.6% to three steel plants, and the remaining 2.3% to a cement factory and other small commercial users.

Trinidad and Tobago became a major global exporter of gas-based products. Total ammonia production reached 5.5 million tons in 2012, methanol 5.5 million tones, and steel billets 1.7 million tons (Central Bank of Trinidad & Tobago 2014). By then, the energy sector generated 81.4% of exports, 54% of government revenue, and 43.7% of GDP. Critically, the petrochemical sector alone was responsible for 17.4% of exports and 8.7% of GDP (Central Bank of Trinidad & Tobago 2014: 8), compared with a 6.6% share of GDP for the rest of the manufacturing and agriculture combined, which generated negligible exports. Yet the petrochemical plants provided barely 1% of total employment, while the rest of the oil and gas sector employed only another 2.5% (representing around 6,700 and 13,500 workers, respectively, in absolute terms). Such figures underline the capital-intensity of the gas sector and the need to diversify the nonenergy sector to provide sustainable employment.

The typical gas-based plant entailed a US$300 million investment for ammonia, US$220 million for methanol, and US$200 million for DRI. Since the average gas-based plant employed only 75–100 workers, the sector created each job at an average investment cost of US$3 million. This was, however, half the US$6 million investment cost per employee in LNG. Another problem emerged, along with low employment creation, namely the efficiency of gas usage as gas prices fell and the accumulation of gas reserves slowed. The newer fertilizer plants consumed much less gas per ton of output than older plants (almost half as much comparing the oldest and newest plants in Trinidad and Tobago, which span four decades in terms of their vintage), while ammonia converts gas into final product less efficiently than methanol.

Still more critically, the viability of the petrochemical sector depends on a continued supply of natural gas at a competitive price, neither of which is assured through the long term due to reduced exploration activity linked to the expansion of fracking in the US. The price of gas from the state-owned gas company varies considerably among the LNG plants, the petrochemical plants, and locally owned gas-consuming firms. The latter claimed they struggled to pay a gas price set initially at US$1.59/million Btu (one-million British thermal units), with an escalator of 4%, which they argued was higher than the base rate of the earlier foreign-owned petrochemical exporters. However, the actual prices for gas paid by foreign firms are linked to the export price, and during the 2004–08 energy boom the rate that they paid rose to US $3.12/million Btu (McGuire 2014: 132). The LNG plants operate under yet another system, which links the price to the gas netback after covering marketing, shipping, and liquefaction expenses.

With respect to government revenue, the first three Atlantic LNG plants, with a production capacity of 9.6 million tons per year (1,400 million ft^3/d), was projected to confer US$6 billion in revenue on the government over its twenty-year operating life. This is an average annual rate of US$300 million or some US$31.50 per ton produced. McGuire (2014: 54–55) noted that through 1998–2006 three LNG trains delivered 1.7 cents per dollar of export revenue in taxes to the government. Given the variations in gas conversion efficiency and in the social return among the different applications, there is scope for reallocating gas when existing contracts fall due for renewal. Reduced incentives for gas exploration arising from lower gas prices since 2014 have prompted the search for gas imports into Trinidad and Tobago to replace domestic supplies. Yet imported gas seems unlikely to be able to discount prices to domestic processors and consumers.

4.5.3 *Limited Diversification through Production Linkages*

Petrochemicals not only represent a highly capital-intensive, minimal diversification from rent-driven growth, but also have generated disappointing downstream linkages, mostly urea, steel, and steel construction products to meet local demand. The small size of the economy of Trinidad and Tobago creates obstacles in supplying the inputs for petrochemical derivatives on an adequate scale and of sufficient variety, and confers limited domestic and regional demand. Most primary petrochemical producers find it more efficient to expand downstream derivatives production at brown-field plants in established major markets within the Americas and Europe rather than in a remote green-field location like Trinidad and Tobago. This is because products requiring bulk shipment incur cheaper freight rates than derivative products, which are manufactured and sold in smaller quantities.

Foreign investors are mainly attracted to Trinidad and Tobago to produce upstream bulk products using cheaply priced natural gas and utility inputs. The scale of gas production hitherto has comfortably generated the large commodity cargoes required to capture the economies of scale in shipping bulk commodities, but foreign investors are unlikely to invest further down-stream in Trinidad and Tobago. Nor has much progress been made with diversification into more sophisticated hydrocarbon-related activity like geo-logical modelling, deep-sea drilling technologies, and energy equipment manufacturing (Artana et al. 2007: 7). Consequently the structure of the economy of Trinidad and Tobago is skewed so that the hydrocarbon sector (including petrochemicals) accounts for 45% of GDP compared with almost 49% in services, within which government services generate 14.6% of GDP. The nonhydrocarbon tradeable sectors, namely agriculture and manu-facturing, generated 6.6% of GDP in 2013.

Additional evidence of Dutch disease effects is provided by comparing the structure of the economy of Trinidad and Tobago against benchmarks for sector employment in market economies at a similar level of per capita income (Raiser et al. 2004). After Syrquin and Chenery (1989), market economy data are assumed to reflect the norm for a reasonably efficient economy. They are applied to Trinidad and Tobago after converting its 2004–08 per capita income into constant 1995 US dollars as US$8,150 to allow direct comparison. The benchmarks reveal that agriculture in Trinidad and Tobago, with a mere 4% of the workforce, was well short of the benchmark employment ratio of 22%. Industry employed 32% compared with a benchmark ratio of 26%, but of this only one-third was in manufacturing and the rest in construction and utilities. Combined, these figures suggest a net 'underperformance' of the tradeable sector of Trinidad and Tobago during the 2004–08 boom of 12% of its expected share of employment. The corollary is that the service sector share is larger than expected, accounting for 64% of employment against the benchmark of 52%.

Raiser et al. (2004) derived benchmarks for the contributions of market services and nonmarket services. At the income level of Trinidad and Tobago they estimate that market services will provide 29% of total employment and nonmarket services 23%. Although, public sector employment data are lack-ing from official statistical sources for Trinidad and Tobago, the IMF (2007: 17) noted that in 2001, on the eve of the energy boom, the public sector employed one-third of the workforce (and in tiny Tobago more than half the workforce, where tourism-related activity, including government services, generates 60% of jobs).[5] This is 50% above the expected norm. Rojas-Suarez et al. (2006: 78) drew on the Inter-American Development Bank (IADB) data to confirm the elevated share of public sector employment.

Some reports suggest that the public sector increased its share of the total workforce of Trinidad and Tobago by 6% during the boom. This was about twice the rate of growth of the service sector as a whole. Finally, if the

---

[5] In Tobago the public sector employs over half the workforce.

boom-linked expansion of construction employment in Trinidad and Tobago is assumed to be temporary, then the combined employment contribution of agriculture and industry drops to 28%, barely three-fifths of its expected share. It seems reasonable to conclude that the benchmark employment data are consistent with strong Dutch disease effects in Trinidad and Tobago. This outcome is not surprising after three decades of underinvestment in the nonenergy private sector, along with repeated surges in the real exchange rate. Within the private service sector, tourism grew relatively slowly, and although finance expanded it failed to match the dynamism of Mauritius (Chapter 5).

The persistence of Dutch disease effects through the LNG boom reflects a strategy of rent deployment that pays insufficient heed to the lessons of the 1974–81 oil booms. At the beginning of the LNG boom, the IFI-backed policies adopted in the downswing were still in place and targeted poverty reduction, health, and education. The 2004–08 boom saw windfall absorption become more narrowly targeted. Higher absorption into the public sector included higher civil service remuneration, as well as an expansion of subsidies like those on fuel[6] and the bailing out of state-run firms such as the sugar producer Caroni (Chapter 3). More specifically, public sector wages grew by almost 1.5% of GDP during 2004–08, while transfers over the same period rose by 4.7% of GDP, pushing them to 8% of GDP in total. The transfers included a 1.4% of GDP increase in energy subsidies,[7] along with a 1.1% rise in subsidies to state-owned enterprises and utilities, a rise of 1.2% of GDP in education and health, and a doubling in unspecified transfers. In addition, private consumption grew by almost 5% of nonenergy GDP, spurred by reductions in the share of nonenergy taxation in GDP, which effectively transferred one-eighth of the windfall to the private sector.

The increased investment during the LNG boom directed almost one-tenth of the 2004–08 rent windfall to raise public investment more than fourfold. Public sector investment reached parity with private sector investment. Unfortunately, the rapid rate of expansion increased the likelihood of wasteful deployment via capacity constraints within the public sector, which had a poor reputation for resource allocation. The government justified the scale of expanded public investment as necessary to reduce the backlog in transport infrastructure and utilities. But the IADB (2009) expressed concern over the efficiency of public investment. It also queried a trend towards off-budget expenditures. The IMF (2013b: 15–16) concurred and blamed the poor performance on failings within the civil service that both impeded its capacity to

---

[6] The 2008 fuel subsidy was projected at TT$2.5 billion or 10% of nonenergy government revenue (IADB 2009: 7).

[7] Petrol prices rose 50% during 2001–03 to around US$1.50 per gallon, at which they were frozen while US prices doubled to over $3 per gallon (IMF 2007: 22), with the difference representing the added subsidy.

invest productively and created bureaucratic obstacles that deterred private investment in the nonenergy sector. Numerous senior government officials remained unconfirmed in positions that they had held for years, while many functions were undertaken by staff on short-term contracts. Such staffing practices lower morale, boost job turnover, and erode institutional memory.

Nevertheless, the deployment of the 2004–08 windfall conferred political dividends on the government, which, having been elected in 2003, won re-election in 2007. In 2003 the incoming government awarded a 15% increase in public sector wages. This exerted an inflationary demonstration effect throughout the private sector and, as in previous booms, stimulated economy-wide wage gains that outstripped productivity. Moreover, labour shortages emerged in the energy and finance sectors, even as surplus labour persisted elsewhere, indicating that overall the workforce of Trinidad and Tobago is underskilled. Total employment expanded by 10% during 2000–08, but it shifted away from tradeable activity as the real exchange rate strengthened (Table 3.2).

A further factor hampering diversification into nonenergy tradeables, aside from misdirected rent deployment, has been the business environment. The economy of Trinidad and Tobago lags well behind comparator economies, outranking only Uganda (Table 4.5). It is especially deficient not only in market size but also innovation enhancers and technological readiness, along with the efficiency of financial and labour markets. It may be recalled that Trinidad and Tobago also underperforms in respect to the quality of governance (Table 3.1), which shows deterioration in key indices such as control of corruption, the reverse of expectations where per capita income has risen.

The underperformance of institutions in Trinidad and Tobago is a critical obstacle to the goal of achieving developed country status by 2020, according to a comprehensive review of the country's energy-driven development undertaken for the IADB (Rojas-Suarez et al. 2006: 5–15). Deficient human capital exacerbates this weakness, as evidenced by the fact that enrolment in tertiary education is barely one-fifth that of developed economies. Meanwhile, a large fraction of the unskilled workforce is underemployed on government make-work programmes such as landscape improvements. These workers are assigned to the International Labour Organization (ILO) classification of community, social, and personal services sector. This group increased its share of total employment from 31% to 34% from 1995 to 2012, even as the sub-sector's share of total GDP shrank from 18% to 9%. Moreover, hourly wages in make-work public sector employment exceed the minimum wage, which makes it difficult for private firms to hire unskilled and low-skilled labour.

Not surprisingly, a study of revealed comparative advantage found that, aside from energy, there were few other prospects for growth for Trinidad

Table 4.5 Global Competitiveness Index, 2015, comparator economies

	South Korea	Saudi Arabia	Trinidad and Tobago	Chile	Mauritius	Brazil	India	Uganda
GDP per capita (US$)	27,105	21,014	17,322	13,469	9,115	8,811	1,616	630
World ranking[1]	26	25	89	35	46	75	55	115
Overall index[2]	5.0	5.1	3.9	4.6	4.4	4.1	4.3	3.7
Basic requirements	5.7	5.7	4.6	5.1	5.0	4.1	4.4	3.8
Institutions	3.9	5.1	3.4	4.6	4.5	3.2	4.1	3.4
Infrastructure	5.8	5.1	4.5	4.6	4.8	3.9	3.7	2.4
Macroeconomy	6.6	6.6	4.9	5.6	4.7	4.0	4.4	4.8
Health and primary education	6.3	6.0	5.9	5.6	6.1	5.1	5.5	4.5
Efficiency enhancers	4.8	4.7	3.9	4.7	4.2	4.2	4.2	3.5
Higher education and training	5.4	4.7	4.3	5.0	4.6	3.8	3.9	2.7
Market efficiency	4.8	4.7	4.1	4.6	4.9	3.7	4.2	3.9
Labour market efficiency	4.1	4.3	4.0	4.3	4.3	3.7	3.9	4.6
Financial market sophistication	3.6	4.3	4.0	4.6	4.4	4.0	4.1	3.7
Technological readiness	5.5	4.7	4.2	4.8	4.1	4.4	2.7	2.8
Market size	5.6	5.4	3.0	4.6	2.8	5.8	6.4	3.4
Innovation enhancers	4.8	4.2	3.5	3.8	3.8	3.6	3.9	3.3
Business sophistication	4.8	4.5	3.9	4.1	4.4	4.1	4.2	3.5
Innovation	4.8	3.8	3.1	3.5	3.2	3.2	3.6	3.2

[1] Ranking out of 128 countries.
[2] Index scores range from 1 to 7, with 7 high.
Source: World Economic Forum (2016).

and Tobago. In this respect, the country performed worse than any other economy in the Latin American and Caribbean region (IADB 2009). The service sector dominated nonenergy growth through the 2004–08 boom, which reflected government expenditure of energy revenue. Moreover, within the service sector, public expenditure grew to reach almost 50% of nonenergy GDP, discouraging private investment in nonenergy activity. Private investment is further constrained by apprehension over rising crime,[8] underinvestment in both efficient infrastructure and human capital, the appreciating real exchange rate, inadequate bank regulation,[9] and the ballooning nonenergy fiscal deficit (Artana et al. 2007: 9). When energy prices faltered after 2009, it became clear that the nonenergy tradeable sector of Trinidad and Tobago has yet to achieve the ability to drive the economy through an energy downswing. The rate of growth in GDP per capita fell to average 0.8% annually 2010–14, compared to 3.4% in Mauritius (World Bank 2017a).

---

[8] The annual homicide rate quadrupled during 1999–2008 to 41/100,000 (mostly in the poorer Port of Spain suburbs), almost four times the rate of Barbados, and crime absorbed 3% of GDP in the mid-2000s, although detection rates are weak (IADB 2009).
[9] Banking is adequately capitalized in Trinidad and Tobago, due in large part to strong reliance on domestic saving rather than external borrowing, despite the strong presence of foreign banks (Artana et al. 2007).

91

4.6 Conclusions

The disappointing outcome of Trinidad and Tobago's deployment of its three large hydrocarbon revenue windfalls can be explained by the staple trap model. The tapering sugar rents and modest hydrocarbon rents initially encouraged a developmental state government in newly independent Trinidad and Tobago. The government built a consensus for a pro-growth strategy that combined export-oriented gas-based industrialization with an inherited import substitution policy. However, an extra-parliamentary challenge in 1970 from protesters against unemployment encouraged a nationalistic expansion of state-led gas-based industrialization. The implementation of the strategy slipped out of government control during the rent windfalls of the 1974–78 and 1979–81 oil booms, which elicited sharp increases in the rates of both investment and consumption. The rate of rent absorption into the domestic economy outstripped absorptive capacity, causing acute implementation problems, not least for the steel plant, the flagship of gas-based industrialization, while its downstream multiplier failed to generate significant employment.

Consistent with the staple trap model, the government absorbed rent over-rapidly through the 1979–81 boom, partly to subsidize employment that markets would not support and partly to boost consumption to win votes. The increased domestic rent absorption outstripped absorptive capacity, which accelerated inflation and intensified the appreciation of the real exchange rate. This compounded Dutch disease effects as the share of nonenergy tradeables in GDP contracted. Although joint-venture petrochemicals expanded successfully, such gas-based industry affords a minimal diversification from rent dependence since it relies on cheap inputs of finite gas for its viability. When oil revenues faltered in the early-1980s and fell short of the burgeoning rent demands of the subsidized activity, economic growth collapsed.

The growth collapse proved protracted because rent recipients resisted reform. Initial policy responses aggravated the situation by drawing down the accumulated financial reserves to sustain wages that could no longer be justified. Successive governments struggled to stabilize the economy until the financial reserves were almost exhausted. The government requested assistance from the IFIs, which provided loans conditional on reforms to open trade policy and cut public expenditure. The reforms sharply reduced per capita income and boosted the rate of unemployment to one-fifth of the workforce. Trinidad and Tobago was a long way from its labour market turning point in 1990, whereas low-rent Mauritius was just reaching its turning point.

The economic recovery was lagged and eventually driven by massive investment in natural gas exports rather than investment in the nonenergy tradeables sector. This was despite the failure of gas-based industrialization to sustain economic growth when the oil rent faltered in the 1980s. The lessons from the 1973–78 and 1979–81 windfalls were too easily disregarded during the LNG boom. Initial IMF-backed caution on domestic rent deployment gave way to excessive rent absorption, which led to a second growth collapse, albeit initially milder than that of 1981–93.

The use of natural gas to drive economic growth in Trinidad and Tobago has rapidly depleted the gas reserves, which have become insufficient to stimulate further growth in the industry (Energy Chamber 2011, 2012). The scale of the proved hydrocarbon reserves suggests that in the absence of a major technological breakthrough in deepwater exploration, gas production has entered the mature stage of the production cycle. Energy scenarios indicate that by 2025, Trinidad and Tobago may be required to cut back hydrocarbon exports and ramp up energy imports, not just to meet household and commercial needs, but also to sustain its manufacturing sector. The minimal diversification conferred by gas-based industry will compound the shock of ceasing to export oil and LNG, rather than cushion the transition from energy exporter to energy importer.

The government of Trinidad and Tobago needs to assemble a coalition of interest groups to fast-track policies for competitive diversification into manufacturing and export services that can sustain GDP growth through the long term, as Mauritius did in the late-1960s. Chapter 5 shows how low-rent Mauritius deployed modest geopolitical, crop, and regulatory rents to expand a globally competitive market economy alongside the rent-driven plantation economy, which eventually absorbed the latter into the increasingly dominant market economy.

5

Low-Rent Mauritius as a Developmental Counterfactual for High-Rent Trinidad and Tobago

5.1 Introduction

This chapter compares the post-independence development trajectory of Mauritius with that of Trinidad and Tobago in order to explain why economic development can be more effective with limited rents.[1] The comparison elaborates on the reasons for the relative underperformance of high-rent economies like Trinidad and Tobago. We demonstrate that not only did Mauritius deploy its initially small and tapering rent stream to reduce the original 1960 income gap between the two economies, but it also completed the process of diversifying its economy away from rent dependence, whereas Trinidad and Tobago remains heavily rent dependent. Moreover, the fact that Mauritius has also achieved greater maturity in both its economy and institutions renders its gains in welfare more sustainable than those of Trinidad and Tobago.

In the immediate post-war decades, however, the political economies of Mauritius and Trinidad and Tobago shared much in common. Both were small and remote monocrop island economies that were running short of land. They shared a similar colonial heritage and ethnically mixed populations that were governed as youthful parliamentary democracies. A critical difference was their rent: the potential rent of Trinidad and Tobago from hydrocarbons was three or more orders of magnitude greater than the modest and tapering rent that Mauritius derived from cropland and foreign aid. Moreover, the rent of Trinidad and Tobago was more volatile. It was also deployed less effectively, which is why the income gap between the two economies

[1] Auty (2017) is an earlier condensed version.

narrowed. The rent from oil had initially lifted the per capita GNI of Trinidad and Tobago above that of Mauritius. Although Mauritius's per capita GNI was relatively high for sub-Saharan Africa in 1962 at around US$230, it was only 36% that of Trinidad and Tobago. By 2014, however, Mauritius's per capita GNI was US$18,150, which was 57% that of Trinidad and Tobago (World Bank 2017a).

The remarkably similar initial conditions, other than rent potential, render Mauritius an informative counterfactual for how Trinidad and Tobago might have evolved without its hydrocarbon resources. Mauritius followed rent cycling theory's low-rent competitive diversification model, in contrast to Trinidad and Tobago's staple trap trajectory. A comparison of the two economies identifies four key reasons for Mauritius's superior performance, two of which arise out of different political incentives and two from differences in the economies' comparative advantage. First, limited prospects for rent motivated the Mauritius elite to form a developmental government that set economic growth as an early priority, which, critically, the elite maintained (Table 2.2). Second, the Mauritius elite also espoused a dual track political strategy to grow a market economy (Track 1), while reforming the rent-distorted sugar economy (Track 2). The dual track strategy managed the political risk of reform, namely that as reforms shrink scope for rent extraction, the reforming government becomes vulnerable to termination by wary rent-seekers. The dual track strategy expands a dynamic market economy, Track 1, alongside the existing rent-distorted economy (Track 2) until the market economy achieves sufficient size and political strength to absorb and neutralize the rent-seeking interests in Track 2.

Third, with respect to the comparative advantage, the priority given by Mauritius's developmental government to efficient economic growth led the economy to pursue its comparative advantage in labour-intensive manufactured exports, which drove rapid economic growth. Finally, the resulting rapid absorption of surplus labour into competitive manufacturing triggered rising wages that drove self-sustaining structural change, which diversified the economy into productivity-driven growth (Table 2.2). The competitive diversification trajectory also built self-reliant social capital and spawned new political groups capable of opposing factions seeking to capture policy. In contrast, the staple trap model prioritizes rent-seeking and skips the labour-intensive growth path and thereby foregoes the developmental benefits that it confers. In Chapter 7, we draw upon the competitive diversification and staple trap models to explain why the low-rent East Asian economies overcame the high-rent Latin American economies' head start on economic development.

The remainder of this chapter is structured as follows. Section 5.2 compares initial conditions in Mauritius and Trinidad and Tobago in the mid-1960s in more detail. It establishes that Mauritian rent was modest and tapered, compared with the larger and volatile rent of Trinidad and Tobago. Section 5.3 examines how initial conditions affected the policy choice of the Mauritian elite. It first explains what motivated the elite to switch early from industrialization by import substitution to industrialization by labour-intensive manufactured exports. It then analyses Mauritius's dual track political strategy for economic reform, which expanded a dynamic market economy, while delaying reform of the residual rent-distorted economy.

Section 5.4 attributes Mauritius's short growth collapse through 1979–81 to the overexpansion of subsidies to the rent-distorted sector during the sugar boom of 1972–75. The growth collapse resulted in the pro-growth coalition briefly losing office, but it quickly returned to power and took advantage of the growth collapse to make the case for accelerating reform by merging Track 2 into Track 1, as the dual track strategy had originally envisaged. Section 5.4 analyses how the recovery in per capita GDP growth ushered in the Lewis labour market turning point by the early-1990s. Section 5.5 then demonstrates how the turning point raised real wages that accelerated Mauritius's competitive diversification into service exports.

Section 5.6 concludes by using Mauritius's development trajectory to identify the benefits foregone by Trinidad and Tobago as a result of overrapid rent absorption, which fed Dutch disease effects and leapfrogged the phase of labour-intensive manufacturing that was critical in launching Mauritius into sustained competitive diversification of its economy (Warner 2015).

5.2 Comparing Initial Conditions in Mauritius and Trinidad and Tobago

From the end of the eighteenth century, Mauritius and Trinidad and Tobago shared similar experiences of economic development as small monocrop island economies colonized by the UK, largely through the expansion of sugar cane plantations.[2] By the time of independence in the 1960s they resembled twin economies, their mineral endowments aside.

5.2.1 The Shared Legacy of Plantation Society

As Chapter 3 explains, the UK conferred geopolitical rents through preferential access to imperial markets and by facilitating the import of cheap labour from South Asia to encourage the expansion of plantations on both islands. These developments shaped the size of the two economies, the structure of

---

[2] The UK governed Trinidad and Tobago from 1797 to 1962 and Mauritius from 1810 to 1968.

society, and also the ethnic composition of their populations. Sugar production grew faster in Mauritius than in Trinidad and Tobago, rising to 130,000; tons by 1860, when it supplied almost one-tenth of world cane sugar. Mauritius's production reached 200,000 tons by 1910 (Macmillan 1914), compared with 50,000 tons in Trinidad and Tobago (Chalmin 1990: 310), where cacao was briefly more important.

The political power of the plantocracy began to weaken in Mauritius from the 1870s and 1880s, as it did in Trinidad and Tobago. This reflected the rise of a Creole professional class and the expansion of Indian-owned small farms to occupy one-third of the cane land by the early twentieth century in Mauritius (North-Coombes 1988). The same symbiosis of plantation and small farm as emerged in Trinidad and Tobago helped maintain cheap labour for the Mauritian plantations. Cane farming also provided a buffer for the sugar factories against price volatility because small farmers tended to expand onto poorer quality land in booms and to withdraw during downswings (North-Coombes 1988). However, as in Trinidad and Tobago, the deterioration in living standards during the Great Depression sparked riots in Mauritius in 1937 that led to the establishment of a Commission of Enquiry, which legalized trade unions and spurred progress towards full democracy.

The CSA boosted geopolitical rent, which attracted investment in sugar production and worker welfare. Total sugar production in Mauritius reached 530,000 tons in 1953, after which expansion slowed due to the worsening land shortage (World Bank 1968). But in contrast to Trinidad and Tobago, sugar in Mauritius continued to expand through gains in productivity, and peaked at 710,000 tons in 1973, almost three times the peak output of Trinidad and Tobago. Large plantations still dominated the economy in the 1960s, managing just over half the cane land, while the rest was run by smaller estates of up to 80 hectares. On the eve of independence, however, sugar still supplied 98% of Mauritian exports, generated 35% of GNP (and the rest of agriculture just 10% of GNP), and employed 35% of the workforce. Manufacturing generated only 7% of GNP, mainly beverages, clothing, and wood products for domestic consumption (Findlay and Wellisz 1993).

The higher geopolitical rent under the CSA boosted the welfare of estate workers through gains in social security and the eradication of malaria. Income gains were diffused through the broader economy by introducing a progressive taxation system and a minimum wage. The welfare gains helped raise life expectancy above sixty years, well ahead of Africa and also higher than the high-growth economies of north-east Asia (Subramanian 2009). The gains accelerated annual population growth to 3% from 0.5% in the 1930s, however. The population reached 1 million in 1968 on an area of 1,865 km^2, only half of which was arable land. With a doubling rate of just over twenty years, the population was projected to reach 2.4 million by 2000, which raised fears of a Malthusian future that profoundly influenced political developments (Findlay and Wellisz 1993).

Mauritius evolved via home rule to full political independence in 1968, when the economy was even less diversified than that of Trinidad and Tobago. Sugar dominated totally in Mauritius, whereas Trinidad and Tobago had begun to diversify into oil extraction. South Asians dominated the population of Mauritius, comprising two-thirds, compared with two-fifths in Trinidad and Tobago. Some 297,000 indentured Indian workers migrated to Mauritius, twice the rate of immigration from South Asia to Trinidad and Tobago. A majority of the population was Hindu but some were Muslim. The plantation owners were mainly French-speaking, while Britons ran the government and Chinese immigrants moved into commercial services.

Increases in both sugar prices and output slowed from the late-1950s while population continued to grow rapidly, so the mean per capita income began to decline. In contrast, Trinidad and Tobago initially avoided falling living standards by deploying hydrocarbon rent to subsidize employment (Chapter 3). Mauritius's first election under universal suffrage in 1959 voted in the left-leaning Labour Party, which won two-thirds of the seats thanks to its core vote from the Indian majority. The South Asian population favoured independence, but many others were opposed. Mauritius therefore embarked on independence in 1968 as a polarized democracy. Consistent with rent cycling theory, however, the straitened circumstances of a political economy under existential threat led to the formation of a pro-growth centrist coalition government in the 1967 election, which edged a more radical redistributive party into opposition.

5.2.2 The Modest Scale of Mauritian Rents

Mauritius had modest potential rent when it gained independence, comprising mainly cropland rent and geopolitical rent from trade preferences, which tapered off through the 1990s and 2000s. In comparison, the rent of Trinidad and Tobago was several orders of magnitude greater and highly volatile, being almost wholly derived from offshore hydrocarbon reserves. The World Bank provides time series data for mineral rent since 1970, but its estimates of crop rent are available only from 1996. In 2000, Mauritius's cropland rent generated a mere 0.8% of GDP (World Bank 2006) and more recently 0.5% in 2014 (Lange et al. 2018). Estimates of cropland rent in prior years must rely on secondary sources, primarily commodity prices, which include an element of geopolitical rent arising from preferential market access (Greenaway and Lamusse 1999: 214).

Data on overseas development assistance (ODA) are available for Mauritius from 1980 and indicate a steady phasing out of an initially modest flow, averaging 3.9% of GNI in 1981–85 and dropping to 0.4% in 2001–05 (World Bank 2017a). Mauritius also drew geopolitical rent from its favoured access to overseas markets for sugar and textiles. Subramanian and Roy (2013) estimated the annual rent from sugar averaged 4.5% of GDP during 1977–2000, based on comparing the price actually received with world prices. In addition, as sugar rent tapered off, the Multi-Fibre Agreement on textile exports yielded rent that rose slightly from 0.5% of GDP in 1984 to 2.9% of GDP in 1996 as clothing exports expanded (Subramanian and Roy 2003: 223, 235).

Finally, the Mauritian government generated regulatory rent through price intervention, which is difficult to measure (Krueger 1992). It tends to be proportional to the degree of trade closure and the share of government expenditure in GDP. Trends in Mauritian economic policy imply higher levels of regulatory rent prior to the IFI-backed reforms of the 1980s, followed by decline as the economy became increasingly market-oriented and government intervention eased.

Overall, Subramanian (2009: 13) estimates that the combined rents for Mauritius from preferential access to markets for sugar and textiles averaged 7% of GDP per annum through the 1980s, with ODA adding a further 3.5% of GNI per annum in that decade; and then in the 1990s, 4.5% annually, with aid adding 1.3% of GNI per annum (Table 5.1). The decline continued and the rent stream ceased in the 2000s when the WTO removed privileged market access. Mauritius's rent was therefore initially modest and declined, compared with the hydrocarbon windfalls of Trinidad and Tobago, which the World Bank (2017a) estimated at 17.5% of GDP in 1975–79, 15.6% in 1980–84, and 18.9% in 2005–09 (Table 3.2). The hydrocarbon rent of Trinidad and Tobago has been more volatile and therefore more challenging to manage. For instance, compared with boom-time highs of 16–19% of GDP, the rent was 3.4% of GDP in 1970–74 and 8.3% in 1985–89.

5.3 Policy Response to Initial Conditions

Mauritius was widely perceived to face Malthusian prospects at independence. An intensifying shortage of cropland slowed the growth in sugar production, so that mean per capita income declined in the face of rapid population growth. Since unionized sugar workers experienced real gains in incomes courtesy of higher CSA rent, the broader workforce bore the brunt of falling incomes. The threat of a Malthusian outcome motivated the elite to form a centrist coalition to prioritize rapid economic growth, as rent cycling theory predicts (Table 2.2).

Table 5.1 Selected economic indicators, Mauritius, 1960–2014

	1960–64	1965–69	1970–74	1975–79	1980–84	1985–89	1990–94	1995–99	2000–04	2005–09	2010–14
Rent proxies											
Total natural resource rent (% GNI)	n.a.	n.a.	n.a.	0.1	0.1	0.0	0.0	0.0	0.0	0.0	0.0
Mineral depletion (% GNI)	n.a.	n.a.	n.a.	n.a.	0.0	0.0	0.0	0.0	0.0	0.0	0.0
ODA (% GNI)	n.a.	n.a.	n.a.	3.0	4.0	3.1	1.8	0.8	0.4	0.9	1.2
Regulatory rent	n.a.	n.a.	n.a.	n.a.	n.a.	n.a.	n.a.	n.a.	n.a.	n.a.	n.a.
Remittances	n.a.	n.a.	n.a.	n.a.	n.a.	n.a.	n.a.	3.9	0.8	0.0	0.0
Arable land per capita (ha)[1]	0.1	0.1	0.1	0.1	0.1	0.1	0.1	0.1	0.1	0.1	0.1
Economy openness											
Exports (% GDP)	n.a.	n.a.	51.3[2]	46.1	47.5	61.2	60.3	62.7	60.5	54.6	51.4
FDI (% GDP)	n.a.	n.a.	n.a.	0.3	0.2	1.0	0.7	0.8	1.4	2.6	3.6
REER	n.a.	n.a.	n.a.	n.a.	n.a.	n.a.	n.a.	n.a.	n.a.	n.a.	n.a.
Terms of trade[3]	n.a.	n.a.	86.5	63.4	82.8	90.7	91.9	92.3	99.6	84.2	73.4
Absorption (% GNP)											
Fixed capital	n.a.	n.a.	18.3[2]	27.2	20.4	21.9	28.5	25.6	23.0	23.6	22.0
Final government consumption	n.a.	n.a.	12.1[2]	15.1	14.4	12.6	12.8	13.1	13.2	13.6	14.0
Private consumption	n.a.	n.a.	69.9[2]	65.8	71.3	62.9	62.0	61.9	62.1	71.4	74.6
Structural change (% GDP)											
Agriculture	n.a.	n.a.	19.8[2]	20.7	15.4	15.3	11.6	9.1	6.7	5.1	4.0
Industry	n.a.	n.a.	22.1[2]	26.0	25.5	31.8	33.0	31.4	30.4	22.1	23.8
Manufacturing	n.a.	n.a.	14.7[2]	15.3	16.4	23.7	23.9	23.5	22.6	17.8	15.6
Services	n.a.	n.a.	55.2[2]	53.3	59.1	53.0	55.4	59.0	62.9	68.9	72.2

Growth

Per capita GDP (US$, 2010)[4]	n.a.	n.a.	n.a.	2,469.6	2,415.5	3,127.5	4,008.3	4,831.4	5,813.3	7,046.5	8,581.3
GDP (%/year)	5.9[2]	0.4[2]	8.4	6.9	1.3	7.4	5.5	4.7	4.6	4.8	3.8
Per capita GDP (%/year)	3.3	–1.8	6.8	5.3	0.0	5.0	4.3	4.3	3.8	4.4	3.6
Population (%/year)	2.8	1.9	1.6	1.5	1.3	0.8	1.1	0.5	0.8	0.5	0.2
Crop output index[5]	89.9	102.6	107.4	108.4	101.3	110.2	106.2	102.8	104.8	93.3	85.7

[1] Cropland rent 2014 (% GDP) = 0.5 (Lange et al. 2018).
[2] According to Findlay and Wellisz (1993).
[3] According to World Bank (1989).
[4] In 1968 the per capita GNI of Mauritius was one-third that of Trinidad and Tobago.
[5] 2004–06 = 100.

Source: World Bank (2017a).

5.3.1 *Malthusian Conditions Shape Elite Incentives at Independence*

Mauritius's per capita cropland endowment of 0.13 hectares at independence matched that of densely settled north-east Asia and was barely half that of 'overpopulated' Bangladesh. Prospects for further expansion of sugar were dim due to stabilizing quotas in preferential markets as well as the worsening land shortage. Nor did the prospects for export manufacturing seem initially promising: Mauritius lacked mineral resources and was unusually isolated, being 25% further from major global markets than the average African country and 30% further than the average developing country (Sachs and Warner 1997). Some sugar planters responded by investing in plantations on the African mainland, notably Kenya, which had more than three times the per capita cropland endowment of Mauritius.

The UK commissioned an evaluation of the island's growth prospects, which in 1961 recommended measures to control population growth, restrain wages, and diversify the economy by taxing sugar in order to subsidize import substitution industry behind protective tariffs. The import substitution policy was launched in 1964 and a Development Bank was set up to provide long-term finance for industry. It was hoped that industrial development certificates would induce domestic capital to remain in the island rather than flow offshore. The certificates granted tax holidays, duty drawbacks, and protection, initially in the form of tariffs and then, from 1969, by import quotas. Meanwhile, the export sector (basically the sugar industry) was taxed through a levy on exports of 5%. In addition, controls on capital outflows were steadily tightened.

A left-leaning government deployed part of Mauritius's 1963–65 sugar windfall to ease social discontent. It sanctioned wage increases in the export sector that rippled through the rest of the economy, creating modest Dutch disease effects. A 25% increase in the minimum wage was granted, although such rises reduced employment opportunities. For those in employment, real wages rose by 50% during 1958–68, while the cost of living increased by just 12% (Findlay and Wellisz 1993: 234). The rapidly growing workforce outstripped the growth in jobs, however, depressing mean incomes and prompting the government to introduce a public works programme. By 1967 the programme employed one-sixth of the workforce, which pushed public expenditure into deficit. In that year the sugar industry employed 38.5% of the workforce, but the civil service employed 20.3%, while state-funded relief work employed a further 22.3%. Such subsidized employment is associated with the high-rent staple trap trajectory and was unsustainable.

The attempt to diversify the economy through import substitution industrialization was disappointing. By 1970 only 70 infant industry plants had been set up and they were mainly high-cost, producing foods, furniture, plastics, and paints for the local market. The manufacturing sector employed less than 3% of the workforce (Yueng 1998: 7–8), which was barely half its relative contribution to GDP and indicative of its capital intensity. Yet unemployment was approaching 20% of the workforce (Yueng 1998: 6). Nevertheless, Findlay and Wellisz (1993) concluded that the deployment of the rent from the sugar boom helped to maintain social peace, while the cost to the economy in terms of lower profits and reduced investment in the sugar sector had minimum economic impact, at least through the medium term.

The achievement of independence in 1968 coincided with riots that were rooted in declining per capita incomes, mounting unemployment, and the polarization of the political system. Ethnic friction was heightened by the fact that a sizeable minority opposed Mauritius's independence. However, the fears of ethnic minorities had also spawned an electoral system that encouraged their participation in the political process, which in turn placed a premium on political compromise. A majority among the Mauritian elite recognized that the pro-labour squeeze on profits and investment was incompatible with an expanding workforce and rising incomes. Factions within the elite backed a coalition of three political parties, including the dominant Labour Party that formed the first independent government. The coalition commanded sufficient votes to prevent a radical redistributive party, the Parti Mauricien Social Democrate (PMSD), from taking power.

The coalition government negotiated a political deal with the Hindu majority. Both sides agreed that rent should be extracted from the sugar sector to sustain the civil service and social protection, which benefited mainly Hindus, but that such transfers would not be allowed to reach a scale sufficient to damage the competitiveness of the principal industry. In 1968 the newly elected government sent a delegation to Taiwan, which returned convinced of the need to prioritize growth through exporting labour-intensive manufactured goods (Yueng 1998; Baissic 2011). In contrast to Trinidad and Tobago, the Mauritian elite maintained its new developmental policy, which prioritized long-term growth over immediate rent extraction and distribution[3] and sustained that priority, consistent with the low-rent competitive diversification model (Table 2.2).

The coalition government cancelled the 1972 election due to the political instability arising from ongoing social unrest, but it still managed to win sufficient seats in the 1976 election to form a government. This prompted the radical Mauritian Militant Movement (MMM) opposition, which had won the most seats of any party, to moderate its stance and back growth-oriented policies over redistribution. In this way, the emerging economic success of the

---

[3] A similar compromise was reached in Malaysia, a successful resource-rich economy, between the sizeable Chinese business community and the lagging Malay majority.

export manufacturing strategy helped to mature the Mauritian political state through the first fifteen years of independence from a polarized democracy towards a consensual democracy.

5.3.2 Rationale for the Dual Track Rent Deployment Strategy

Subramanian (2009) struggled to explain Mauritius's successful development. He rejected Sachs and Warner's view that it arose from the country's open economy, since high import tariffs persisted into the 1990s. He thereby underestimated the dominant role within the economy of investors in the export processing zone (EPZ) and the plantations whose exposure to international competition incentivized them to deploy inputs efficiently. Rather, Subramanian (2009) leant towards Rodrik (1999), who argued that Mauritius pursued a heterodox trade policy. This policy required the government to intervene to ensure that investment in export-oriented activity was fully compensated for any costs over and above world prices that were incurred by using protected domestic goods and services.

The focus on trade policy is overly simplistic. Lau et al. (2000) provided a more nuanced formulation of the Mauritian policy, which they term dual track economic reform. Basically, a dynamic market economy is created within economic zones (Track 1), while reform of the rent-distorted economy (Track 2) is postponed until the economic and political strength of interest groups in Track 1 is sufficient to dominate and co-opt Track 2 groups. The dual track strategy allowed Mauritius's coalition government to prioritize economic growth while reducing the risk of its dismissal by aggrieved rent recipients. Post-Mao China also espoused this strategy for dealing with reform of its state enterprises.

The competitive diversification strategy, implemented through dual track reform, contrasted with the policies of most newly independent governments, especially in sub-Saharan Africa (Chapter 6), which tended to be land-rich and to allocate rent for political objectives at the expense of markets and economic efficiency. Most governments in sub-Saharan Africa sought to industrialize through import substitution, which as it expanded demanded subsidies that eventually exceeded the available rent. This prompted many resource-rich governments, wary of offending powerful rent-seekers, to tax away not just the economic rent from politically weak commodity exporters but also the returns to capital and labour (Krueger 1992).

More specifically, the Mauritian coalition government established Track 1 as an EPZ in 1970. Although technically an EPZ is a defined geographical area, in practice the EPZ of Mauritius extended anywhere on the island, reflecting Mauritius's very small size. EPZ investors also initially benefited from regulatory rent. They were given a ten-year tax holiday on dividends and profits, along with exemption from import duties on productive machinery, equipment, spare parts, and raw materials if they produced solely for export. In addition, factory buildings on fully serviced land were available at low or subsidized rates, while charges for electricity and water were also subsidized. A state enterprise provided critical services to the EPZ, such as training, investment credits, and negotiation of trade agreements. Finally, labour laws were more flexible and pay was lower in the EPZ than within the rent-distorted sector. This resulted in female labour dominating the EPZ workforce, exceeding two-thirds of the total (Rodrik 2001: 24).

Foreign companies were allowed unrestricted repatriation of their capital investment (other than capital appreciation), as well as all their profits and dividends. They also received guarantees against nationalization and were assured of easy access to residence visas and work permits. These terms attracted firms from Hong Kong, the UK, and France, although the scale of FDI rarely exceeded 2% of GDP (Table 5.1). A location in Mauritius conferred privileged access to developed country textile markets, which encouraged Hong Kong firms to invest in joint venture factories to circumvent restrictions on exports from Hong Kong to the EU and US. Romer (1993) argued that the resulting infusion of expertise was critical to the success of Track 1 by introducing a new and important mode of wealth creation to the island and teaching local investors how to succeed. The hotel industry was granted similar privileges to Track 1 and it too began to expand through the 1970s.

Investment of some of the 1972–75 sugar industry windfall rent, mostly by private firms, helped stimulate the export economy in Track 1. The sugar boom conferred an extra 7.4% of GDP annually in the early-1970s. Most developing country governments at the time taxed away the bulk of such windfalls, which they deployed inefficiently (Auty 2001). Rather unusually, the government of Mauritius left the bulk of the rent with the planters, taxing away only 5–12% of the windfall. Consequently, Mauritius's rent deployment remained relatively diffuse, which both limited scope for government patronage and relied more on markets to allocate it than was typical in sub-Saharan Africa. This improved the efficiency of deployment. The planters invested much of the windfall in the EPZ, where it was exposed to global competition, initially in joint ventures with Asian partners but increasingly in locally owned firms.

Within the wider economy, gross saving jumped from 15.2% of GDP in 1970–72 to 34.2% of GDP during 1974–75 (Findlay and Wellisz 1993). The rate of increase in investment lagged somewhat, but it still rose by one-half to average 23% of GDP on a rising trend. The sugar planters invested some of their windfall in the hotel sector as well as in Track 1 and the domestic sugar industry. As the 1972–75 sugar boom faded, Track 1 still grew rapidly and, along with tourism, accelerated economic diversification. Whereas in 1971 just nine Track 1 firms had generated 1% of exports and employed 640 workers, by 1980 101 firms generated 27% of exports, employed 21,600 workers, and produced 4.3% of GDP (Yueng 1998: 10–11). Meanwhile tourist arrivals tripled through 1970–80 to reach 115,000, marking the broadening of diversification into the export service sector. In these ways the expansion of Track 1 helped drive per capita GDP growth at 6% per annum through the 1970s, which undermined the appeal of the radical redistributive policies of the political opposition.

Developments in Track 2 almost derailed the export-driven development strategy, however. The rent-distorted sector included the import substitution industry, which had led the diversification strategy prior to the launch of Track 1, but had degenerated into a vehicle to accommodate rent-seeking. Social groups with a vested interest in perpetuating rent-seeking included the unions, civil servants, and owners and workers in the import substitution industry. The protection given to infant industry discouraged maturation and imposed costs on domestic consumers, who not only paid more for high-cost locally made goods, often of inferior quality, but also needed to substitute for the import tax revenue that was foregone by protecting infant industry. With no incentive to mature, rent still subsidized rates of effective protection in Mauritian import substitution manufacturing and averaged 185% as late as 1980 (Findlay and Wellisz 1993). Such ratios prompted the IMF to classify Mauritius as a highly closed economy based on its index of trade openness (Subramanian 2009).

The import substitution industry was not only inefficient but also capital-intensive, so it created few jobs, prompting the government to overexpand public sector employment in the civil service and worker relief programmes, as Trinidad and Tobago did. The policy originated in the 1960s but extended into the 1970s as part of the dual track strategy of deferred reform. Protected from competition, wages in the rent-distorted Track 2 sector were around 50% higher than those in Track 1. Additional social policy initiatives included subsidies on basic household commodities. Critically, the policy contributed to growing public debt in the 1970s and became unsustainable after the 1979 oil shock. Track 2 therefore acquired characteristics of the staple trap model (Table 2.2) and threatened to destabilize the entire macroeconomy and derail Track 1's competitive industrialization, despite a decade of rapid GDP growth.

5.4 From Short Growth Collapse to Labour Market Turning Point

This section explains both the growth collapse of the early-1980s, which was shorter than the collapse in Trinidad and Tobago, and how a re-elected pro-growth coalition government turned Mauritius's growth collapse to advantage by using the threat of a recurrence to accelerate economic reform.

5.4.1 Destabilization by the 1972–75 Sugar Boom

Most commodity-driven developing economies mismanaged the rent from the booms of the 1970s. Like Trinidad and Tobago, they invariably absorbed the rent too rapidly into the domestic economy, boosting rent-seeking activity and amplifying Dutch disease effects. By the time the booms had subsided, governments had established patterns of consumption that proved hard to cut back. Many governments initially borrowed to sustain the rate of absorption after the boom, an action that tended to compound the original misallocation of capital and labour, further distorting the economy. In search of additional revenue, governments often squeezed the commodity exports to extract not just rent but returns to capital and labour as well. This weakened the commodity sector even as the economy depended increasingly upon it, which is the essence of the high-rent staple trap (Table 2.2), causing many economies to experience growth collapses that were protracted.

In Mauritius, rising public expenditure within Track 2 to appease rent-seeking interests lay behind the growth collapse. The expanded transfers during the 1970s proved difficult to rein back when sugar prices eased. The coalition had expanded social spending by two-thirds through the 1970s, raising the share of social spending in GDP from 6% to 10% by boosting public expenditure on health and education and increasing food subsidies for the poorest. The extra public expenditure outstripped revenue and widened fiscal deficits. It also sparked inflation as wage rises in the booming plantation sector rippled through the entire economy, irrespective of sector differences in productivity growth. This process was exacerbated by the establishment of a wages council, which automatically indexed wages to inflation. The inflationary pressures received a further push from the 1979 oil shock, which the government responded to unwisely by extending price controls.

Although data on the real exchange rate for 1963–2014 show that the volatility of the Mauritian rate was less than half that of Trinidad and Tobago (Bruegel 2017), which facilitated macro policy, inflation still eroded competitiveness (Yueng 1998). The loss was exacerbated by government retention of the export tax on sugar that it had raised to 6% as a temporary measure during the boom. The levy imposed losses on the hitherto efficient sugar sector that risked decapitalization. By 1979, public sector borrowing had reached 13% of GDP and external debt topped 50% of GDP. Although the debt/GDP ratio was lower than in many contemporary developing economies, it was deemed unsustainable (Findlay and Wellisz 1993). Foreign exchange reserves shrank to just two weeks of coverage and forced the government to approach the IFIs for assistance.

The IFIs provided assistance to stabilize economies after their growth collapses and to reduce their external debt, on condition of economic reform. In many cases, rent-seeking interests sought to capture the reform policy in order to substitute geopolitical rent for the reduced natural resource rent and regulatory rent. This initially retarded reform, thereby rendering the growth collapses protracted in many countries, as in the case of Trinidad and Tobago. In contrast, the growth collapse of low-rent Mauritius was, like that of low-rent South Korea (Chapter 7), brief and lasted through the early-1980s.

5.4.2 Speedy Macroeconomic Stabilization and IFI-Backed Recovery

The IFI reforms strengthened Mauritius's dual track development strategy. The IMF and World Bank granted assistance in exchange for the adoption of orthodox economic policies that reduced social expenditure and dismantled trade controls. The resulting economic retrenchment shrank GDP by 10% in 1980, which sapped the coalition government's political support and helped the opposition MMM to win a landslide victory at the general election of 1982. However, by then Mauritius had evolved from a polarized democracy at independence into a consensual democracy because the radical opposition party strengthened its commitment to democracy and abandoned its former prioritization of nationalization and worker self-government.

Instead, the MMM pledged to promote investment while planning a wealth tax to meet higher social spending along with higher minimum wages and expanded employment opportunities. By then its ambitious nationalization plans had been scaled down to sustaining two loss-making sugar mills and holding half the equity in the hotel sector. On taking office following its 1982 victory, the MMM party adhered to the principal tenets of the economic reforms agreed with the IFIs. The new government focused on economic stabilization while also promoting domestic and foreign private investment. The stabilization policies split the MMM government, however, which led to an early general election in 1983 that saw a new pro-growth coalition take power, comprising a splinter group of the MMM along with the PMSD and the Labour Party, which adhered to the IFI-backed developmental policy.

The new pro-growth government inherited falling inflation (down to 6.4%) and a shrinking deficit (5.6% of GDP), but with unemployment still very high at 17% of the workforce, far from the labour market turning point (Yueng 1998: 19). However, external conditions improved as energy prices fell in real terms and the global economy recovered. The government curbed social expenditure, so that by the late-1980s it channelled one-third of its geopolitical rent (some 2.5–3% of GDP annually by then) into a social safety-net.

Food subsidies which had accounted for more than 2% of GDP were cut by two-thirds. On the revenue side, a value added tax was introduced at 5% in 1983. Tax rates were streamlined and reduced from penal levels down to 35% for the maximum rate on both profits and income in order to further encourage saving and investment for wealth creation. After an initial decline, tax revenues began to expand in the mid-1980s. Overall, the budget deficit fell from 12.6% of GDP to 2.1% through 1982–87 and taxes diversified away from trade and high earners.

Private firms invested in wealth-generating activity, in response to partly the rebalancing of taxation and partly incentives for wealth creation such as the encouragement of import substitution firms to export. Firms that were hitherto domestically oriented were offered lower taxation on the share of output that they exported. In addition, trade liberalization phased out import quotas along with domestic price controls. A further move to harmonize conditions across the two tracks of the economy saw the Track 1 tax holiday replaced by a 15% profit tax, which was still relatively low but aimed to encourage long-term investment rather than short-term profit-taking. Track 1 firms were also exempted from minimum wage legislation in 1985, which caused male employment to expand in Track 1 from its low level of one-fifth of the total.

In contrast to Trinidad and Tobago, Mauritius's growth collapse was brief and gave way to boom. The share of investment recovered to 30% of GDP, although the efficiency of investment was somewhat disappointing, yielding an ICOR of five compared with three to four in Taiwan and South Korea at a similar income level. Through 1980–90 the number of Track 1 firms rose from 101 to 570 and EPZ employment quadrupled to 89,900, which was 31% of the total employment. In macroeconomic terms, Track 1 contributed in 1990 some 12% of GDP and 64% of exports (Yueng 1998: 19–20). Meanwhile, the number of tourists increased from 115,000 in 1980 to 295,000 in 1990 when direct expenditure on hotels and restaurants comprised 3.1% of GDP (IMF 2005b: 35).

Mauritius's labour-intensive manufactured exports increased rapidly from one-quarter of total exports in 1980 to two-thirds in 1990, finally ending sugar's two centuries of economic dominance. Whereas many Track 1 firms in the 1970s had been joint ventures, the investment in the 1980s was mainly by domestic firms, which specialized predominantly in textiles. Apparel comprised more than 80% of production (Baissic 2011). At its peak the Mauritius textile industry was the second largest world producer of knitted textiles, the third largest exporter of pure wool tissues, and the fourth largest exporter of T-shirts to Europe.

The rapid growth in textile exports helped to transform the trade deficit into a surplus in the mid-1980s and, after a phase of depreciation, the exchange rate began to strengthen. However, Subramanian (2009: 16) calculated that compared with the developing countries as a group, Mauritius sustained a significantly undervalued exchange rate for an unusually prolonged period. Labour-intensive textiles and clothing still provided 84% of exports in the early-1990s, of which three-quarters were shipped to markets providing concessional entry, namely the three largest EU economies (51%) and the US (32%). The next most important export, clocks and watches, accounted for only 3.9% of exports.

The speedy recovery from the recession of the early-1980s merely cut the rate of per capita GDP growth through 1980–84 to 0%, before it rebounded to grow at 5.0% in 1985–89 (Table 5.1). However, economic growth was still driven mainly by the accumulation of capital and labour: productivity growth contributed just one-tenth to the growth rate (Subramanian 2009: 4). In consequence, rapid economic growth boosted total employment, which tripled in the EPZ during 1980–90, while the national rate of unemployment fell from 21% to 4%. Labour shortages began to prompt some firms to import low-cost labour. By the early-1990s Mauritius had therefore reached the Lewis labour market turning point, whereas in high-rent Trinidad and Tobago the prolonged growth collapse had caused unemployment to balloon to 20% of the workforce (Chapter 4).

5.5 From Labour-Intensive Manufacturing to a Service Economy

This section examines Mauritius's rapid structural change after it reached its labour market turning point. Consistent with the competitive diversification model, we note first the shift into productivity-driven economic growth and then the rise of service exports.

5.5.1 *Elimination of Surplus Labour and Shift into Productivity-Driven Growth*

The arrival of the labour market turning point intensified wage pressures. Wage rates in spinning had reached US$1.40 per hour in Mauritius by the early-1990s compared with US$1 in Thailand, US$0.56 in India, and US$0.36 in China and Vietnam. By the mid-1990s, Mauritian textile wages were four times those of China and Vietnam and this exerted pressure to raise productivity, as the low-rent model predicts (Table 2.2). The rate of growth of textile production within the EPZ slowed to average only 6% in 1989–93 compared with four times that rate in 1984–88 (Financial Times 1994a).

The responses of textile firms to the elimination of surplus labour differed. Some Mauritian firms relocated the production of low-value textiles to cheap-labour locations like Madagascar and China, while others expanded into higher-value products such as textile design, spinning, weaving, and knitting. This shift into higher-value items contradicts the common criticism that EPZs merely employ low-wage labour. From 1982 to 2007 Track 1 exports grew at an average annual rate of 11%. By 2007 the importance of the EPZ to the economy resembled that of sugar production a generation earlier: Track 1 generated 66% of exports and 26% of GDP with 36% of the labour force and 19% of the capital stock (Subramanian 2009: 14). At its peak, the zone employed 60,000 workers in 500 firms generating US$1.2 billion in exports. However, constant change was required.

Track 1 firms also diversified into more skill-intensive industries and services through the 1990s, including information technology (IT) (Chernoff and Warner 2002). The growth in total factor productivity accelerated to contribute one-quarter of the economic growth rate, or 1.4%, compared with one-tenth previously. The economy grew by around 5.0% per annum through the 1990s, even as the erstwhile dominant textile sector began to slow and shed employment. The pace of decline in the two key staples accelerated through the late-2000s: employment in textile production fell by 36,000 and in sugar by 22,000. By then their contributions to GDP had shrunk below 6% for textiles and 4% for sugar (Joseph and Troester 2013: 24). The decline in each case was accelerated by world trade negotiations, which cut the remaining geopolitical rent by removing preferential market access on textiles in 2005 and sugar in 2009. The government responded in two ways. First it encouraged new export clusters, including financial services, ICT, and fish processing. Second, it prioritized competitiveness so as to prolong a viable sugar sector by lifting previous restrictions on more productive practices that had aimed to sustain employment.

As the WTO phased out preferential market access for crops like sugar, the Mauritius government took advantage of the buoyancy of the broader economy to restructure the sugar industry. In the early-1990s, sugar production had fallen to just over 600,000 tons, down from the peak of two decades earlier. But it still accounted for 12% of GDP, qualifying as one of the four pillars of the economy along with textiles, tourism, and financial services. However, having initially taken advantage of the rent conferred by favourable access to markets to maintain employment (by restricting mill closure, taxing sugar exports, and banning imports of harvest machinery), the government reversed course.

The Mauritian sugar industry maintained the competitiveness of most of its output through the commodity super-cycle, whereas the Trinidad and Tobago sugar industry collapsed. Whereas the real exchange rate of Mauritius appreciated by 10% from the late-1990s to the early-2010s, that of Trinidad and Tobago strengthened by more than 50% (Bruegel 2017). Mauritian sugar production costs under the CSA regime were 25% above world levels, compared with three times higher for Trinidad and Tobago, which was hopelessly uneconomic. The Mauritian government cut costs further. It abolished the sugar export tax, which had previously been cut from 6% to 4%, and promoted measures to lower production costs from 40 cents/kg to 26 cents/kg. Seven of the eleven sugar factories were closed (already down from 21 at peak production in 1973) so as to increase average factory size and capture the internal economies of scale. In addition, cane production and cane harvesting were mechanized, which entailed some loss in output on marginal land that was released for tourism and IT activity (IMF 2002). To counter friction with the workforce and discourage rent-seeking, workers were given the opportunity to take a 25% share-holding in the surviving efficient sugar factories.

5.5.2 Expanding Services

By the late-1990s, services rather than manufacturing had become the main driver of the Mauritian economy. Tourist arrivals had tripled through 1983–93 to reach 375,000, when the sector employed 11,000 workers directly (Financial Times 1994b), but arrivals then doubled to 700,000 in 2003, when the sector contributed more than one-tenth of GDP for the first time (Baissic 2011). Tourists generated around one-quarter of export earnings by then, helping total service exports to exceed those of goods exports (Joseph and Troester 2013: 23). Yet the Mauritian tourist industry, like that of Reunion, remained overly reliant on Europe, especially France, echoing the pattern of colonial or neocolonial dependence that had started with sugar and continued with textiles. This proved unfortunate when the global financial crisis struck in 2008. Tourist arrivals stabilized and were 965,000 in 2012, whereas a projection made on the eve of the financial crisis had forecast 1.5 million tourists by then. Since the hotel sector had expanded capacity by one-third on the basis of such growth projections, room occupancy rates languished at around 60%, increasing to 76% in the mid-2000s (Financial Times 2013).

The slowdown in tourism contributed significantly to a halving in the rate of GDP growth through the late-2000s. Mauritius considered diversifying towards Asian tourists, including Chinese. But this risked shifting towards mass tourism, which the environment of a small island like Mauritius would struggle to accommodate, especially with respect to congestion. In 2011 tourism contributed 12.6% of GDP directly, a figure that more than doubles to 28.6% when indirect effects are included (World Travel and Tourism Council 2012a). The addition of induced effects lifts the figure to just above 30% of GDP. With respect to employment, those directly employed by tourism totalled 67,500 (12% of the total), but consideration of indirect employment boosted the workforce to 151,000 (26.5%).

Even as tourism boomed and then slowed, finance and insurance expanded to become the fourth pillar of the economy. The sector already contributed directly an estimated 5% of GDP in 1990 (Joseph and Troester 2013), which increased to 10.3% of GDP by 2012 (Financial Services Commission 2013). The sector employed around 12,000 workers directly, which was only 4% of total employment, but it employed a much larger number indirectly in outsourced legal, accounting, technology, administration, processing, and other services. The institutional inheritance from the UK and its subsequent adaptation contributed strongly to the lead in financial services that Mauritius built within the region. In 2015 Mauritius ranked forty-sixth out of 128 countries in the Global Competitiveness Index, second highest within the African region and well ahead of Trinidad and Tobago (Table 4.5).

A major source of business growth for Mauritius arose from channelling capital into the Indian economy, taking advantage of a double taxation treaty to compound the benefits that Mauritian firms enjoyed from the island's low-tax regime. Some US$75 million of FDI was injected into India from 2003, using Mauritian skills and advantageous tax breaks. Faced with tension over Indian charges that Mauritius permits investors to exploit a 'tax haven', the Mauritian financial sector sought to diversify by becoming an investment conduit for sub-Saharan Africa. This entailed Mauritius competing directly with the Seychelles and Singapore as well as Luxembourg and the Netherlands in this regard (Financial Times 2013). However, by 2010, Mauritius had agreed taxation treaties with twelve African governments (Googoolye 2012).

The Mauritian government aimed to emulate Singapore and boost scope for logistics businesses by facilitating trade between Asia and Africa. With this in mind it engineered a low-tax environment for international business. It realigned its tax rates at 15% for both export-oriented and domestic-oriented activity. In addition, the mean tariff level was reduced from 19.9% in 2001 to just 6.6% six years later (Baissic 2011: 242). These measures have their roots in the 1994 launch of the drive to establish a low-tax, free trade area when Mauritius created two free zones at the international airport and the seaport. Such measures proved timely, given the subsequent decline in exports of textiles and sugar.

Mauritius continued to find new diversification options, notably within ICT and fish processing. By 2012, ICT was estimated to generate 6% of GDP and to be growing at around 8% annually (Joseph and Troester 2013: 61). It employed 17,000 workers, depending on the definition used for ICT work, and contributed around 3% of export revenue. This is well short of the ICT export ratio achieved by India of 47%, indicating considerable growth potential. While low-order services through call centres dominated export sales, IT outsourcing firms began to expand. Future employment growth is expected to be rapid and draw especially on younger workers and also women as they are discharged from the shrinking textiles industry.

The 2008–13 financial crisis prompted the Mauritian government to consider further economic reform and to reorientate the economy geographically, not only within Asia but more especially to Africa. The government concluded that Mauritian finance could perform four functions for Africa by acting as: (i) a channel for FDI, building on its financial sector, quality of institutions, and low-tax advantage; (ii) an entrepot for trade between Africa and Asia; (iii) a source of investment and expertise in sugar production and other agribusiness; and (iv) an investor in textiles of various levels of sophistication, which were relocating from Mauritius to the neighbouring continent (Financial Times 2013). To varying degrees, Mauritius performed these roles for India in the 2000s, drawing upon the increasing sophistication of the Mauritian financial and legal sectors.

5.6 Conclusions: Drivers of Mauritian Success

The low-rent competitive diversification trajectory of Mauritius exhibits three critical advantages compared with the high-rent staple trap trajectory. First, Mauritius demonstrates that a modest and tapering rent stream may improve welfare at a faster rate than a larger rent stream. Rather like the tortoise in the fable of the tortoise and the hare, the Mauritian economy has sustained a higher average rate of economic growth since independence than the more erratic Trinidad and Tobago hare. The rent-driven economy of Trinidad and Tobago advanced spectacularly during booms but slipped backwards when rents subsided. Moreover, the greater economic gains of Mauritius are more securely underpinned because they are generated by a diversifying economy that is buttressed by maturing institutions and is globally competitive. By contrast, in most high-rent economies, commodity booms trigger Dutch disease effects that discourage investment in competitive diversification, so that gains from rent windfalls may prove transient.

Second, Mauritius shows that policy counts. After independence, both Mauritius and Trinidad and Tobago downgraded inherited policies of industrialization by import substitution in favour of export-oriented industrialization in line with their comparative advantage. The labour-intensive competitive industrialization of Mauritius proved far more effective than the resource-based industrialization of Trinidad and Tobago, however. The superiority of labour-intensive manufacturing derives from its self-sustaining internal dynamic that confers a singular pattern of structural change, which is summarized by the low-rent competitive diversification model (Table 2.2). It rapidly expands labour-intensive manufacturing to absorb surplus labour and reach the labour market turning point, whereupon rising wages exert pressure to boost productivity through diversification into more capital-intensive and skill-intensive activity. The diversification process is self-sustaining and driven by structural change rather than being driven by industrial policy, which at most is accommodating. In addition, rapid structural change spawns new groups in society that are ready and able to contest policy capture by rent-seeking interests. Together they help to embed into policy the allocation of resources by efficient markets at the expense of political allocation via patronage networks. In comparison, the resource-based industrialization pursued by Trinidad and Tobago furnishes a minimal diversification from commodity dependence: the downstream products, whether metals or petrochemicals still depend on subsidized energy.

Third, dual track reform reduces the risk that a reforming government will be dismissed mid-reform (before it can embed competitive diversification) by rent recipients who are the potential losers from reform. The dual track strategy postpones confrontation with the rent-seeking groups in Track 2, until the dynamic market economy in Track 1 gains sufficient size and political strength to absorb the rent-distorted economy and channel erstwhile rent-seeking groups into productivity-driven growth. In addition, the early success of the dynamic economy drives political maturation from an initially polarized democracy into a consensual democracy that maintains policy continuity despite changes in government.

In an echo of the high-rent model, however, Track 2 of Mauritius's dual track strategy generated features of the staple trap by the late-1970s that threatened to destabilize the economy. These features arose from increased social expenditure, boosted by rents from the 1972–75 sugar boom, which created entitlements that proved difficult to both sustain and cut when the boom subsided. The resulting growth collapse proved brief, however, and prompted the pro-growth government to use the threat of a further growth collapse to justify accelerating reform of rent-dependent Track 2. The reforms merged Track 2 into the competitive, low-tax economy in Track 1, thereby subjecting Track 2 activity to market discipline. In contrast, successive governments of Trinidad and Tobago failed to recognize, and more importantly to proactively respond to, intensifying rent dependence and the need for policy reform. The 1981–93 growth collapse in Trinidad and Tobago was ended by a massive expansion of natural gas exports, while the nonenergy sector continued to be starved of the investment required for much-needed economic diversification.

Finally, Mauritius's experience suggests that the self-sustaining structural change triggered by the labour market turning point is the principal driver of the competitive diversification model. In contrast, the demographic components of the model appear to have a much smaller role (Table 2.2). Both

Table 5.2 Population growth and dependency ratio, Mauritius and Trinidad and Tobago, 1960–2010

	1960	1970	1980	1990	2000	2010
Mauritius						
Population growth (%/year)	2.9	1.7	1.5	0.9	1.0	0.5
Age dependency, old	4.9	4.6	6.0	7.1	9.0	10.9
Age dependency, young	91.5	81.6	58.6	43.7	37.8	29.3
Age dependency, total	96.4	86.2	64.6	50.8	46.8	40.2
Trinidad and Tobago						
Population growth (%/year)	2.3	0.9	1.5	0.7	0.3	0.4
Age dependency, old	6.6	7.6	9.0	9.5	9.6	11.7
Age dependency, young	79.8	76.2	56.1	55.4	37.7	29.2
Age dependency, total	86.4	83.8	65.1	54.9	47.3	40.9

Source: World Bank (2017a).

Mauritius and Trinidad and Tobago display similar trends in demography and dependant/worker ratios (Table 5.2), albeit Mauritius started its demographic transition later and proceeded faster. Moreover, the gini coefficient of Mauritius, having declined from 0.500 in 1960 to 0.389 in 2006, was not much lower than the coefficient for Trinidad and Tobago of 0.403 (Vandermoortele and Bird 2011; Joseph and Troester 2013). However, the experience of sub-Saharan Africa examined in Chapter 6 identifies the circumstances under which the demographic cycle plays a much more crucial role. It does so as the opening chapter of Section 3, which applies the rent-driven models to explain trends in the economic development in five major global developing regions.

Section 3
Differential Rent-Driven Development in Global Regions

6

Agricultural Neglect and Retarded Structural Change in Sub-Saharan Africa

6.1 Introduction

Section 3 applies the rent-driven models to explain trends since the 1960s in the economic development of five major global developing regions, namely sub-Saharan Africa, Latin America, East Asia, South Asia, and the Gulf states. It does so in three chapters, each of which also evaluates the role of the dominant economic sector in the regions' development. We argue that post-war policy in the developing countries outside East Asia prioritized manufacturing with adverse consequences for both agriculture, whose growth potential was frequently neglected, and export services, which also continue to be undervalued. We elaborate on the costs of agricultural neglect in sub-Saharan Africa; query the pessimism of Rodrik (2018) regarding the consequences of premature deindustrialization in Latin America; and evaluate the rise of export services in South Asia. We draw these threads together in Chapter 9 (Section 9.4) to make the case for a sector neutral development policy based upon emerging comparative advantage.

This chapter applies the rent-driven models to explain the persistence of a large but low-productivity agricultural sector in most economies in sub-Saharan Africa. At independence, the majority of sub-Saharan African economies were classified as small and resource-rich. They were mostly reliant upon small-scale farming, but a handful were mineral-dependent (Auty 2001: 24). We focus here on crop-driven growth and defer consideration of mineral-driven growth until the chapters dealing with Latin America and the Gulf states where mining has played a more prominent role. Farming in sub-Saharan Africa initially generated diffuse rents with potentially favourable development linkages, whereas mining yielded concentrated rents, which have proved more challenging to manage (Table 2.1).[1]

It may be recalled that Baldwin's (1956) yeoman farm model suggests that the diffuse economic linkages and flexible production functions of the crop-exporting economies of sub-Saharan Africa favoured competitive diversification of the economy. Yeoman farming rewards modest increments in investment with rising productivity and incomes to drive a rural multiplier that stimulates local manufacturing of simple household goods and farm equipment, some eventually for export (Mellor 1976).

Yet, the crop-driven economies in sub-Saharan Africa traced a staple trap trajectory instead. We attribute this predictive failure to the neglect of Baldwin's model to specify two key pre-conditions, namely a developmental political state and effective institutions, which most countries of sub-Saharan Africa lacked, apart from Botswana and Mauritius. The result has been that most economies traced a staple trap development trajectory. The resulting false start of sub-Saharan Africa on economic development underlines the very high cost of a retarded demographic transition, which the competitive diversification trajectory avoids.

6.2 The Global Regional Context

Section 2 identified the central role played in successful economic development of rapid and self-sustaining structural change, driven by the efficient pursuit of comparative advantage. Most traditional societies embark on development with around 80% of their workforce in low-productivity agriculture, 10% in artisanal manufacturing, and a further 10% in service activity. Incomes should rise partly as a consequence of gains in productivity—both 'within-sector' gains, which result from the accumulation of capital, technological change, and shifts of resources between firms; and 'structural reallocation' that arises from transferring labour from low-productivity activity, initially agriculture, into higher-productivity employment. Advanced economies tend to employ around 80% of their workforce in services with a mix of productivity—17% in high-productivity industry and 2% in high-productivity agriculture. All too often, high-rent economies falter in making the transition to a high-productivity economy, however, and intensify their dependence on rent, from whatever source, instead of achieving competitive diversification.

---

[1] World Bank (2012) provides a useful snapshot of sub-Saharan Africa's mineral economies during the commodity super-cycle.

6.2.1 *Rent Streams*

Most countries in sub-Saharan Africa were land-rich at independence, but around one-tenth of Africans lived in mineral-rich economies (Ndulu et al. 2008). In addition, a third small group of economies, mostly in the Sahel, were initially resource-poor, but some nevertheless accumulated sizeable composite rent streams. For example, as noted earlier, Mauritania generated rent from minerals (10% of GNI) in its first independent decade, but from the early-1970s received geopolitical rent in response to drought, and then rent from fishing licences taken by EU ships, conferring total rent equivalent to two-fifths of GNI for over forty years (Auty and Pontara 2008). In sub-Saharan Africa overall, total natural resource rent rose from 4.7% of GDP per annum in 1970 to 8% in 2015 as the super-cycle commodity boom faded. But in twenty-three countries, natural resource rent exceeded 10% of GDP, and in a further eleven it comprised between 5 and 10% (World Bank 2017a). Estimates of cropland rent from case studies such as Cuddington (1989) for Kenya and Ghanem (1999: 145) for Cote d'Ivoire suggest that it can be 5–10% of GDP. For example, the World Bank (Lange et al. 2018) provided an estimate of cropland rent for Uganda in 2014 of 9.6% of GDP, four times the ratio for India.

Geopolitical rent in the form of ODA in sub-Saharan Africa expanded from US$3 billion in 1970 to US$18 billion in 1987, at which time inflows of nonconcessional loan capital were slightly larger (Sundberg and Gelb 2006). Thereafter, nonconcessional loans fell abruptly while ODA stabilized at US $20 billion, until a major expansion in the 2000s lifted the annual total to US$40 billion by 2011–15. The recent expansion incorporated improvements in aid delivery after criticism that much aid fed rent-seeking activity. Thereafter, development aims were prioritized over political objectives in deploying ODA. The importance of aid in sub-Saharan Africa varied between countries. For example, in 2015 it exceeded 10% of GNI in twelve countries; lay between 5 and 10% of GNI in twelve more; and was less than 5% of GNI in twenty-six (World Bank 2017a).

Estimates of regulatory rent are drawn from case studies (Krueger 1992; Sharpley and Lewis 1990). It may be recalled that regulatory rent is a function of state intervention and proportionate to the degree of trade closure. This implies for sub-Saharan Africa that regulatory rent expanded steadily after independence through the late-1960s and 1970s as the adoption of what Ndulu et al. (2008) described as antigrowth syndrome policies (discussed in Section 6.4.2) intensified, before levelling off during the IFI reforms that commenced in the 1980s. Finally, remittances reached US$38 billion in 2017 (World Bank 2017a) but tend to be diffuse and beneficial in low-income economies like those of sub-Saharan Africa.

Resource endowments have changed over the period studied: mineral discoveries tripled the ratio of Africans living in mineral-driven economies to 30% (Ndulu et al. 2008). The remaining economies, most of which were initially land-rich, experienced sustained rapid population growth that transformed many into land-poor economies. The average per capita cropland endowment in sub-Saharan Africa shrank from 0.57 hectares in 1961 to 0.22 hectares in 2014 (World Bank 2017a). Rent cycling theory predicts that the resulting rent squeeze will encourage elites in the most land-poor economies to promote economic growth by pursuing their emerging comparative advantage in labour-intensive exports. Mauritius is an early example, but when the initially land-rich sub-Saharan African countries subsequently approached land scarcity they struggled to make that adjustment (Ndulu et al. 2008: 84–87) due largely to chronic neglect of the agricultural sector (reviewed in Sections 6.4 and 6.5).

6.2.2 The Broad Pattern of Development: Lagging and Skewed Long-term Structural Change

The basic pattern of development for sub-Saharan Africa is one of a brief promising start at independence, giving way to sluggish overall growth through 1960–75, and then a growth collapse into the 1980s and 1990s, in most cases cancelling out the earlier income gains (Ndulu et al. 2008: 78–79). The IFIs responded to government requests for assistance from the mid-1970s and into the 1980s by making loans conditional on structural adjustment programmes to rebalance the heavily distorted economies. The reforms took longer than expected to revive economic growth, however, due in part to opposition from rent-seeking interests. Overseas aid initially struggled to improve growth prospects (World Bank 2012), partly because it functioned to some extent as a substitute for shrinking regulatory rent, until the aid was more carefully targeted.

The reforms were eventually sufficiently effective for most countries to benefit from the 2004–14 commodity super-cycle, which conferred rapid annual GDP growth on sub-Saharan Africa of around 6%. Long-term structural change in sub-Saharan Africa diverged from the broad global pattern, however: it displayed a pronounced lag, and manufacturing generates a much smaller share of GDP than Asia or Latin America, despite the contraction of agriculture (Diao et al. 2017). Moreover, agriculture still employs almost two-thirds of the workforce, and at low levels of productivity. Nevertheless, gains in poverty reduction in the crop-driven economies outstripped those of the mineral economies as the latter continue to battle against increased rent dependence. Those Africans living in extreme poverty in the mineral economies failed to benefit from rapid economic growth, and the rates of extreme poverty actually increased in Gabon, Angola, and Congo-Brazzaville (World Bank 2012).

During the commodity super-cycle, the number of countries in sub-Saharan Africa classified as middle income (with a per capita income exceeding US$1,000) rose to twenty-two out of forty-eight, with a total population of 400 million. However, Africa's middle income countries have struggled to escape the middle income trap, which only a handful of developing economies, including the East Asian Dragons, have succeeded in achieving. The mid-income countries of sub-Saharan Africa have struggled, like many others, including relatively successful economies like Brazil, Indonesia, and Malaysia. Swift progress to middle income status during the commodity super-cycle gave way to decelerating economic growth, and at a lower per capita income than in most mid-income economies (Flaaen et al. 2013). The competitive diversification model suggests that the fastest gains in productivity and welfare occur when surplus labour is absorbed into globally competitive activity, notably labour-intensive manufacturing. In sub-Saharan Africa, however, it is labour-intensive services within the informal sector that dominate the absorption of surplus rural labour from low-productivity agriculture (McMillan 2012).

The causes of the middle income trap appear to be linked to deficiencies in manufacturing in some countries, mainly in sub-Saharan Africa and Latin America, but in others like Malaysia it is linked to an unreformed service sector. The middle income trap has also revealed a strong association with inadequate institutions (Eichengreen et al. 2013). However, another group of countries, including India, Indonesia, and Vietnam, struggles with deficient infrastructure, notably transportation and telecommunications. Eichengreen et al. (2013) concluded that the middle income trap is associated with three main factors: tardy economic diversification, low productivity growth, and lagging secondary and tertiary education. All three characteristics are evident in sub-Saharan Africa.

Uganda provides an example of the sub-Saharan African development trajectory (Auty 2017b). It exhibited favourable prospects at independence as a land-rich peasant farm economy endowed with moderate natural resource rent comprising mostly beneficially diffuse crop rent. It also had an enterprising Asian business community capable of facilitating economic diversification. However, ethnic tension between northern herders and wealthier southern farmers prompted northern elites to capture the government, confiscate Asian business assets, and manipulate crop prices to extract rent. A protracted growth collapse through 1974–86 retarded the demographic transition, so that high population growth transformed the economy from land-rich to land-poor (Table 6.1). Although natural resource rent along with sizeable geopolitical rent drove economic recovery during 1990–2015, boosted public

Table 6.1 Selected economic indicators, Uganda, 1960–2014

	1960–64	1965–69	1970–74	1975–79	1980–84	1985–89	1990–94	1995–99	2000–04	2005–09	2010–14
Rent proxies											
Total natural resource rent (% GDP)	n.a.	n.a.	8.6	14.9	28.8	9.6	20.1	15.5	15.1	14.6	11.8
Energy depletion (% GDP)	n.a.	n.a.	0.0	0.0	0.0	0.0	0.0	0.0	0.0	0.0	0.0
Ore depletion (% GDP)	n.a.	n.a.	0.8	0.7	0.0	0.0	0.0	0.0	0.0	0.0	0.0
Forest depletion (% GDP)	n.a.	n.a.	2.6	3.5	7.8	2.6	9.4	6.0	6.1	4.8	11.7
Aid (% GNI)	4.5	2.3	2.0	1.4	7.2	5.9	20.1	11.7	14.9	13.5	7.6
Regulatory rent	n.a.	n.a.	n.a.	n.a.	n.a.	n.a.	n.a.	n.a.	n.a.	n.a.	n.a.
Remittances (% GDP)	n.a.	n.a.	n.a.	n.a.	n.a.	n.a.	n.a.	n.a.	5.0	4.3	4.0
Arable land per head (ha)[1]	0.46	0.45	0.39	0.35	0.32	0.31	0.26	0.23	0.20	0.18	0.18
Economy openness											
Exports (% GDP)	26.8	24.4	18.8	12.5	13.1	10.1	7.9	11.8	12.3	18.8	18.9
FDI (% GDP)	n.a.	n.a.	(0.2)	0.1	0.1	0.0	1.0	2.5	3.0	5.4	4.1
Net barter terms of trade[2]	n.a.	n.a.	n.a.	n.a	236.0	235.4	129.0	154.1	95.7	96.7	113.9
REER[1]	n.a.	n.a.	n.a.	n.a	560.1	237.9	112.5	119.8	91.5	88.0	118.1
Absorption (% GDP)											
Fixed capital formation	12.2	12.6	11.9	6.1	8.6	9.7	14.7	17.1	19.8	22.3	27.2
Final government consumption	8.7	10.4	n.a.	n.a.	10.8	9.3	9.8	12.4	14.5	12.9	9.4
Household consumption	75.3	75.9	n.a.	n.a.	86.3	87.7	88.8	80.4	78.7	75.8	75.4
Structural change (% GDP)											
Agriculture	51.5	51.1	58.3	71.9	59.3	55.9	52.5	43.4	33.8	24.7	27.5
Industry	13.4	13.4	11.6	6.4	8.6	10.2	12.7	17.2	20.9	25.8	21.7
Manufacturing	8.2	8.6	8.0	5.3	5.1	6.0	6.0	8.5	9.6	7.7	10.5
Services	35.2	35.6	30.3	21.8	32.1	33.9	34.9	39.4	45.3	49.5	50.7
Growth											
Per capita GDP (US$, 2000)	n.a.	n.a.	n.a.	n.a.	177.1	162.3	180.6	222.7	253.3	338.2	356.1
Population growth (%/year)	3.3	3.5	3.0	3.1	3.2	3.6	3.3	3.0	3.3	3.2	3.3
GDP growth (%/year)	4.0[3]	5.4[3]	1.0[3]	-3.2[3]	2.7	3.2	6.0	7.7	5.4	8.0	5.5
Per capita GDP growth (%/year)	0.7[3]	1.9[3]	-2.0[2]	-6.3[3]	-0.6	-0.4	2.5	4.5	2.0	4.8	2.2
Crop output index[4]	42.2	48.1	76.0	74.2	59.9	63.4	80.1	89.9	104.6	105.6	109.1

[1] Cropland rent 2014 = 9.6% of GDP (Lange et al. 2018).
[2] 2000 = 100 (Chenery and Syrquin (1975).
[3] According to Kazekende and Antingi-Ego (2008).
[4] 2004–06 = 100.

Source: World Bank (2017a).

investment, and bridged fiscal and current account gaps, self-sustaining growth remains elusive.[2] Competitive diversification lags (Table 6.1) and Uganda has experienced agricultural involution as manufacturing remains stunted, which has left agriculture and the informal sector to absorb the expanding workforce at low or subsistent incomes.

The rest of this chapter is organized as follows. Section 6.3 compares structural change in sub-Saharan Africa with that in the other major developing regions in more detail. The remaining sections explain the African pattern. Section 6.4 identifies the important role played by a transition sector of low productivity informal activity in managing sub-Saharan Africa's rural labour surplus and explains how maladroit rent deployment brought this about. Section 6.5 evaluates alternative explanations for and solutions to sub-Saharan Africa's lagged structural change. Section 6.6 summarizes the findings and considers their implications.

The staple trap model identifies three principal reasons for sub-Saharan Africa's distinct structural change. First, the elite prioritized immediate rent extraction over long-term growth in response to initial conditions that include ethnic diversity, youthful democracies, and weak institutions. Second, cumulative economic distortions triggered growth collapses through 1975–99 that retarded the demographic transition, so that population growth outstripped job creation, exacerbating the rural labour surplus. Third, disadvantageous agroclimatic conditions combined with low farm productivity, reflecting sustained rural neglect, to render food expensive. This boosts wages sufficiently to remove any potential global competitive advantage, as opposed to regional advantage,[3] from low-cost labour.

6.3 Structural Change in High-Rent Sub-Saharan Africa

In the 1950s, Ghana was deemed to be destined for successful development, whereas South Korea was viewed as a development basket-case. The outcome is the opposite of what was predicted, both for the individual countries and for their respective regions. This section draws on rent cycling theory, along with three stylized facts African development trajectories identified by Timmer

[2] McKinsey (2016) classified Uganda, Botswana, Cote d'Ivoire, Kenya, Mauritius, and Rwanda, among others, as stable economies that maintained economic growth through the early-2010s above 4% annually and diversified away from resource dependence. They generate one-fifth of regional GDP. In contrast, growth in the unstable economies decelerated from 2010. They comprise most mineral economies, generate 43% of regional GDP in aggregate, and need to diversify away from resources. Slow growers (Maghreb and Southern Africa) generate 38% of GDP.

[3] McKinsey (2016) saw scope for manufacturing to expand via competitive import substitution and regional exports, albeit limited global export potential.

(2012) to describe sub-Saharan Africa's lagged and skewed structural change and to analyse the forces that mould it.

6.3.1 Structural Change and Productivity: Sub-Saharan Africa in Comparative Perspective

Binswanger-Mkhize (2012) traced structural change in sub-Saharan Africa from 1961 to 2007 (Table 6.2). Over the entire period, there is a modest net gain in per capita GDP, measured at purchasing power parity (PPP), of just 16%, or 0.35% per annum. Manufacturing initially stagnated and then contracted after 1990, falling from 17% of GDP to just 14% by the early-2000s. Over the same period, the share of agriculture in GDP, which was initially low compared to the global pattern, shrank by just 3%, to 17%. Critically, however, the ratio for agricultural *employment* is very different: employment in agriculture doubled to 198 million in 2007, which comprised 63.8% of the total workforce. Agriculture therefore remains by far the principal source of employment but is characterized by remarkably low productivity, which in 2010 was one-quarter that of services and manufacturing (Table 6.3).

McMillan (2012) compared recent trends in productivity growth in the three principal developing regions through 1990–2005. She noted that developing Asian economies followed the mature economies' pattern of structural change and productivity growth more closely than the other principal developing regions. Chapter 7 attributes East Asian success to the pursuit of the low-rent competitive diversification trajectory, stressing labour-intensive industrialization that sustained *employment*-expanding structural change. The trajectory was also more productive: average regional labour productivity growth rates through 1990–2005 ranged from 3.9% in Asia through 1.4% in Latin America to just 0.9% in sub-Saharan Africa (Table 6.4).

Table 6.2 Structural change in Africa, 1961–2007

Structure of the economy	1961–70	1971–80	1981–90	1991–2000	2001–07
Population growth (%/year)	2.5	2.8	2.9	2.7	2.4
Per capita GDP (US$ constant 2005 PPP)	1,451.0	1,775.0	1,643.0	1,516.0	1,685.0
Per capita GDP growth (%/year)	2.40	0.80	−1.13	−0.40	2.43
Agriculture share of GDP (%)	21.0	20.0	18.0	18.0	17.0
Industry share of GDP (%)	31.0	33.0	34.0	30.0	30.0
Manufacturing share of GDP (%)	17.0	17.0	17.0	16.0	14.0
Services share of GDP (%)	48.0	48.0	48.0	53.0	52.0
Agriculture labour force (millions)	96.6	114.4	139.4	170.0	198.4
Agriculture share of labour force (%)	82.9	78.2	73.1	68.2	63.80

Source: Binswanger-Mkhize (2012: 10).

Table 6.3 Economic structure (% GDP) and productivity ratios, sub-Saharan Africa, 1990 and 2010

Sector	Value added 1990	Value added 2010	Labour share 1990	Labour share 2010	Labour productivity 1990	Labour productivity 2010
Agriculture	24.9	22.4	61.6	49.4	0.4	0.4
Industry	32.6	27.8	14.3	13.4	3.5	2.6
Mining	11.2	8.9	1.5	0.9	23.9	19.5
Manufacturing	14.0	10.1	8.9	8.3	2.4	1.6
Other	7.3	8.8	3.9	4.2	5.3	2.9
Services	42.6	49.8	24.1	36.8	2.4	1.6
Distribution	28.1	34.0	12.9	23.5	3.0	1.8
Finance and business	5.4	8.6	1.5	3.4	10.4	8.1
Government	11.5	12.2	6.4	8.7	2.5	1.7
Other	2.9	3.5	5.3	5.4	1.0	1.0

Source: de Vries et al. (2013).

Table 6.4 Decomposition of productivity growth (%/year), by main global region, 1990–2005

	Total productivity growth	Growth within economic sectors	Growth from intersector transfer
Latin America	1.35	2.24	−0.88
Africa	0.86	2.13	−1.27
Asia	3.87	3.31	0.57
High-income economies	1.46	1.54	−0.09

Source: McMillan (2012: 3).

McMillan (2012) broke the productivity gain into its two prime components, namely within-sector gains and structural reallocation, and identifies failing intersectoral transfer of labour as a marked feature of sub-Saharan Africa. She found that through 1990–2005 the within-sector productivity growth rate for sub-Saharan Africa averaged 2.1% annually, whereas intersectoral transfer contributed −1.3% for the very low net gain in productivity of just 0.9% per annum. The negative intersectoral rate reflects labour transfers being mainly from sectors with productivity somewhat higher than average, namely *formal* sector wholesale and retail trade, and into lower-productivity services, mostly within the informal economy such as community help, personal services, and government. Meanwhile, productivity in manufacturing grew by a negligible 0.25% through the entire fifteen-year period studied. In sharp contrast, the within-group labour productivity growth for developing Asia was 3.3% per annum, while labour transfer between sectors *added* 0.6% per annum for an overall annual gain of 3.9% (Table 6.4).

Latin America occupies an intermediate position between East Asia and Africa: its within-group gain in productivity averaged 2.2% per annum through 1990–2005, while the contribution of intersector labour transfers was –0.9%, to give an overall productivity gain of just 1.4% (Table 6.4). Yet Latin America data for 1950–75 suggest that whereas the growth of the within-sector component of productivity was similar to that of 1990–2005, the rate of growth of the intersector productivity component was positive and also relatively high at 2%, but it subsequently collapsed.

McMillan (2012) attributed the decline to economic reforms following the growth collapses of 1975–90, which closed the least competitive manufacturing plants in Latin America or dismissed excess labour. Critically, the discarded labour tended to shift into less productive activity through 1990–2005, whereas in the earlier period it gravitated towards more productive activity. The switch to a negative contribution of the labour transfer component in productivity growth occurred around the mid-point of the period covered (early-1980s) and accounts for the marked slowdown in both Latin American productivity growth and the region's manufacturing-led structural change.

6.3.2 *Sub-Saharan Africa's Lagged Transition*

Rent cycling theory suggests that mineral-driven economies are more at risk of growth collapses than peasant farm economies because their rent is concentrated and easier to steal, whereas cropland rent is more diffuse, being spread across many economic agents, and therefore more effectively deployed and less vulnerable to theft. However, as noted earlier, many governments in sub-Saharan Africa abused their crop marketing boards to extract rent by retaining significant fractions of the world price. This practice converted the diffuse cropland rent into concentrated rent, squeezing real returns so that farmers became vulnerable to growth collapses.

Nevertheless, the staple trap model predicts that without new rent streams, such as a mineral discovery, growth collapses will be self-correcting. This is because by prolonging the demographic transition, growth collapses shrink per capita rent to a level that eventually incentivizes the elite to grow the economy and accrue wealth by promoting efficient economic growth. Widespread growth collapses did occur in sub-Saharan Africa through 1974–86 and beyond (Ndulu et al. 2008: 63) and, as the staple trap model predicts, they did retard the demographic transition and perpetuate rapid population growth. But labour-intensive manufacturing failed to expand. Much of the additional population therefore remained in the rural sector, which led to vigorous land colonization that eroded initial land abundance and rendered many countries land scarce.

The slow pace of reform prolonged passage through the demographic cycle and further postponed the arrival of the Lewis labour market turning point, with adverse implications for rural productivity. Without rapid growth in labour-intensive manufacturing for export, surplus labour in sub-Saharan Africa remained trapped in low-productivity agriculture or else seeped into the transition sector. The transition sector comprises small, informal, labour-intensive firms engaged in varied manufacturing and service activity geared towards domestic demand. It lacks the in-built momentum of a productivity-boosting export sector that drives the competitive diversification model. Rather, during the reforms, geopolitical rent played an important role in sustaining living standards (Rodrik 2018 within a trisector economy that comprised: low-productivity agriculture; the closed, informal transition sector; and an open, modern formal sector that swung between exporting and serving the domestic market in response to shifts in the real exchange rate and access to regulatory rent.

During the stalled demographic transition, the rapid increase in the work-force in most sub-Saharan African countries was largely accommodated by extending the cultivated area for subsistence agriculture. Table 6.2 indicates that the *agricultural* workforce of sub-Saharan Africa doubled in the four decades from the 1960s to the 2000s. Nevertheless, some very modest redistribution of labour away from agriculture also occurred, so that despite the large absolute increase in agricultural workers, the sector's share of the total workforce declined from 83% in 1961–70 to 64% in 2001–07 (Table 6.2).

The corollary of sub-Saharan Africa's expanded transition sector is a marked underdevelopment of manufacturing. Through 1950–2006, in the developing countries as a whole, rising productivity within industry combined with inter-sector transfer from agriculture into industry to explain 50% of the catch-up with mature economies in total productivity, according to Duarte and Restuccia (2010). Sub-Saharan Africa diverged markedly from this pattern, however: for more than four decades the share of manufacturing in GDP remained constant or declined slightly, depending on the database. For example, using a different database from Binswanger-Mkhize (2012), de Vries et al. (2013) estimated that in 2000 manufacturing generated just 10% of GDP, slightly less than in the 1970s and less than half the average share of manufacturing in GDP in the developing countries as a whole. Moreover, unlike the developing countries as a group, the share of manufacturing in GDP in sub-Saharan Africa has been declining, so that manufacturing output per capita is around one-third that of the developing country average (Page 2012).

6.3.3 Timmer's Three Stylized Facts Models of African Structural Change

Timmer (2008) investigated the stalled agricultural transition in sub-Saharan Africa in some depth, and usefully summarized his findings in terms of three stylized facts trajectories of structural change (Table 6.5). The three trajectories are differentiated according to the rate at which they transfer low-productivity agricultural workers into higher-productivity services and manufacturing. They comprise: (i) a rapid transfer with labour-intensive manufacturing; (ii) an intermediate rate of transfer, mainly into informal manufacturing and services; and (iii) a minimal labour transfer out of agriculture. In each of the three trajectories the economy is assumed to grow for two decades, with sector growth rates of 7.5% in manufacturing, 5% in services, and 3% in agriculture (just ahead of population growth). The differences between the three basic

Table 6.5 Three stylized facts trajectories of structural change in sub-Saharan Africa, 1990–2010 (% GDP, except where stated)

	Industry	Services	Agriculture	GDP
Start condition (year 0)				
Output	20.0	30.0	50.0	100.0
Share of GDP	20.0	30.0	50.0	100.0
Number of workers	7.0	15.0	50.0	72.0
Labour productivity	3.0	2.0	1.0	1.4
Share of workers (% of total)	9.7	20.8	69.5	100.0
Sectoral growth rates (%/year)	7.5	5.0	3.0	4.5
Contribution to growth in year 0	1.5	1.5	1.5	4.5
End outcome (year 20)				
Output	85.0	80.0	90.0	255.0
Share of GDP	33.3	31.4	35.3	100.0
Number of workers				
(i) Labour-intensive model	28.0	40.0	39.0	107.0
(ii) Intermediate	14.0	24.0	69.0	107.0
(iii) Minimal labour absorption	7.0	15.0	85.0	107.0
Labour productivity				
(i) Labour-intensive model	3.0	2.0	2.3	2.4
(ii) Intermediate	6.8	3.3	1.3	2.4
(iii) Minimal labour absorption	12.7	5.3	1.1	2.4
Share of workers in total workforce				
(i) Labour-intensive model	26.2	37.4	36.4	100.0
(ii) Intermediate	13.1	22.4	64.5	100.0
(iii) Minimal labour absorption	6.5	14.0	79.5	100.0
Contribution to GDP growth in year 20	2.5	1.6	1.1	5.2
Memo item				
Inequality index: labour productivity ratio	Top 20%: low 20%			
Start ratio	2.6			
End ratio				
(i) Labour-intensive model	1.5			
(ii) Intermediate	4.0			
(iii) Minimal labour absorption	7.2			

Source: Timmer (2012, 2008).

sectors in their growth rates reflect differences in technological progress on the supply side and the operation of Engel's law on the demand side. Over the entire two decades of observation, total GDP with rapid transfer expands 2.5 times for an average economic growth rate of 4.8%, but on an accelerating trend that commences at 4.5% per annum and ends at 5.2%. The workforce is assumed to grow by 2% annually, so that the aggregate labour productivity increase is 70%, which implies an annual rate of growth of 2.7%.

Timmer's rapid-growth trajectory resembles the competitive diversification model from rent cycling theory, being driven by labour-intensive manufactured exports. It confers the fastest rate of labour absorption out of agriculture. The model holds labour productivity constant in both the manufacturing and service sectors as those sectors draw labour from agriculture at the same annual rate as the growth of each sector. One interesting consequence of the rapid pace of absorption of labour from agriculture is that after two decades, labour productivity is higher in agriculture than in services and only 23% below that of manufacturing.

At the other extreme, the minimal labour absorption model sees sector productivity in manufacturing and services grow at the same rate as the sectors themselves, so neither sector absorbs new workers. New workers therefore remain confined to the agricultural sector which must accommodate the entire increase in the workforce. However, because agricultural productivity growth rises slightly faster (albeit only marginally) than the growth of the farm workforce, the agricultural sector manages a 0.3% annual gain in productivity in Timmer's model.

Timmer's minimal labour absorption model most closely matches the aggregate pattern for sub-Saharan Africa, but not exactly. Importantly, in his model, not only does the size of the agricultural workforce expand substantially, but also its share of the total workforce increases, rising from 69.5% at the outset to 79.5% after twenty years (Table 6.5), contrary to the data analysed by Binswanger-Mkhize (2012). In fact, the minimal labour absorption model most closely matches the shift in labour experienced during African growth collapses, as for example with Uganda during 1974–86 (Auty 2016a) and Rwanda through 1980–94 (Auty 2016b).

Finally, the intermediate scenario assumes labour productivity in manufacturing and services grows at half the rate of sectoral output growth. The absolute size of the agricultural workforce expands by 38% over the twenty years, when it employs 64.5% of the total workforce, and labour productivity in agriculture grows at 1.4% annually. This set of outcomes is closer to the pattern exhibited by sub-Saharan African economies like Ghana and Nigeria, after they had revised their official statistics to take fuller account of activity in the informal transition sector. It also captures the outcome for economies recovering from growth collapses following IFI reform and in receipt of sizeable inflows of geopolitical rent.

The memo item in Table 6.5 shows the productivity ratios of Timmer's three trajectories after twenty years, which provide an index of income inequality. Consistent with rent cycling theory's competitive diversification model, the data indicate that the most equitable distribution of income is associated with the rapid structural change of Timmer's labour-intensive trajectory, with a ratio of just 1.5:1.0 for the incomes of the richest one-fifth to the poorest one-fifth. This compares with an income ratio of 7.2:1.0 for the minimal labour absorption trajectory.

The critical insight from Timmer's models is that the faster and more labour-intensive the rate of structural change, the swifter the decline in the share of low-productivity agriculture not only in the economy as a whole, but also in the total workforce. The fastest rate of structural change is associated with the fastest growth in agricultural productivity, even though the rate of growth in agricultural GDP remains the same in all three of Timmer's scenarios. The development trajectories therefore underline the central role of structural transfer in raising rural labour productivity and thereby reducing poverty.

The broader conclusion, which is elaborated in Section 6.4, is that the failure of sub-Saharan Africa's crop-driven economies to match the promise of Baldwin's (1956) crop-driven model with its beneficially diffuse linkages and structural change reflects policy failure. Most crop-driven economies followed a staple trap trajectory. That model attributes the failure to politically driven rent deployment that neglected agriculture in favour of subsidized urban activity, notably protected manufacturing, a prime source of rent extraction, triggering growth collapses that prolonged the demographic transition. Farmers responded to the lack of competitive diversification and scope for nonfarm employment by extending the cultivated margin rather than by intensifying yields (Binswanger-Mkhize and Savastano 2018), engendering a process of agricultural involution (Geertz 1963) in place of the productivity-boosting structural change that Baldwin predicted and that effective economic development demands.

6.4 Sub-Saharan Africa's Transition Sector

This section analyses the dynamics of the sub-Saharan African economies' transition sector and its role in the pattern of lagged structural change. Timmer (2012) argued somewhat controversially that rapid industrialization had not been achieved by any developing country, although he conceded that several East Asian countries (Hong Kong, Singapore, South Korea, and Taiwan) have come close. He considered that most countries of sub-Saharan Africa fell well short of such an outcome, but made exceptions for South Africa, which made an early start on industrialization, and two well-governed countries, Mauritius and Botswana. In fact, neither Botswana nor South Africa developed vibrant outward-oriented manufacturing sectors, but Mauritius did, as Chapter 5 confirms. Instead, for the vast majority of sub-Saharan African economies, the transition sector has filled the void left by the underdeveloped manufacturing sector.

6.4.1 *The Nature of the Transition Sector*

Diao and McMillan (2014) showed that much economic growth in sub-Saharan Africa has taken place within the transition sector, which comprises informal, labour-intensive, multisector activity that is orientated towards the domestic market. They argued from data on economic growth for 2000–12 that structural change has been greater than official statistics suggest due to underrecording of informal activities. In particular, workers are moving out of agriculture and into nonagricultural activity within the transition sector. The transition sector therefore substitutes to some extent for the role played in East Asia by manufactured exports in the absorption of labour from low-productivity agriculture. It is, however, by no means as effective in raising productivity as export manufacturing.

The full extent of transitional activity has been masked because it is performed by numerous small firms within the informal sector that are difficult to monitor. Lewis (1979) identified the sector as an 'in-between' sector that typically comprises many small, labour-intensive firms with one to five employees, some of which engage in simple manufacturing, but others in construction, transport, and a wide range of services that are mostly aimed at domestic consumers. Diao and McMillan (2014) viewed the transitional sector as a predominantly 'closed' component of the evolving economy. It produces similar goods and services to the formal modern sector, albeit of lower quality and price and, critically, is aimed overwhelmingly at domestic demand rather than exports. This reduces the competitive stimulus to higher productivity compared with export activities.

The informal transitional sector exerts a strong multiplier effect within the mainly 'closed' domestic economy. However, incomplete official data significantly understate the size of the transition sector and therefore total GDP in many sub-Saharan African economies. Recent measurements of this hitherto underrecorded sector have resulted in major additions to the total GDP of, for example, 60% for Ghana and 89% for Nigeria. In this context, the modern formal sector comprises the 'open' component of the evolving African economy, which trades on global as well as domestic markets. Activity within the modern sector moves between domestic and foreign markets according to shifts in the real exchange rate. The shifts are a function of the scale and pace of external capital absorption, including natural resource rent from exports. But it also includes geopolitical rent, which it may be recalled has often been sizeable in the aftermath of the 1974–85 growth collapses (OECD

2017), and exhibits similar properties and similar consequences to natural resource rent (Rajan and Subramanian 2011).

The transition sector injects some flexibility into the economy by allowing many workers, especially those with primary and post-primary education, to move out of low-productivity agriculture and into mixed services and manufacturing activity with higher productivity (Table 6.3). As a result of this process, Benin and Nin-Pratt (2016: 50–51) reported steady gains in total factor productivity for sub-Saharan Africa since the mid-1980s, in contrast to the minimal advance through the first generation of independent development. The gain has been assisted by the IFI-backed economic reforms, which brought substantial improvements in development policy from the late-1990s (Ndulu et al. 2008: 63; Radelet 2016).

de Brauw et al. (2014) confirmed that in recent decades, by far the most important gain in rural productivity in sub-Saharan Africa, accounting for one-half, came from small farmers switching their main source of income to farm-related activity in rural towns in either self-employment or public sector jobs.[4] A further one-third of the gain came from raising land productivity through higher yields. Finally, rural–urban migration accounted for barely one-sixth of the gain in rural productivity. However, whereas many educated workers may have benefited from moving between sectors, workers with little or no education remain for the most part trapped in low-productivity agriculture with shrinking per capita land resources (Diao et al. 2017).

6.4.2 How Rent Deployment Distorted Sub-Saharan African Economies

The low productivity of agriculture in sub-Saharan Africa is not an inevitable outcome of the development process, but reflects flawed policies. Agriculture can play a significant role in the early stages of economic growth (Johnston and Mellor 1961). The sector can provide cheap food and cheap labour to the expanding cities, along with inputs for manufacturing, as well as foreign exchange and tax revenues. Critically, but often ignored, farmers furnish an important source of domestic demand, because at low income levels during the early stages of development they comprise by far the bulk of the population (Mellor 1976). Farmers can therefore provide a large market for locally manufactured farm inputs and household goods, provided the development strategy boosts farm productivity so that rural incomes rise. An additional benefit conferred by a robust agricultural sector is that it is more pro-poor than industrial growth (Diao and McMillan 2014), mainly because farming offers the poor greater participation in driving the economy.

---

[4] Many younger men undertake long-distance migration to accumulate capital and send back remittances (Bahiigwa et al. 2005).

Rent cycling theory suggests that without the institutional and policy discipline required for effective deployment of mineral rents, the prospects for economic development in sub-Saharan Africa appeared more favourable for the high-rent crop-driven economies. This is because small cash-crop exporters generate diffuse economic linkages that deploy resource rents effectively (Baldwin 1956; Bevan et al. 1987), whereas large mines exhibit concentrated linkages that are vulnerable to policy capture and maladroit rent deployment, especially if the mines are state owned. Unfortunately, as noted in Section 6.3.2, most sub-Saharan African countries embarked on independence with less mature political economies than Baldwin's model assumes or that many Asian and Latin American countries possessed. Dumont (1966) recognized early on that most former French colonies in sub-Saharan Africa had made a false start on economic development after independence by prioritizing indigenization of the civil service and promoting industrialization over efficiency gains in peasant farming. We attribute the disappointing development outcome in sub-Saharan Africa to this post-independence policy failure.

Ndulu et al. (2008: 12) concurred and usefully recognized four antigrowth syndromes arising from maladroit rent deployment in sub-Saharan Africa, namely: espousal of regulatory regimes that distort productive activity to benefit rent-seeking; ethnoregional redistribution that sacrifices efficiency to garner resource transfers to local political groups; intertemporal redistribution that cycles resources to present citizens at the expense of citizens of the future; and state breakdown or civil strife and local insecurity. Krueger (1992) adds that policy in sub-Saharan Africa became too complex for governments to comprehend the full consequences of their own myriad interventions.

Ndulu et al. (2008: 63) measured the deterioration in development policy in sub-Saharan African economies in terms of the percentage of time through the years 1960–2000 that the economies as a group exhibited one or more of the four antigrowth syndromes. On the eve of independence, policies were syndrome-free for 65% of the time, but the ratio declined to below 20% during 1975–88, before improving only slowly thereafter. A sharp rebound commenced in the late-1990s which by 2000 lifted the incidence of syndrome-free policy to 58% of the time. The improvement reflects the structural adjustment programmes and economic reforms that were a condition of the IFIs for providing loans to help stabilize sub-Saharan African economies after the post-1974 growth collapses and to reignite economic growth.

Policy error deflected most sub-Saharan African countries away from Baldwin's diffuse linkage development trajectory and onto a staple trap path. Many governments in sub-Saharan Africa squeezed not only natural resource rent from peasant farms and nationalized mines but also regulatory rent in the form of part of the return to capital and labour. The total rent was invariably absorbed into the domestic economy too rapidly and in line with political objectives rather than economic considerations, so that its deployment was economically inefficient. Fearful that urban unemployment might lead to violence, governments expanded urban jobs in industry and public sector services that depended on subsidies from the primary sector, which was, meanwhile, relatively neglected. This meant that small farmers needed to make their own adjustments in order to raise productivity and incomes.

Most sub-Saharan African governments favoured industrialization by import substitution to help expand employment, which proved an inefficient solution because much of the industry was capital-intensive and created few jobs. In addition, domestic demand was typically inadequate to support factories of minimum viable size, which therefore ran inefficiently below capacity and with little incentive to mature. For example, as one of the larger African economies, Kenyan GDP was only US$1.6 billion in 1970 (World Bank 2017a), which was still less than one-quarter the size of a large economy, which is defined in Table 1.1 after Chenery and Syrquin (1975) as having a domestic market in 1970 greater than US$7 billion. Only resource-rich South Africa and at that time resource-poor Nigeria met the domestic market requirement. Yet other governments persisted with the policy, driven by concern that growing urban unemployment threatened violence. Gelb et al. (1991) showed how counterproductive this strategy is, with reference to Zambia, where the neglect of agriculture fed rural–urban migration, which the government accommodated by providing subsidized urban jobs in the public sector. The creation of urban jobs that were superior to farm employment merely encouraged further rural–urban migration.

Manufacturing became a burden on the domestic economy: the sector was relieved from paying most taxes, unable to earn foreign exchange for the imported inputs that it required, but able to sell products on the domestic market at higher cost despite quality below that of imports. Sharpley and Lewis (1990) provided a measure for Kenya of the scale of transfer of regulatory rent from the rural economy to the urban economy. Kenya was by no means the worst offender, having initially opted for growth-promoting policies because many of the Kenyan elite were cash-crop farmers, notably producing coffee, and benefited from a relatively open trade regime. This delayed the closure of trade policy compared with many African economies and encouraged crop-driven growth through the 1960s. However, a debt crisis resulted in legislation in 1971 that encouraged black ownership of manufacturing, triggering a steady shift of the elite out of farming and into import substitution manufacturing, catching up on developments elsewhere in the region.[5]

---

[5] This section draws upon Auty (2010).

Thereafter, the internal terms of trade of Kenya steadily shifted in favour of manufacturing, except for a brief pause during 1976–79 when a coffee boom boosted resource rent by 8% of GDP annually (Cuddington 1989). The World Bank (1987) calculated that the rate of effective protection of Kenyan manufacturing doubled from the early-1970s to the mid-1980s. By 1985 the average effective rate of protection for manufacturing was 51% of value added, with a range from 37% for private domestic firms to 57% for multinational firms and 65% for parastatals. The expansion of quota restrictions pushed the rate of effective protection on items like rolled steel, with a relatively low domestic added value, to 160%.

Sharpley and Lewis (1990) measured the scale of the subsidies by comparing Kenyan manufacturing value added at world prices with its value added at domestic prices: the difference reflects the burden of the subsidy on other sectors of the economy. Through 1964–84 the increase in the subsidy was equivalent to almost 60% of manufacturing value added, which was also equal to 28% of the increase in agriculture's value added. An analysis of the sources of economic growth reveals that barely 5% of the increased manufacturing output during 1964–84 is explained by exports. Rather, just over one-quarter of the increase is due to import substitution and two-thirds of the increase is due to the expansion of domestic demand. The result was that, as in most of sub-Saharan Africa, Kenyan manufacturing regressed and became less outward oriented and less competitive, while agriculture bore much of the cost, the reverse of what economic development required.

6.4.3 IFI Reforms, Rent Streams, and Agricultural Neglect

The cost of policy failure fell mainly on the rural community. Many African governments exploited the weak political clout of small farmers in isolated rural areas to extract from them not only the resource rent from cropland, but also regulatory rent. Crop marketing boards withheld from farmers part of the export revenue ostensibly to cover the costs of marketing and input supplies, but in fact to also generate revenue with which to bestow favours on political allies. Krueger (1992) estimated that in sub-Saharan Africa, the abuse of marketing boards allowed the state to capture half or more of the world price from crops, double the levels observed in Latin America and Asia. Such punitive revenue extraction repressed farmers' returns to land and labour, encouraging a retreat into low-productivity subsistence farming where returns were meagre but harder to steal. In this way, maladroit policy converted the potentially beneficial diffuse rents of peasant farming in sub-Saharan Africa into concentrated/point source rents. The agricultural sector slipped into the basic roles of absorbing the unemployed and providing a reservoir of unskilled labour at subsistence levels.

The inefficient allocation of rent distorted the economy and weakened it, as the high-rent staple trap model explains, rendering the economy increasingly vulnerable to price shocks and a growth collapse. The oil price hikes of 1973–74 and 1979–81 duly triggered such shocks. Each transferred 2% of global GDP per annum from oil consumers to oil exporters (Chenery 1981) and interacted with volatile markets for other commodities. The first oil shock inflicted growth collapses in those indebted sub-Saharan African countries deemed unable to manage additional loans. The more resilient African economies, like Cote d'Ivoire, Kenya, and Mauritius, along with many Latin American economies were deemed sufficiently creditworthy to be able to borrow recycled petro-dollars. However, many governments deployed the loans for current consumption rather than investment in wealth-generating assets that were capable of servicing the debt. These economies collapsed when the 1979–81 oil shock destabilized their external accounts and led to higher interest rates that sharply raised debt service charges. Kenya, for example, experienced a protracted growth collapse through much of 1980–2004 (Auty 2010: 425). Finally, the oil exporters experienced growth collapses when the oil price plummeted in 1985 due to global consumers conserving energy in response to sustained high oil prices.

The growth collapses were associated with a period of lower natural resource rent as commodity prices eased. In addition, scope to extract regulatory rent subsequently shrank (but not entirely) as IFI-backed reforms reduced state intervention and created greater reliance on competitive markets. Although, as noted, new mineral discoveries expanded the fraction of the population living in mineral-driven economies in sub-Saharan Africa from 10% of the total in 1960 to 30% by 2000 (Ndulu et al. 2008), the majority of sub-Saharan African economies had become land poor. Defining mineral-rich economies as having at least 25% of exports from mining yields twenty such economies, of which seven are oil exporters (Lundgren et al. 2013: 6). Based on data from 1963–2007, Lee and Gueye (2014) found that through the short-run, mineral windfalls enhance welfare by raising incomes and lowering inequality, but the gain for sub-Saharan African countries is small, and almost negligible in countries with weak institutions. Moreover, Lee and Gueye (2014) reported that there are no long-run welfare gains from resource windfalls deployment in most of sub-Saharan Africa, unlike in other global developing regions.

Nevertheless, rent in one form or another continued to play an important role. It helped to boost post-reform regional economic recovery, so that a significant part of sub-Saharan Africa's economic growth remained rent-driven rather than productivity-driven. More specifically, the IFI reforms (Diao and McMillan 2014) were accompanied by a sharp expansion of geo-political rent through the 1980s that was sustained into the mid-2010s in many cases (OECD 2017). Within individual countries the scale of foreign aid could match and even exceed natural resource rent and regulatory rent. Moreover, during the commodity super-cycle, resource rent expanded and augmented foreign aid in stoking Dutch disease effects (Rajan and Subramanian 2011) that inflated real wages at the expense of competitiveness. As explained in Section 6.5.2, this reinforced the role played by rising food costs in boosting real wages and weakening the competitiveness of labour-intensive activity within the now more 'open' reformed modern formal sector of sub-Saharan African economies.

Overall, however, economic distortions were reduced. IFI reforms rebalanced the terms of trade in favour of farmers by dismantling the import substitution industrial policy and transferring to them a much higher fraction of export crop prices. Much import substitution manufacturing in sub-Saharan Africa shut down during the IFI-backed economic reform. Rodrik (2016, 2018) lamented such 'premature deindustrialization', but he assumed that the protected manufacturing plants will eventually mature, which few showed signs of doing. The reforms also weakened the rent-seeking lobby's support for an overvalued real exchange rate, which had cheapened the cost of imported inputs required by domestic manufacturers. Yet rent-seeking persisted: the expansion of foreign aid prompted them to attempt to manipulate it for personal advantage. For example, rent-seekers supported privatization and bought state-owned companies at a discount, but then exerted pressure to retard trade policy reform so they could exploit the monopoly rents of the domestic market conferred by their newly acquired firms.

Critically, the growth spurt driven by higher rents during the commodity super-cycle left many sub-Saharan African economies, and especially the mineral economies, reliant on rent-driven growth rather than productivity-driven growth. In addition, structural change in sub-Saharan Africa has continued to lag other regions and to be skewed against manufacturing, compared with earlier industrialized economies in the advanced countries and East Asia.

6.5 Constraints on Structural Change in Sub-Saharan Africa

Ndulu et al. (2008) concurred in assigning maladroit rent deployment the central role in skewing structural change in sub-Saharan Africa. They identified accommodating preconditions in sub-Saharan Africa as: resource endowments that encourage narrow commodity specialization, which provides large and volatile rents to political incumbents; the diversion of productive resources into rent-seeking and other forms of distributional struggle, including civil wars; and politically driven distortions in the composition of investment and the allocation of labour and capital across sectors and firms. In addition, there is evidence that sub-Saharan Africa has an inherently less favourable physical environment for crop production than the temperate zone environments of both the mature economies and the north Asian economies. Finally, low-productivity food production boosts both prices and wages and thereby erodes the region's potential to benefit from the cheap labour phase of the global development cycle, as some lagging countries in Asia have done.

6.5.1 *Environmental Constraints*

Eberhardt and Vollrath (2014) analysed the environmental constraints. They argued that differences in potential agricultural productivity within the major agroclimatic zones confer diverse propensities for structural change. Using data from 128 countries through 1961–2002, they demonstrated how the elasticities of agricultural output vary with respect to labour in each of the three basic climatic zones, namely temperate/cold, equatorial, and tropical highland climate zones. They also showed that variation in technology helps to determine the differential speeds of structural transformation in response to changing agricultural productivity and demographic pressures.

Eberhardt and Vollrath (2014) used data for 1963–2005 for South Korea, which is located within the temperate zone, to calibrate a model that captures the experience of the economies that were undergoing early structural change during the post-war period of the globalizing world economy. In 1963, 63% of South Korea's workforce was employed in agriculture, but by 2005 only 8% were so employed. Between these dates agricultural output per worker rose by a factor of 7.4 whereas nonagricultural output per worker increased 3.5-fold. The total population grew 1.8 times (Eberhardt and Vollrath 2014: 17), indicating rapid passage through the demographic cycle. Eberhardt and Vollrath (2014) concluded that for a given amount of productivity change, shifts in labour allocation between economic sectors and gains in living standards occur two to three times faster in temperate agroclimatic zones than in either equatorial or tropical highland zones.

Fox et al. (2016) lend support to Eberhardt and Vollrath (2014): they argued that structural change is inherently slower in sub-Saharan Africa than in other developing regions, due to low productivity growth in sub-Saharan African agriculture. As the rent-driven models explain, the combination of low productivity growth and the associated lag in the demographic cycle causes the workforce to expand much faster than wage-paying employment can be created. Fox et al. (2016) showed that through 2000–10 the labour force grew in sub-Saharan Africa by 2.6% per annum compared with 1.7% in South Asia and just 1.2%% in East Asia (Fox et al. 2016: 5). Moreover, wage growth occurs mainly in sophisticated services rather than manufacturing or basic services, so that, as noted, many workers remain trapped in semisubsistence employment within low-paying, low-productivity agriculture and nonwage services (Section 6.4.1).

This pessimistic view of African agriculture has not gone unchallenged, however. The World Bank (2013) concluded that Africa holds almost half of all the unused land available for sustained agricultural production. Moreover, the prolonged period of often extreme policy discrimination against African agriculture (Anderson and Masters 2009) has left much of the region's farming well behind the production frontier, which confers considerable scope to boost productivity now that IFI reforms have eliminated the anti-agriculture policy bias. Significant gains can be made from unused and underused irrigation, especially for small farms, while rain-fed agriculture can also improve yields substantially with access to moderately priced productivity-boosting inputs along with efficient transport to regional markets in burgeoning local cities as well as overseas. Critically, the overall package of inputs can be effectively coordinated through participation in value chains run by dynamic small and medium-sized enterprises. With such coordination, rural production, productivity, and incomes can all improve considerably and trigger strong multiplier effects.

6.5.2 Explanations for Retarded Industrialization

Gelb et al. (2014) argued that low agricultural productivity erodes the potential competitive advantage in global manufacturing promised by the low wages that sub-Saharan Africa's delayed start on development might have been expected to confer, but has failed to do (Page 2012). Gelb et al. (2014) attributed sub-Saharan Africa's modest manufacturing growth to relatively high labour costs that stem from rising food costs. Food typically comprises half of household expenditure, so that gains in food prices can be sufficiently large as to inflate wages relative to those of competitors. Grabowski (2015) concurred: he found that although African labour may be abundant, it may not be cheap and may rise in cost over time. This is basically because much food in low-income economies is virtually nontradeable due to the dominance of subsistence demand. This renders the food market thin and thereby makes prices sensitive to even modest shifts in demand.

The sensitivity of the domestic food prices to minor shifts in demand means that if the modern sector draws labour from the traditional sector at a faster rate than subsistence food can be increased, then food prices rise and erode the cheap labour advantage that is required to sustain labour-intensive export growth. This causes production in the modern sector to become increasingly capital intensive. This outcome in turn shrinks the share of GDP in labour-intensive manufacturing, while the share of GDP in modern sector services rises. In addition, the competitiveness of primary product exports weakens, especially if the export is labour intensive. The economy will grow, but, according to Fox et al. (2016), structural change will be far slower than in, for example, East Asia. Rather, production will shift from agriculture to services, skipping manufacturing, although much of the workforce remains in the traditional sector comprising subsistence farming and nonwage services. The economy will therefore expand employment in the modern sector only slowly, losing the strong dynamic that the rapid absorption of surplus labour bestows on the competitive diversification model.

Grabowski (2015) drew upon Taiwan, Indonesia, and Uganda as representative of the three main developing country regions to demonstrate how gains in agricultural productivity helped to contain labour costs in both Taiwan and Indonesia. This facilitated beneficial structural change in both GDP and labour allocation. However, this was not so for Grabowski's (2015) African case study, Uganda, where lagging gains in food productivity kept labour costs high. Gelb et al. (2017) estimated the cost differential versus Bangladesh (Table 6.6). Relatively high-cost labour has impeded manufacturing growth compared to services and repressed structural change in both GDP and employment.

Gelb et al. (2014) identified additional reasons why sub-Saharan Africa has consistently failed to nurture dynamic industrial firms that are capable of extending investment and thereby diffusing high productivity throughout the economy. Productive firms within the region tend to remain constrained within a narrow band because Africa's geography and colonial history have shaped state formation and market structure in three important ways. First, a complex political economy of business–government relations encourages rent-seeking within Africa's small economies, intensifying resource misallocation. Second, the poor business climate constrains the allocation of production factors between sectors and enterprises. Third, the distribution of firm capabilities is skewed towards a handful of relatively large and well-connected companies with proportionate access to political favours. The latter contributes to a markedly uneven distribution of human capital among the population, which is exacerbated by slow productivity growth. This combination of

Table 6.6 Comparative labour costs (US$) in four African economies and Bangladesh

Economy	Labour cost/worker	Capital cost/worker	GDP per capita
Bangladesh	835.31	1069.84	853.02
Kenya	2118.01	9775.45	1116.69
Tanzania	1776.65	5740.99	1094.95
Senegal	1564.64	2421.98	775.45
Ethiopia	909.28	6137.98	471.19

Source: Gelb et al. (2017: 10).

forces has spawned a political economy that sustains a dysfunctional and high-cost business culture, which represses the productivity of individual firms and retards the convergence of sector-wide and economy-wide productivity.

One further disadvantage arises out of excessively high overland freight charges, which shrink margins for farmers and manufacturers alike, especially in landlocked locations. Uganda's transport costs per ton-mile to ocean-going ports are double those in Brazil or the US. Assuming cropland rent amounted to one-tenth of GDP, not untypical in a small land-rich developing economy (Auty 2001: 131), the transport cost on export crops would absorb 5% of GDP (Teravaninthorn and Raballand 2009: 15). Yet the prime reason for high freight rates is not high operating costs, which along Africa's four main transport routes are similar to those in western Europe. Rather, African transport costs are among the highest worldwide, notably in West Africa and Central Africa, because trucking cartels set prices to yield profits that are twice operating costs. Regulation inflates costs, albeit to a lesser degree, on East African routes, whereas transport in southern Africa functions the most efficiently.

Overall, despite Rodrik's fears about premature deindustrialization and inherent lags in structural change in sub-Saharan Africa, land-scarce, mineral-deficient coastal African economies in particular may yet embark on low-rent competitive diversification. Table 6.6 suggests that Ethiopia may already be close to pursuing such a strategy. More countries may follow in response to a combination of lower commodity prices, continued population pressure on increasingly scarce land, and economic reforms that shrink regulatory rent and improve the deployment of other forms of rent, especially into agriculture. A competitive real exchange rate and efficient sector neutral resource allocation within effective markets may boost rural productivity and constrain wage costs.

6.6 Conclusions

Most countries of sub-Saharan Africa were resource-rich at independence. The majority were small, land-rich, crop-driven economies, although a handful were mineral economies that, with the notable exception of diamond-rich Botswana, struggled to benefit from resource rent (Acemoglu et al. 2002; Auty 2009). Baldwin's (1956) diffuse diversification model suggests that crop-driven economies with diffuse linkages and flexible production functions can develop successfully. Baldwin convincingly argued that the farming system responds to incremental increases in investment with modest gains in productivity and incomes, which trigger a rural multiplier that stimulates diversification into competitive manufacturing and services, some for export.

Critically, however, Baldwin took for granted resilient institutions and sound economic policies, the absence of which throughout much of sub-Saharan Africa resulted in the abuse of crop marketing boards to convert the favourably diffuse linkages of sub-Saharan Africa's small farm agriculture into concentrated linkages that facilitate theft of crop rents. The resulting switch from Baldwin's crop-driven competitive diversification trajectory towards a staple trap trajectory reflects policy error arising out of adverse initial conditions. In sub-Saharan Africa these conditions include youthful political states, malleable institutions, and ethnic tensions that incentivized elite rent-seeking and the associated flawed economic policies.

The cumulative distortions of the staple trap trajectory weakened the primary sector and rendered the crop-driven sub-Saharan African economies vulnerable to economic shocks. The heightened commodity price volatility of 1974–85 triggered growth collapses lasting into the 1990s that largely eliminated the initial post-independence gains in income of 1960–75. The growth collapses also retarded the demographic transition, so that persistent rapid population growth transformed many initially land-rich economies into land-scarce ones. In consequence, the neglected agricultural sector changed from a potential growth motor into a reservoir of surplus low-productivity labour. However, contrary to rent cycling theory, the growth collapses failed to incentivize the elite to pursue the potential comparative advantage in labour-intensive exports. Within sub-Saharan Africa, only Mauritius responded to increasing land scarcity by reform to espouse the competitive diversification trajectory.

The staple trap growth collapses in sub-Saharan Africa contributed to a pattern of structural change that markedly lagged the global pattern and by 2016 had limited the share in GDP of manufacturing to 10.5%, well below that of the other major developing regions. Agriculture still employed a large fraction of the population (55%), but generated only 17.5% of GDP at a very low level of productivity (World Bank 2017a). This reflected failure to complete the demographic transition, so that the growth in the workforce outstripped job creation. In the absence of labour-intensive export manufacturing in sub-Saharan Africa, a transitional informal sector expanded to provide employment that comprised simple fabrication along with basic services and nonwage household tasks. Since these activities are oriented towards the domestic market, they face little international competition and the pressures it exerts to raise labour productivity.

At the root of Africa's false start on development has been the early and widespread adoption of the fashionable post-war strategy of industrialization by import substitution, despite its unsuitability to the small domestic markets of most countries in sub-Saharan Africa at that time. The continuing failure of surplus labour in low-productivity agriculture to trigger labour-intensive manufacturing in sub-Saharan Africa appears to owe much to the tight food markets, which react to small increases in demand by sharply raising prices. The resulting high cost of food boosts wages to levels that erode any cheap labour advantage vis-à-vis low-income Asia, not least for export manufacturing.

In addition, however, the agroclimatic potential of much of sub-Saharan Africa lowers farm productivity compared with temperate developing regions. Nevertheless, policy-makers should redouble their efforts to boost farm productivity, especially in areas of reliable water supplies and superior soils, such as the rift valley lakes region, coastal West Africa, and conflict-free areas of the Sudd (Economist 2016).

Chapter 7 analyses the role of manufacturing in development in more depth with reference to Rodrik's (2018) concern about premature deindustrialization in Latin America and its absence in East Asia.

7

The Evolving Role of Manufacturing in Economic Development

7.1 Context: Persistent Prioritization of Manufacturing-Led Development

In Chapter 6 we attributed the underperformance of agriculture and manufacturing in sub-Saharan Africa to policy failure, namely the prioritization of manufacturing through import substitution and the associated neglect of the considerable growth potential of agriculture at low income levels. In this chapter we focus more specifically on the role of manufacturing and in particular the erosion of Latin America's head start on development by the East Asian dragon economies. We attribute the divergence to the early rejection by East Asian governments of industrialization by import substitution in favour of labour-intensive export-oriented manufacturing. In contrast, Latin American governments persisted with import substitution, partly at the urging of the Economic Commission for Latin America (Prebisch 1950) and partly through rent-seeking inertia.

Most Latin America countries embarked on industrialization earlier than countries in other developing regions. Their governments were forced to industrialize by the economic hardship arising from the disruption of global trade during 1913–45. As the global economy re-emerged in the 1950s, Latin American governments sustained industrialization by import substitution voluntarily. This partly reflected the widespread belief that the terms of trade for primary product producers were deteriorating through the long term (Singer 1950). Manufacturing also appeared to offer faster productivity growth than either agriculture or services due to the strong positive externalities associated with learning by doing (Matsuyama 1992; Sachs and Warner 1997). Since the head start of the advanced economies was believed to constrain entry into manufacturing by developing country producers, state intervention seemed necessary to overcome this.

In fact, most developing country governments opted for industrialization by import substitution, especially the smaller countries, even though their domestic markets for most products were invariably too small to support factories of minimum viable size. The larger developing economies like Brazil, Mexico, India, and China pursued heavy industry big pushes (Auty 1994a), while mineral-rich economies favoured resource-based industrialization (Auty 1990), including hydrocarbon-rich Malaysia, Nigeria, the United Arab Emirates (UAE), and Trinidad and Tobago. Resource-poor economies also initially pursued import substitution, but a handful, including Mauritius, South Korea, and Taiwan, reformed early and deployed their shrinking natural resource rent, geopolitical rent, and regulatory rent to promote an emerging comparative advantage in labour-intensive manufactured exports.

The deterioration of the US military position in Vietnam created an existential crisis that incentivized the East Asian elite to form pro-growth developmental political coalitions and prioritize the efficient allocation of resources for long-term development. In contrast, Latin America governments persisted with import substitution industrialization under soft budget constraints into the 1980s, although this fed rent-seeking and deployed rent less efficiently. The protected industry failed to mature or matured only slowly, and distorted the economy, creating recurring foreign exchange and fiscal gaps that led to volatile economic growth, with growth spurts punctuated by inflation and contractionary stabilizations. The policy repressed comparative advantage; proved vulnerable to policy capture; and extended industry maturation rates by decades. It played a central role in causing most economies to follow a staple trap trajectory that triggered protracted growth collapses during the 'lost decade' of the 1980s and beyond.

Petreski and Wong (2014: 2) summarized the principal outcomes of the two contrasting trajectories. Whereas globally the share of manufacturing in GDP for upper middle income countries peaked at 29% around 1982 and declined to 22.5% by 2010, the share of manufacturing in Latin American GDP peaked at just below 27% in 1988 and declined rapidly to stand at 17.5% in 2010. This one-third decline was considerably larger than the 10% decline averaged by other developing regions, and led Rodrik (2015) to decry 'premature deindustrialization'. In respect to labour productivity, Ungor (2017: 26) showed that whereas South Korea and Taiwan raised their economy-wide productivity from 14% of the US level in 1963 to around 70% by 2011, Latin America raised its productivity through 1961–81 from 35% of the US level to 42% but then retreated to 25% of the US level by 2011. Ungor attributed the difference to policy and institutional failure rooted in the ambivalence of Latin American governments to the private sector, but, as referred to in Sections 7.2.2, 7.3.1, and 7.4.3, IFI-backed policy reform is the more likely cause.

The remainder of the chapter is structured as follows. Sections 7.2 and 7.3 analyse how two Latin American economies of contrasting size, Chile and Brazil, respectively, struggled with reforms aimed at espousing competitive manufacturing. Mineral-driven Chile embarked relatively early and boldly on orthodox economic reform, and consequently presents a longer time frame for evaluation. Brazil reformed later and more reluctantly, after two disappointing industrial big pushes failed to establish sustainable economic growth. Both countries face doubts about the sustainability of post-reform economic growth.

Section 7.4 critically evaluates South Korea's rapid competitive diversification via its controversial heavy industry big push. We note the continuing costs of South Korea's more aggressive reform strategy compared with Taiwan's more cautious policy in terms of welfare foregone and persistent rent-seeking. Section 7.5 concludes by rejecting Rodrik's (2015) thesis of premature deindustrialization in Latin America and sub-Saharan Africa. We argue that recent structural trends reflect a correction of earlier policies of forced industrialization. Moreover, recent innovations in IT and global value chains (Hallward-Driemeier and Nayyar 2017) strengthen the case for dethroning manufacturing in favour of sector neutral development. The innovations accelerate long-term trends in business specialization (Haig 1926) and more recent growth in the productivity of export services, which are the focus of Chapter 8.

7.2 Chile: Does Successful Reform of a High-Rent Economy Cause Deindustrialization?

Through 1973–90 Chile transformed its economy from one struggling with the legacy of prolonged import substitution, which had heightened mineral dependence, into a model of mineral-driven development and best practice political economy in high-rent Latin America. The transformation was associated with significant welfare gains: in 1973 the per capita income of Chile was 82% of the Latin American regional average but rose to 91% in 1989 and 143% by 2013 (Ffrench-Davis 2014: 21). This section critically evaluates this outcome in three parts, explaining: pre-reform trends; the protracted learning curve of economic reform; and whether Chile is an outlier of the Asian Dragon economies or a victim of premature deindustrialization.

7.2.1 Pre-1973: Increasing Mineral Dependence and a Populist Boom

In the early-1970s the per capita income of Chile was close to the Syrquin and Chenery (1989) norm for a country of its size and level of development.

Hitherto, development policy had aimed to raise domestic revenue retention from mining (Auty 1993) while deploying import tariffs to protect nonmining tradeables, namely manufacturing and agriculture, from Dutch disease effects. The economy experienced chronic inflation and frequent fiscal crises that delivered modest growth in per capita GDP of around 2% per annum (Table 7.1). By the early-1970s, mining generated one-tenth of GDP (including 7.7% of GDP in mineral rent) and was the major source of both foreign exchange, a critical requirement for the purchase of inputs for import substitution manufacturing, and government revenues. Agriculture produced barely half the share of GDP predicted by the Syrquin and Chenery (1989) norms for an economy of Chile's size and level of development (Table 7.1), whereas the share in GDP of manufacturing was slightly larger than the norms predicted. However, most manufacturing required protection, with the average tariff above 100% and extensive nontariff barriers on exports as well as imports (Dornbusch and Edwards 1994).

Chile functioned as a factional democracy, but a rift between centrist and centre-right political parties resulted in the election in 1970 of a leftist leader, Allende, with just 36% of the vote. Discontent over income inequality prompted Allende's government to: sanction a sharp increase in real wages; undertake wholesale land reform; and nationalize the mines, banks, and industry. The radical programme ignited a populist boom, which Sachs (1989) argued traces a distinctive four-stage trajectory. First, a brief period of rapid economic growth occurs as wage rises outpace inflation and boost demand, so that idle productive capacity is fully utilized. Second, inflation accelerates and creates worsening trade and fiscal deficits. Third, economic stabilization is required whose deflationary measures cause a sharp economic contraction. Fourth, incomes fall below pre-boom levels before economic growth resumes. In Chile, the socioeconomic turmoil that accompanied the populist boom culminated in a coup that established an authoritarian military regime under Pinochet. The metamorphosis of the military regime into a developmental state, which has the aim of long-term development and the capacity to achieve it (Lal 1995), was not widely foreseen.

7.2.2 The High Cost of Protracted Economic Reform 1973–89

The Pinochet regime adopted bold orthodox reforms, which were implemented by economic technocrats shielded from political pressures by repressing dissent. The reforms aimed to improve manufacturing efficiency and reorient the economy from import substitution to competitive export manufacturing. Faced with inflation of 100%, the stabilization programme was severe and the economic restructuring entailed high social costs. Cuts shrank public spending from 45% of GDP to 24% through 1973–78 and reduced the

Table 7.1 Selected economic indicators, Chile, 1960–2014 (% GDP, except where stated)

	1960–64	1965–69	1970–74	1975–79	1980–84	1985–89	1990–94	1995–99	2000–04	2005–09	2010–14
Rent proxies											
Total natural resource rent	n.a.	n.a.	8.3	10.6	7.8	10.4	8.4	6.5	7.9	18.1	16.7
Mineral rent	n.a.	n.a.	7.7	8.9	6.0	9.2	7.3	5.9	7.3	17.5	16.1
Net ODA received	2.0	1.6	0.4	0.4	0.0	0.1	0.3	1.3	0.1	0.1	0.1
Regulatory rent	n.a.	n.a.	n.a.	n.a.	n.a.	n.a.	n.a.	n.a.	n.a.	n.a.	n.a.
Remittances	n.a.	n.a.	n.a.	n.a.	n.a.	0.0	n.a.	n.a.	0.0	0.0	0.0
Arable land per head (ha)[1]	0.5	0.4	0.4	0.4	0.3	0.2	0.2	0.1	0.1	0.11	0.1
Economy openness											
Exports	12.1	14.3	13.5	21.9	20.4	29.6	29.0	27.2	34.2	41.5	35.0
FDI	n.a.	n.a.	n.a.	0.6	0.9	2.9	2.6	6.8	5.6	7.5	9.1
Terms of trade[2]	n.a.	n.a.	n.a.	n.a.	211.4	156.7	110.5	111.0	104.2	175.0	204.5
REER[2]	n.a.	n.a.	n.a.	n.a.	152.2	93.1	85.8	101.7	90.1	96.1	100.2
Absorption											
Gross fixed capital formation	15.6	15.0	15.2	16.1	16.3	19.6	23.9	25.5	21.1	22.2	23.6
Central government consumption	9.7	10.6	13.9	13.9	13.2	10.7	8.9	10.9	11.8	10.9	12.2
Household consumption	78.1	72.1	72.1	71.6	72.6	64.3	63.7	63.4	62.5	57.6	61.2
Structural change											
Agriculture	9.5	8.5	7.3	8.3	7.0	9.3	9.4	6.5	4.9	4.2	3.9
Industry	38.9	41.8	42.7	39.3	39.6	42.2	40.9	37.0	36.1	40.6	36.0
Manufacturing	23.7	24.8	26.9	22.9	22.7	19.5	20.9	18.8	18.6	13.4	12.0
Services	51.6	49.8	49.9	52.4	53.4	48.5	49.7	56.5	59.0	55.2	60.1
Growth											
Population growth (%)	2.2	2.1	1.8	1.5	1.5	1.7	1.6	1.3	1.2	1.0	0.9
GDP growth (%)	4.4	4.7	1.5	3.5	0.5	6.6	6.8	5.4	4.6	3.8	4.6
Per capita GDP growth (%)	2.1	2.4	(0.3)	1.9	(1.0)	4.8	5.1	4.1	3.4	2.7	3.7
Per capita GDP (US$, 2010)	3996	4760	4725	4362	4938	5204	6782	8775	9977	12045	13948

[1] Cropland rent 2014 = 0.6% of GDP (Lange et al. (2018).

[2] Base year = 2000.

Source: World Bank (2017a).

fiscal deficit from 25% of GDP to 0.8% over the same period (Ministry of Finance 1989). Spending curbs included a public sector wage freeze, redundancies, and the privatization of 400 smaller state enterprises through 1973–79 (Harvey 1980). Labour market reforms weakened trade unions and wage indexation lagged rapid price increases in basic consumer goods.

Trade policy reform lowered the average import tariff from over 100% to 10% by 1979. It also depreciated the real exchange rate by two-thirds and espoused a crawling peg to compensate for subsequent inflation and maintain external balance. The resulting realignment of prices aimed to restructure the economy in line with Chile's comparative advantage in resource-based activity. Table 7.1 traces the recovery in the share of exports in the country's GDP through the 1970s and the relative decline in manufacturing as the level of protection fell.

The costs of adjustment were substantial and fell disproportionately on the poor: Chile's mean per capita income did not regain its 1970 level until 1978, and the poorest fifth of the population experienced declines in income, health, nutrition, housing, and education. The ratio of the income of the richest quintile to the poorest quintile widened from 12 in the late-1960s to 18 in the early-1990s (World Bank 2017a). Meanwhile, the military government strengthened its autonomy by retaining state ownership of copper mining and extracting 10% of the copper revenue for itself.

During 1978–82, reforms became increasingly doctrinaire and proceeded too quickly, leading to a serious policy error. The government assumed a copper boom would commence in 1979 and attract FDI, but it lacked a mineral revenue stabilization fund (MRSF) to manage revenue volatility. Moreover, the government let the exchange rate appreciate to repress inflation, which attracted foreign capital that policy-makers relied on to augment public saving in financing investment. Private domestic saving was barely 3% of GDP because potential domestic investors preferred to consume rather than invest, which raised imports while exports flagged, widening the trade gap. In addition, changes in the terms of trade and the interest rate over 1979–82 inflicted a strong negative shock that intensified in 1982 when copper prices fell further and interest rates rose sharply. Corbo and de Melo (1987) estimated the combined negative shock was 12.2% of GNP in 1982–83, with higher interest rates responsible for almost two-thirds of the 12.2% of GNP negative shock. Foreign capital inflows abruptly reversed, causing the near-collapse of the domestic financial system. By 1985, Chile had the highest per capita foreign debt in Latin America at 140% of GDP and debt service absorbed 48% of export earnings. A government with less autonomy might have abandoned economic reform, but the military government persisted with IMF assistance.

The Chilean government once more espoused economic stabilization, cutting public spending while devaluing the exchange rate. This time, however, it raised average import tariffs to 35% for two years 1982–84 both to temporarily shield manufacturers from foreign competition and to boost government revenues. The government also intervened to avert a banking collapse and belatedly established an MRSF in 1985 to smooth revenue inflows through the mineral cycle. Having stabilized the economy by 1985, government policy re-emphasized export-led growth, aided by an unexpected upswing in copper prices that pushed rents above 10% of GDP annually through 1985–89 (Table 7.1).

The copper boom might have destabilized the economy but for the MRSF. The MRSF set a reference price for copper each year and divided the differential between the long-term price and the actual price into three bands. Revenues up to 0.4 cents/lb higher required no deposit into the MRSF; revenues 0.4–0.6 cents/lb higher required 50% to be saved; and revenues 0.10 cents/lb higher required 100% to be deposited. During the 1988–92 boom, the funds deposited averaged 2.2% of GDP per annum (Marfan and Bosworth 1994), which was associated with a modest appreciation of the real exchange rate in 1988–90.

The copper boom expanded FDI and helped push GDP growth to average 6.3% through 1985–99. Unemployment initially fell sharply from 25% in 1982 to less than 10% by 1987 and the rate of domestic saving recovered from its lows in the early-1980s to average 24% during 1987–95 on a rising trend (Morande 1996). Economic restructuring reduced mineral dependence, so that minerals shrank to just 45% of exports compared with 85% in the early-1970s. Manufacturing accounted for one-third of exports as resource-based industry, notably timber products and metals (Gwynne 1985), replaced import substitution activity. Agricultural exports also grew, especially out-of-season fruit geared to northern hemisphere markets.

The military dictatorship proved a turning point: through 1960–73, Chile's growth had been below the global average and the volatility of per capita GDP was higher, whereas through 1984–2003 Chile's growth was faster than 150 world economies and its volatility significantly lower (Schmidt-Hebbel 2006). The sustained rapid economic growth established a new political consensus in Chile based upon the post-1982 policy of competitive diversification and public subsidies targeted on the neediest. Chile elicited favourable comparison with the East Asian Dragons. Yet although Chile achieved the highest rate of labour productivity growth in Latin America through 1963–2010 at 2.0% per annum (Ungor 2017: 30), with agriculture (4.8%) and mining (3.0%) outstripping manufacturing (2.3%), productivity in Taiwan and South Korea grew faster and by 5.6% annually.

7.2.3 *Moderating GDP Growth: Economic Maturity or Deindustrialization?*

Helped by steady economic growth, democratic Chile deployed its revenues to maintain public expenditure around one-quarter of GDP and make significant progress in reducing poverty. The poverty rate fell to 14% in 2011 and extreme poverty to less than 3%, compared with 39% and 13%, respectively in 1991 (IADB 2016). Indices of the quality of institutions (Table 3.1) and global competitiveness (Table 4.5) are high, even for an economy with Chile's per capita income. Schmidt-Hebbel (2006) identified Chile as an outlier with respect to levels of institutional development that are superior, often substantially so to comparators at its per capita GDP. Chile also scores well on indicators of competitiveness, ranking thirty-fifth out of 128 countries with high readings for basic economic requirements and efficiency enhancers, but lower ones for innovation (Table 4.5).

Although economic growth decelerated, it still averaged 3.8% per annum through 1990–2015. Productivity data available for 1990–2005, when GDP growth averaged 5.3%, indicate that more than half the economic growth rate (some 3.1%) reflected gains in productivity. Capital investment also contributed significantly, whereas labour accumulation contributed least (Schmidt-Hebbel 2006). In contrast, under the military government of 1974–89, GDP grew by 2.9% while total factor productivity had *declined* and labour accumulation was responsible for three-quarters of growth. Nor during the pre-reform years of 1961–73 did gains in total factor productivity contribute to the modest GDP growth rate of 3.1%, which reflected equal contributions from physical capital and labour.

Nevertheless, Chile's spectacular growth spurt of 1985–99 was not sustained. This appears to be characteristic of a mature mid-income economy that follows a comparative advantage in resource-driven growth. The contribution of copper to Chile's economic development has fallen, albeit the decline was interrupted by the 2005–14 copper boom (Table 7.1). More typically, copper has been a solid source of taxation and foreign exchange rather than of production linkages. Specifically, copper mining earned 42% of export earnings during 1990–2010 and also furnished 13% of total tax revenues via state-owned Codelco (between one-tenth and one-third of taxes if private mines are included). However, mining generated just 6.2% of GDP in 1980–2010 on average and contributed only 50,000 jobs. The maturity of economic management is shown by the fact that when copper rents more than doubled their share of GDP to almost 17% annually during 2005–14, the real exchange rate appreciated only modestly, despite the huge gain in the terms of trade (Table 7.1).

Data on the evolution of Chile's product space 1980–2000 (Hausmann and Klinger 2007) confirm that exports of both mining and agriculture generated limited domestic linkages, curbing scope for sustained structural transformation. The revealed comparative advantage of Chile since the reforms has been in producing primary products and processing them, but is weak in most manufacturing. This includes even low-technology products like textiles, let alone medium technology such as automobiles. Ffrench-Davis (2014) blamed overrapid trade opening and capital market liberalization from the late-1990s for diminished growth prospects. Hausmann and Klinger (2007) argued that more fundamentally, prospects for diversification into more productive activity are diminished by specialization in relatively unsophisticated exports and limited scope for product upgrading.

The decades of economic growth since the mid-1980s exhibit limited upgrading of exports and any expansion of products has involved goods that were present at the outset, notably seafood products and wood products, which afford little scope to progress further. Critically, the per capita value of exports has stagnated, so that Chile is falling behind comparators. Chile's exports also have larger shares of their markets than the exports of most countries at a similar level of income, pointing to limited expansion options in future. The removal of such constraints on long-term growth may require governments to encourage high-technology export options and export services, building on the fact that Chile exports more services per capita than comparator developing economies.

7.3 Brazil: How Debt and Exchange Rate Appreciation Impede Competitive Diversification

Most Latin American countries are resource-rich, but Argentina, Brazil, and Mexico also have potential scale advantages due to their large domestic markets and their extensive geographical areas, which increase their self-sufficiency, diversify their commodity exports, and render them less vulnerable to trade shocks. Yet Perkins and Syrquin (1989) found that large economies perform no better than small ones, especially large resource-abundant economies, a conclusion at odds with a more recent study (Auty 2001). Certainly, prior to the 1980s, large economies favoured high levels of autarky that shield firms from global competition, blunt incentives to deploy resources efficiently, and enhance scope for rent-seeking. This section examines Brazil with reference to: the problems arising from relying upon import substitution to sustain economic growth; the increasing difficulty of achieving stabilization in an overheating economy; and the constraints on post-reform economic performance.

7.3.1 *Brazil's Rapid but Episodic Economic Growth 1955–80*

The post-war development of Brazil exhibits two phases (Firpo and Pieri 2016). First, from 1950 to 1980, trade policy closure was associated with high economic growth, which was, however, episodic and eventually unsustainable. During this phase, Brazil sought to sustain growth through forced industrialization, launching two heavy-industry big pushes to maximize the economies of scale by simultaneously establishing complementary intermediate and downstream activities, so that both sets of factories could operate at the scale required to be efficient (Murphy et al. 1989). However, successive governments struggled to generate sufficient foreign exchange to cover essential imported inputs as well as revenues to close gaps in the funding of investment and public services. The second phase from 1980 to the present is characterized by repeated failure to stabilize the economy until the Real Plan of 1994, which ushered in a period of steady but modest economic growth.

Two key initial conditions that impacted Brazil's pre-reform economic performance are the rent streams and the type of government. Regulatory rent has been substantial in Brazil and directed primarily to promote manufacturing, whereas mineral rent and geopolitical rent were negligible (Table 7.2). Bergsman (1970) estimated that in the mid-1960s, regulatory rent subsidies to manufacturing comprised 20% of GDP annually. Consistent with this, rates of effective protection for manufacturing averaged 118% in 1966 and, despite some trade opening, still 44% in 1981 (Auty 1994b: 85). In contrast, agriculture was a *source* of rent: Krueger (1992: 61) calculated that government interventions during 1969–83 reduced farm revenues by 8% compared with a sector neutral policy. This is modest for a land-rich economy, however: in comparison the discrimination against agriculture in Chile extracted 22% of farm revenue through 1960–83, and in three sub-Saharan African economies in the 1960s and 1970s some 51%. In contrast, agriculture in land-scarce South Korea *benefited* from state interventions through 1960–84 to the extent of 13% of revenues. Nevertheless, Brazil has sustained a leading role in agricultural exports (Firpi and Pieri 2016), despite relatively low productivity, which implies that cropland rents have been substantial, although Lange et al. (2018) data estimate they had fallen to 1.1% of GDP (Table 7.2). The aggregate rent stream has adversely impacted manufacturing, however, both by facilitating soft budget constraints on industrialization and through exchange rate volatility.

The political system in Brazil functioned as a factional democracy after 1951, except for the military governments of 1964–85. Previously, governments had responded to political pressure from propertied interests in coffee, then from manufacturing in the south, and also mining and ranching in the centre, intervening in ad hoc fashion to create regulatory rent for pragmatic

Table 7.2 Selected economic indicators, Brazil, 1960–2014 (% GDP, except where stated)

	1960–64	1965–69	1970–74	1975–79	1980–84	1985–89	1990–94	1995–99	2000–04	2005–09	2010–14
Rent proxies											
Total natural resource rent	n.a.	n.a.	1.5	1.9	2.7	2.0	1.8	1.3	3.1	4.9	4.5
Mineral rent	n.a.	n.a.	0.5	0.7	0.8	0.7	0.6	0.4	1.0	2.4	2.3
Net ODA received	1.0	0.9	0.3	0.1	0.1	0.1	0.0	0.0	0.0	0.0	0.0
Regulatory rent[1]	n.a.	n.a.	n.a.	n.a.	n.a.	n.a.	n.a.	n.a.	n.a.	n.a.	n.a.
Remittances	n.a.	n.a.	n.a.	0.1	0.0	0.0	0.3	0.2	0.3	0.2	0.1
Arable land per head (ha)	0.3	0.3	0.4	0.4	0.4	0.4	0.3	0.3	0.3	0.4	0.4
Economy openness											
Exports	6.7	6.6	7.4	7.1	10.2	10.1	9.6	7.5	13.7	13.5	11.3
FDI	n.a.	n.a.	n.a.	1.0	0.9	0.4	0.4	2.5	3.4	2.3	3.6
Terms of trade[2]	n.a.	n.a.	n.a.	n.a.	63.1	71.9	83.1	112.3	98.7	105.3	125.6
REER[2]	n.a.	n.a.	n.a.	n.a.	77.9	64.7	83.8	87.1	59.3	82.5	94.3
Absorption											
Gross fixed capital formation	n.a.	n.a.	20.6	22.7	20.4	21.6	19.9	18.7	17.7	18.2	20.5
Central government consumption	13.0	11.1	10.6	10.0	9.3	12.2	17.6	19.6	19.1	19.1	18.9
Household consumption	67.5	68.8	69.2	68.5	69.8	61.9	60.7	64.7	62.5	60.5	61.3
Structural change											
Agriculture	18.3	15.4	12.9	12.5	10.5	10.5	8.2	5.5	6.3	5.3	5.0
Industry	37.1	35.3	38.8	39.8	45.3	44.5	39.0	25.8	27.1	27.2	25.9
Manufacturing	28.9	27.4	29.7	30.3	33.6	31.8	25.5	15.3	16.0	16.5	13.2
Services	44.6	49.4	48.3	47.7	44.8	45.2	53.3	68.7	66.6	67.5	69.1
Growth											
Population growth (%)	2.9	2.7	2.4	2.4	2.3	2.0	1.7	1.6	1.3	1.1	0.9
GDP growth (%)	5.6	6.7	11.0	5.9	1.4	4.5	1.6	2.2	3.1	3.7	3.4
Per capita GDP growth (%)	2.0	3.8	8.4	3.4	(0.9)	2.5	(0.1)	0.6	1.7	2.5	2.4
Per capita GDP (US$, 2010)	3,640	3,971	5,647	7,372	7,689	8,268	8,019	8,619	8,940	10,139	11,646

[1] 1965 = 20% of GDP (Bergsman 1970).
[2] Cropland rent 2014 = 1.1% of GDP (Lange et al. (2018).
[3] Base year = 2000.

Source: World Bank (2017a).

ends (Maddison 1992). The extraction of regulatory rent to satisfy wealthy pressure groups persisted, however (Palma 2011: 570), even as state intervention expanded in the post-war years and political parties increasingly campaigned on policy. Technocrats used quasi-market mechanisms to engineer policies to try to mitigate distortions in resource allocation caused by state interventions, while the informal economy and entrepreneurial sleight also facilitated economic exchange. Maddison (1992) concluded that this system worked well until the early-1980s, by which time efforts to prolong economic growth through import substitution had cumulated levels of debt, at both the state and federal levels, that exceeded the capacity of governments to manage them. Mendes (2014) ascribed the subsequent disappointing recovery of Brazilian economic growth to the vulnerability of governments to rent-seeking from all levels of society (see Section 7.3.3).

Brazil launched two big pushes in 1956–60 and 1974–79 but struggled to execute them effectively. The merits of a big push are disputed (Yoo 1990) in part because it tends to outstrip domestic implementation capacity. It typically traces a three-stage sequence (Auty 1992) not unlike a populist boom (Table 7.3). First, the massive scale of heavy industry construction hits the economy like a commodity boom as capital inflows combine with shortages of critical inputs to trigger inflation, strengthening the exchange rate and exacerbating fiscal and trade deficits. Second, stabilization of the overheated economy depresses economic growth below its long-term trend as the heavy industry comes on stream, lowering capacity use and financial returns. Third, successful stabilization revives domestic demand so that the heavy industry rebounds towards full capacity and financial returns improve. Yet, in practice, all too often technical failings, cost overruns, and lack of hard budget constraints extend factory maturation over decades and revenues struggle to cover costs (Auty 1994b).

Table 7.3 Brazil heavy industry big pushes

Stage	Pre-push	Construction	Stabilization	Rebound
Late 1950s big push				
Time period	1951–55	1956–60	1961–67	1968–73
GDP growth (%/year)	6.7	8.1	4.6	11.2
Inflation (%/year)	16.1	21.8	53.7	21.0
Fiscal gap (% GDP)	n.a.	(2.4)	(33.5)	(0.5)
Current account gap (% GDP)	1.3	(1.7)	(0.3)	(2.2)
Late 1970s big push				
Time period	1968–73	1974–79	1980–84	1985–88
GDP growth (%/year)	11.2	5.5	1.5	4.7
Inflation (%/year)	21.0	41.4	132.1	317.2
Fiscal gap (% GDP)	(0.5)	(1.5)	(3.0)	(12.4)
Current account gap (% GDP)	(2.2)	(4.9)	(3.8)	(0.3)

Source: Auty (1994b: 118).

Both of Brazil's big pushes outstripped implementation capacity and forced recourse to external borrowing that further expanded debt and spurred inflation. This led to stop-go macro policies that drove the country's rapid but episodic per capita income growth prior to 1980. The initial 1956–60 big push stressed import substitution to meet domestic demand. It focused largely on steel and automobiles, and neglected hitherto dominant labour-intensive industries like textiles and food processing. Both the competitive diversification model and the experience of sub-Saharan Africa suggest this neglect squandered important contributions to rapid and relatively egalitarian economic growth.

The big push was implemented by technocrats who drafted sector plans, provided protection against imports to guarantee domestic markets, and supplied much of the capital through public investment (Maddison 1992: 29). The 1956–60 big push triggered the three-stage boom–stabilization–rebound sequence. Inflation rose sharply, but weak civilian governments postponed stabilization, which finally commenced under the incoming military government in 1964 (Auty 1994b). A partial opening of trade policy combined with exchange rate controls to stimulate exports and the rebound stage of the first big push to drive Brazil's 'economic miracle' of 1967–73 when GDP grew in excess of 10% annually.

The negative oil shock in 1973 abruptly knocked the military government off course, however. The government responded by launching a second industrial big push to exploit Brazil's natural resources to ease foreign exchange constraints through increased energy self-sufficiency and additional exports. It expanded rents to raise import protection and deployed export subsidies to harness natural resources for the big push. The government also triggered some reversal of trade policy opening and attracted foreign capital, including recycled petro-dollars, which it overoptimistically assumed could be serviced by increased output and exports. Investment flowed into capital-intensive resource-based metal and hydro projects in the Amazon in a vain attempt to sustain rapid growth. State firms played a key role in the heavy industry projects, however, and their performance deteriorated as their investment expanded amid soft budget constraints.

Nevertheless, GDP growth averaged 5.9% annually through 1975–79 and further sustained the high rate of labour productivity growth since 1950, of which structural change contributed 40% (McMillan et al. 2014). As noted in Section 7.1, it also helped raise economy-wide productivity relative to the US from 35% to 43% (Ungor 2017). However, the 1979–82 oil and interest rate shock sharply decelerated economic growth as repeated attempts to subdue inflation failed. After more than two decades, some heavy industry including steel and auto assembly was nearing maturation, but the collapse in domestic demand through the 1980s caused them to regress. The eventual maturation rates of Brazil's heavy industry spanned three decades and more. Meanwhile, total exports remained small at 7% of GDP, resource-dependent, and subsidized (Auty 1994b). Moreover, aggregate debt and debt service had cumulated to excessive levels, while annual inflation reached 100%.

7.3.2 Protracted Struggle for Stabilization and Competitive Diversification 1980–2015

When democracy was restored in 1985, Brazil still lacked a consensus regarding industrial policy, and governments continued to display ambivalence towards private manufacturing. Political parties were numerous and fragmented but campaigned on programmes. Rent extraction persisted, mostly hidden, and facilitated coalition-building, albeit occasionally surfacing to bring down governments on corruption charges (Lisboa and Latif 2013). Repeated failure to achieve stabilization saw inflation accelerate, its momentum sustained by indexed wages and prices until the introduction of the Real in 1994, a new currency fixed at parity with the US dollar. The subsequent adoption of a crawling exchange rate in 1999 along with IMF-backed containment of the fiscal deficit ushered in a period of modest GDP growth through the 2000s. High real interest rates sought to curb inflation and maintain a primary fiscal surplus, but in combination with the commodity super-cycle they strengthened the real exchange rate (Table 7.2), which weakened export manufacturing, repressed investment, and slowed economic growth (Amann and Baer 2012: 416; Palma 2011). The government provided manufacturers with ad hoc assistance through tax relief on domestic inputs used to manufacture exports.

Annual GDP growth through 1980–2014 was slower but more stable at 2.8% (Table 7.2) compared with 7.3% through 1960–79 (McMillan et al. 2016). Growth under a left-leaning government during the commodity super-cycle reduced the incidence of poverty through increased public spending, which doubled to almost one-fifth of GDP compared with military rule (Table 7.2). Yet Brazil's gini coefficient declined only modestly, from 0.60 in 1997 to 0.56 in 2005, and the richest one-fifth of the population still accounted for 60% of income, compared with 48% in China and 45% in India (World Bank 2017a).

Firpo and Pieri (2016) drew upon employment data to query whether IFI-backed liberalization caused structural change to regress as Rodrik claims. They argued that Brazil maintained a diversified industrial structure, although employment data do suggest that structural change slowed, having been fastest under the military governments of 1963–79. The agricultural workforce stabilized at around one-tenth of the total, while manufacturing employment stabilized at around one-sixth. Through 1950–2005, structural change contributed just 16% to labour productivity growth, compared to 84% for within-sector gains

(Firpi and Pieri 2016). However, through 2000–15, manufacturing ceased to lead productivity growth: mining and agriculture recorded higher gains in both productivity and wages. Agriculture thrived in global markets despite relatively low productivity, whereas manufacturing remained mainly oriented to domestic demand (Firpi and Pieri 2016), so that outward-oriented reforms largely failed to trigger competitive manufacturing.

The structure of trade shows that diversification towards manufacturing was not sustained. During the rapid growth phase of 1950–80, commodities remained dominant, supplying 80% of total exports in 1965, with coffee alone supplying two-thirds in 1963. By 1979, however, manufacturing caught up: both primary products and manufactured goods generated 41% of total exports, the residual being semi-manufactures. Manufactured exports then exceeded primary product exports for three decades 1979–2009, averaging around 55% of the total, compared with 30% for primary products. But in 2009, the two main export sectors once again generated 41% of exports each, and thereafter primary exports exceeded manufactured exports during the rest of the commodity super-cycle.

GDP data identify faster structural change than employment data do, however (Table 7.2). They show that manufacturing's share of GDP peaked in the early-1980s after the second big push at 33%, but dropped to 13% by 2014. The latter outcome is similar to the 11% share shown by labour data (Ungor 2017). Brazilian agriculture also experienced a declining share of GDP, which fell to one-quarter of the level of the early-1960s, although the rate of contraction slowed markedly after the reforms of the mid-1990s. In terms of value added, therefore, post-reform Brazil follows the global pattern of structural change, with services rising to dominate the economy at the expense of manufacturing and agriculture (Table 7.2). However, productivity also regressed during 1980–2010, relative to the US. Brazil achieved only 19% of US labour productivity by the mid-2000s, whereas resource-rich comparators Australia and Canada reached 77% of the US level (Castaldi et al. 2008: 44).

Petreski and Wong (2014: 16) confirmed the critical role of rent flows in driving structural change, consistent with the staple trap model. They found that increases in revenue from commodity exports, aid, and remittances caused Dutch disease effects in post-reform Latin American economies like Brazil that negatively impact tradeable sector growth and are strongest during export booms. For example, the Brazilian exchange rate strengthened by 50% comparing 2010–14 with 2000–04 (Table 7.2), reflecting Dutch disease effects attributable to increased commodity rents and also remittances. Inflows of FDI proved neutral, however, due to central bank interventions that: boosted domestic money supply/and or sterilized foreign currency; contained public spending in order to free space for private investment; and operated a crawling peg exchange rate depreciation.

The rent streams distorted the Brazilian economy in a second way, by feeding corruption. Brazil's federal democracy functions with numerous parties that render governments vulnerable to pressure to muster sufficient political support for their agenda. If a government aspires to developmental aims, it struggles to build a coalition to pursue it, even with recourse to copious bribes. Table 3.2 indicates limited control of corruption in Brazil, given its level of per capita income. Mendes (2014) argued that not only the wealthy but also the middle class and workers barter their political support in return for state favours, whether through, respectively, tax exemptions, free higher education, or civil service wages rises.

The net result is a process of rent-seeking that amounts to dissipative redistribution, because it expands public expenditure at the expense of investment, while also reducing the efficiency of public expenditure. The potential scale of distortion through rent-seeking was revealed in 2016 when the chief executive officer of state-owned Petrobras, hitherto a symbol of national pride, announced losses from mismanagement and graft of US$17 billion. He also revealed that in order to restore financial balance Petrobras needed to sell assets valued at a similar amount and to postpone investment plans. The company's cumulated debt totalled US$100 billion and its market value halved. Petrobras acknowledged arrears in paying wages and generating less employment than workers expect.

7.3.3 *Structural Change for Improved Economic Performance*

The persistent failure of Brazil to meet its economic potential reflects the difficulty of sustaining competitive diversification in an economy subject to strong shocks from volatile commodity prices, appreciation of the real exchange rate, and government ambivalence towards the private sector. The debt that Brazil accumulated during its long phase of forced industrialization continues to constrain competitive diversification. Hausmann (2008) identified a lack of capital for investment as the binding constraint on Brazilian economic growth, because, in contrast to Chile, Brazil has more investment options than it has funds to invest in them.

An improved business environment would make projects even more attractive (Tables 4.5 and 7.4), but that would not resolve the investment shortage, which results from excessive borrowing that risks bankruptcy and deters investors from committing further funds. Government capitulation to the rent-seeking pressures identified by Mendes (2014) results in high taxation, high debt service, overexpanded social entitlements, and wasteful public service provision, which all combine to squeeze the domestic resources available for both private and public saving. This suggests that reforms should slim entitlements, notably pensions. This would, however, be politically difficult.

Hausmann (2008) therefore concluded that to speed up economic growth and outgrow the cumulated tax burden, Brazil should stress fiscal consolidation and reduction of public debt, while gradually improving the tax effort and the efficiency of public expenditure.

The Brazilian government deploys public expenditure relatively inefficiently. It struggles to provide effective education and health care, despite expending sizeable shares of GDP on each (Amann and Baer 2012: 421). Moreover, whereas the World Bank estimates developing countries should invest 25% of GDP annually, with 7% of GDP on infrastructure, Brazil invested only 17% of GDP annually and cut government infrastructure investment below 1% of GDP (Economist 2009). One consequence is that 60% of Brazilian freight moves by truck along often poorly maintained roads to reach costly and relatively inefficient ports. Such outcomes reflect the ambivalence of governments towards business: the state seeks increased private sector growth but burdens businesses that conform with complex taxation rules and high tax rates (Table 7.4). Yet the disappointing level of private investment that lies behind the post-1980 deceleration in economic growth and labour productivity also reflects less commendable behaviour by potential investors. Palma (2011: 580) noted, '... in Brazil, like the rest of Latin America, economic reform seems to have unleashed more powerfully the predatory and rentier instincts of the region's capitalist elites (the former especially during the privatization period) rather than Schumpeterian ones'.

Brazilian manufacturing exhibits a dual structure, with world-class firms alongside low-productivity ones. Protracted economic instability through the 1980s and 1990s motivated leading Brazilian manufacturers to reduce their reliance on domestic and regional demand and instead target global

Table 7.4 Doing business: global ranking 2015

	Trinidad and Tobago	Mauritius	Brazil	Chile	South Korea	India	Saudi Arabia	Uganda
Per capita GDP (US$, PPP)	33,377	20,126	15,647	23,579	34,421	6,139	54,118	1,777
Overall rank	79	28	120	41	5	142	49	150
Starting up	71	29	167	59	17	158	109	166
Construction permits	113	117	174	62	12	184	21	183
Getting electricity	21	41	19	49	1	137	22	164
Registering property	159	98	138	45	79	121	20	125
Getting credit	36	35	89	71	36	36	71	131
Protecting minority shareholders	62	28	35	56	21	7	62	110
Paying taxes	113	13	177	29	25	156	3	104
Crossing frontiers	76	17	123	40	3	125	92	161
Enforcing contracts	180	44	118	64	4	186	108	80
Resolving bankruptcy	66	43	55	73	5	137	163	98

Source: World Bank (2017a).

markets (Castro 2009: 261). The most dynamic private firms circumvent persistent overvaluation of the exchange rate by shedding labour to improve competitiveness. Some Brazilian manufacturing boomed through the 2000s, notably automobiles (30% of manufacturing growth), machinery and equipment (12%), and electronics and communication equipment (7%). Indicative of emerging technological prowess, Brazil has the third largest global producer of aircraft (Embraer, privatized in 1994) and significant programmes in space, biofuels, and deep offshore hydrocarbon extraction.

The low-productivity firms are often in the informal sector, which is estimated to generate 40% of Brazilian GDP, compared with 22% in India, 20% in Chile, and 12% in China. Regulation-conforming Brazilian companies find themselves squeezed between spry informal enterprises and a heavy-handed government. Yet although the informal firms are profitable, they have little incentive to invest in expansion because that would raise their profile and attract government attention. Echoing the experience of sub-Saharan Africa, Palma (2011: 590) argued that the high employment elasticity of the informal sector helps accommodate the collapse in the region's productivity growth rate by absorbing not only a large residual of underemployed labour, but also new entrants into the workforce and workers made unemployed by structural change in agriculture and manufacturing.

This pattern of structural change in Brazil lowers labour productivity in contrast to the productivity *boost* that low-income Asia derived from rapid growth in labour-intensive manufacturing. Yet, as with sub-Saharan Africa, but for different reasons, Latin American wages are too high to compete effectively in labour-intensive manufacturing against low-income Asian economies like Vietnam. Latin America's large predominantly low-productivity domestic sector offers little incentive to compete and improve efficiency. Nor do weakened trade unions exert effective pressure to raise real wages that would elicit investment to boost productivity. For a country with its per capita income, Brazil compares unfavourably with Mauritius, Chile, Saudi Arabia, and South Korea in not only the quality of governance (Table 3.1) but also global competitiveness (Table 4.5) and the business environment (Table 7.4).

The structure of Brazil's exports reveals some limited further scope to diversify, if debt is reduced and interest rates fall, so that a weaker real exchange rate spurs private investment in increasingly competitive activity. De la Cruz and Riker (2012) applied Hausmann's export product space analysis to identify emerging comparative advantage between 1998 and 2008. Like much of Latin America, Brazil has a revealed comparative advantage mainly in primary commodities (agriculture and mining), rather than manufactures like machinery, although automobile assembly and aircraft manufacture are significant.

Amann and Baer (2012: 415) concluded from Brazil's economic performance through 1995–2010 that conditions might support GDP growth of 4.5% annually, but no more without higher saving and investment plus substantially improved education and infrastructure. In addition, the experience of the East Asian economies reviewed below suggests that Brazil's big pushes might have been more successful with hard financial constraints underpinned by resistance to the assumption that in the last resort the country's vast natural resources would bail out the economy. Although firms in resource-poor East Asia had access to some rent, their success is rooted in hard budget constraints that helped incentivize efficient allocation.

7.4 Rent Deployment for Competitive Diversification in Resource-Poor South Korea

After World War II, East Asian governments, like developing country governments elsewhere, espoused closed trade policies to force industrialization. The policies also increased scope to extract regulatory rent with which to manage political support and enrich the elite. However, in resource-poor South Korea and in Taiwan the elite prioritized economic growth relatively early. Taiwan embarked on competitive diversification in 1958 and South Korea from 1963, whereas the majority of developing countries were rent-rich and persisted with forced industrialization into the 1980s. The post-war experience of the differing developing regions suggests that the later and slower the reform of industrial policy, the greater the loss of potential welfare (Auty 1994a). Despite flaws in its reform strategy, the experience of South Korea helps explain East Asian success.

7.4.1 *Initial Conditions in South Korea*

In the early-1960s South Korea was regarded as a development basket case. Population pressure had pushed per capita cropland below 0.1 hectares and there were few minerals, while most industry was lost to North Korea after the early-1950s civil war. Manufacturing in South Korea generated only 6% of GNP at partition, despite tariff protection. Nevertheless, total rent was around one-quarter of GDP, and comprised foreign aid that averaged 15% of GNP annually through the 1950s (Castley 1997: 378) together with regulatory rent that during 1953–60 Cho (1996) estimates averaged 11.9% of GNP, which was generated from state intervention to restrict imports and overvalue the real exchange rate. The combined rent stream allowed the government to override markets and remunerate supporters, but investment efficiency and GDP growth remained low.

A military coup in 1961 replaced the aid-dependent regime with an autocratic developmental political state. Fearful of the withdrawal of US aid and threatened by North Korea's apparent economic success, the new regime espoused policies to accelerate competitive industrialization (Lim 2000: 26–7). The gains from opening trade policy benefited from the earlier expansion of primary education and land reform during Japanese colonial rule, which by broadening economic participation helped to diffuse development opportunities across the population.

7.4.2 Rent, Political Incentives, and Economic Outcomes: The Korean Heavy Industry Big Push

From 1963 the military regime responded to a steady decline in aid (Table 7.5) by emulating low-rent Taiwan's trade liberalization to promote competitive industrialization that was initially labour intensive. Through the 1960s the new regime cut the regulatory rent that its predecessor had wrung from import restrictions and exchange rate controls by three-quarters to 3.4% of GNP annually (Cho 1996: 211). It cycled the reduced rent to support labour-intensive exports, notably textiles. GDP growth accelerated sharply to average 10% per annum through 1965–69 (Table 7.5). By the early-1970s the rapid growth in labour-intensive manufacturing had eliminated surplus rural labour (Kuznets 1988), stimulating investment in more productive skill-intensive and capital-intensive activity (World Bank 1993), as rent cycling theory predicts.

Amsden (1992: 198) attributed South Korean economic diversification in the 1970s to government targeting of regulatory rent at heavy industry, rather than to market-driven structural change. Yet Stern (1990) analysed structural change in South Korea and found no evidence that it occurred faster than would have been the case without an active industrial policy, an outcome consistent with the assumption in the competitive diversification model of income-driven structural change. Stern et al. (1995) calculated that the targeted industrial sectors in South Korea yielded poor returns not only in financial terms but also in economic terms (Stern et al. 1995). Auty (1997) confirmed the disappointing financial returns generated by the big push strategy. Finally, Noland and Pack (2003) analysed the costs and benefits of the strategy and concluded it was not efficient. South Korea's reform towards competitive exports succeeded despite its interventionist industrial policy.

In fact, the government motive for accelerating industrial diversification through its big push appears to have been strategic rather than economic: it feared that national defence capability would be inadequate if the Vietnam War led the US to withdraw from the region. To this end, the government quadrupled regulatory rent in the 1970s in support of a heavy industry big

Table 7.5 Selected economic indicators, South Korea, 1960–2014 (% GDP, except where stated)

	1960–64	1965–69	1970–74	1975–79	1980–84	1985–89	1990–94	1995–99	2000–04	2005–09	2010–14
Rent proxies											
Total natural resource rent	n.a.	n.a.	0.3	0.5	0.4	0.1	0.0	0.0	0.0	0.0	0.0
Mineral rent	n.a.	n.a.	0.1	0.0	0.0	0.0	0.0	0.0	0.0	0.0	0.0
Net ODA received (% GNI)	7.3	5.2	2.6	0.6	0.1	0.0	0.0	0.0	0.0	n.a.	n.a.
Regulatory rent	n.a.	n.a.	n.a.	n.a.	n.a.	n.a.	n.a.	n.a.	n.a.	n.a.	n.a.
Remittances	n.a.	n.a.	n.a.	0.3	1.0	1.3	0.8	0.9	0.8	0.6	0.5
Arable land per capita (ha)[1]	0.1	0.1	0.1	0.1	0.1	0.0	0.0	0.0	0.0	0.0	0.0
Economy openness											
Exports	4.2	9.1	17.4	24.5	28.7	30.9	24.5	30.8	39.2	42.1	53.1
FDI	n.a.	n.a.	n.a.	0.2	0.1	0.4	0.3	0.9	1.4	1.1	0.8
Terms of trade[2]	n.a.	n.a.	n.a.	n.a.	16.3	132.6	134.3	123.7	83.1	58.8	46.2
REER[3]	n.a.	n.a.	n.a.	n.a.	n.a.	n.a.	n.a.	n.a.	n.a.	n.a.	n.a.
Absorption (% GNP)											
Fixed capital investment	12.4	22.1	24.5	30.3	30.5	30.7	37.7	34.6	31.0	31.0	29.8
Final government consumption	12.0	9.7	9.8	10.6	11.6	11.0	10.6	11.0	12.1	14.2	14.8
Private consumption	83.6	77.5	71.6	62.5	60.0	51.3	50.3	50.3	53.7	52.2	50.8
Structural change											
Agriculture	42.5	33.8	27.9	23.9	15.1	10.9	7.2	5.2	3.9	2.8	2.4
Industry	19.0	25.3	27.3	31.8	35.9	38.8	39.4	38.5	37.2	36.7	38.3
Manufacturing	13.0	18.1	20.5	23.2	25.0	28.5	26.9	27.4	27.8	28.3	30.9
Services	38.5	41.0	44.8	44.3	49.0	50.4	53.4	56.3	59.0	60.4	59.4
Growth											
GDP growth (%/year)	7.4	11.2	10.4	10.5	7.5	10.1	8.5	5.8	5.7	3.6	3.7
Per capita GDP growth (%/year)	4.4	8.6	8.3	8.8	5.9	9.0	7.4	4.9	5.1	3.1	3.2
Population (%/year)	2.8	2.4	1.9	1.6	1.5	1.0	1.0	0.9	0.5	0.5	0.6
Crop output index[3]	38.9	50.0	57.3	82.1	82.1	90.1	91.3	98.4	101.2	99.6	92.5
Per capita GDP US$, 2010	1,017	1,400	2,135	3,259	4,293	6,623	9,765	10,339	16,509	20,005	23,189

[1] Cropland rent 2014 = 0.2% of GDP (Lange et al. (2018).
[2] 2000 = 100.
[3] 2004–06 = 100.

Source: World Bank (2017a).

push by reducing interest rates to domestic savers and channelling cheap loans to the chaebol (family-owned conglomerates), modelled on Japanese industrial conglomerates (zaibatsu). Cho (1996: 214–15) compared loan rates with kerb market rates to estimate that regulatory rent averaged 12% of GNP annually during 1970–84. Broadly consistent with Cho (1996), Pyo (1989) estimated that rent subsidies tripled, from 3% of GNP annually during 1962–71 to average 10% of GNP during 1972–79.

We argue that the South Korean big push was overambitious and damaged the political economy, but was less problematic than the big pushes of Brazil and Mexico (Auty 1994b). South Korea channelled the regulatory rents as cheap capital to the chaebol, to accelerate heavy industry. The rent lifted the investment rate by 5% of GDP during 1975–79 (Table 7.5), which proved excessive and hit the economy like a commodity boom (Park 1996), outstripping domestic absorptive capacity and briefly triggering staple trap symptoms. The resulting inflation fed Dutch disease effects that sapped export competitiveness and amplified macroeconomic imbalances (Park 1986; Auty 1995), forcing the government to deflate the economy in 1978–79 just as the negative oil shock struck. The rent channelling also stoked social resentment by discriminating in favour of both a well-connected business elite and capital-intensive activity, whereas previously labour-intensive manufacturing had maintained a relatively equitable income distribution (Auty 1995).

Nevertheless, rates of technical and financial maturation suggest that the South Korean big push was significantly more efficient than those of Brazil or Mexico (Auty 1994b). With respect to steel, the minimum viable size of an integrated plant rose fivefold during the post-war decades and exceeded domestic demand in even the largest developing economies. South Korea started building its first steel plant at Pohang in 1972 and completed it in 1982. It relied on Posco, an unusually efficient state-owned firm with high autonomy, to construct and operate its steel plants. The government supplied low-interest loans and cheap labour that helped push construction costs below those of Japan. Posco constructed a second world-scale plant even faster than the first during 1984–92.

In contrast, Brazil began constructing two additional steel plants in the 1950s before its first plant reached full scale, rendering all three suboptimal in size (Auty 1994b). Whereas the Brazilian plants targeted the domestic market, Posco exported around one-fifth of its output to secure sufficient foreign exchange to cover imported inputs and service foreign debt, but also to spur efficiency. Posco's technical standards quickly matched those of advanced economies, while financial returns were low but positive, indicating maturation within eight years. This is only slightly above the five to seven years that Krueger and Tuncer (1982) argued is required in order for the discounted revenues to cover the discounted costs of initial state assistance. In comparison, Brazilian steel took a generation to approach maturity in the early-1980s, and then regressed due to depressed domestic demand during the 'lost' decade of the 1980s as well as through government pressure to subsidize sales to domestic consumers. None of the five steel plants that Brazil eventually constructed reached world scale by the 1990s, yet production costs precluded export. Maturation exceeded four decades (Auty 1994b).

South Korea relied on joint ventures with multinational companies to enter petrochemicals, building two ethylene crackers in quick succession in the 1970s and early-1980s, rapidly achieving technical maturity. However, financial viability proved problematic after the 1979–81 oil shock sharply boosted ethylene feedstock prices. The South Korean government assumed the crackers lacked comparative advantage and began withdrawing support, only to grant a reprieve when oil prices (and ethylene costs) collapsed in 1985–86. In contrast, Brazil repeated its error in the steel sector, adding two new crackers simultaneously, both of which struggled to reach capacity when they came on stream in the 1980s just as domestic demand sagged. Technical maturation was rapidly achieved, but government overpricing of domestically produced inputs postponed financial maturation.

Finally, governments in both countries entered auto assembly prematurely, Brazil in 1958 and South Korea in 1974. By 1980, Brazil produced one million units against South Korea's 120,000, half the minimum viable assembly plant size. However, Brazilian production sank through the 1980s' growth collapse, whereas South Korean output expanded to one million units. Brazil relied on four MNCs to produce cars for the protected domestic market, within which they earned substantial regulatory rents. As with steel, Brazilian automobile assembly neared international competitiveness in 1980, but then regressed as lower domestic demand reduced operating capacity. South Korea incentivized three domestic producers to speedily reach technical and financial maturity, but only Hyundai did so and by the mid-1980s, a decade after start-up.

In common with industrial big pushes elsewhere, the Korean push triggered imbalances, which demanded stabilization that depressed domestic markets during 1979–81, so that the new heavy industry initially operated below capacity. This, along with cost overruns and high debt service, rendered many new plants nonviable and unable to service their highly geared capital. Even the efficient steel plant earned negligible returns on capital, while downstream steel users, like ship building, either lost money or, like automobiles, required import protection (Auty 1995). Meanwhile, the big push neglected light industry, which lost competitiveness through 1974–79 as the inflationary construction boom caused the real exchange rate to appreciate. Acute macroeconomic imbalances caused a growth collapse and deep recession in South Korea through 1979–81.

The recession destabilized the political economy and unseated the long-serving president, but not the military regime, which abandoned the policy of sector targeting in 1979, and after stabilizing the economy much faster than Latin American rivals it embarked on selective economic liberalization. Consistent with the three-stage big push model, successful stabilization quickly expanded demand to levels that allowed the heavy industry to operate at full capacity and improve capital recovery. South Korean industrial policy faltered, but it was still superior to that of Brazil, due basically to hard budget constraints that imposed market discipline and rendered access to subsidized capital contingent on the speedy maturation of investments.

7.4.3 The Inertia of South Korean Rent-Seeking

South Korean economic liberalization in the early-1980s sought to increase the role of markets in allocating credit, mainly by dismantling the heavy industry policy and privatizing banks. GDP growth recovered to prerecession levels, albeit at the cost of consumption foregone during the recession compared with the more efficient capital allocation of Taiwan (Auty 1997). South Korea's incremental capital output ratio, which had deteriorated from 2.9 during 1965–74 to 5.0 during 1980–84, improved to 3.2 during 1985–89 as the surplus industrial capacity of the big push was employed.

Boltho and Weber (2009) drew on data from Maddison (2007) to assess economic progress through the first twenty-five years of economic reform. They showed that South Korea increased its per capita GDP almost sixfold during 1965–90 (at 7.5% per annum), compared with a more than fivefold increase for Taiwan through 1960–85. With respect to manufacturing, Brandt et al. (2008a: 570) showed that South Korea manufacturing grew 25-fold during the initial twenty-five years of reform, while that of Taiwan expanded 17-fold over its equivalent period. Taiwan raised labour productivity relative to the US from 13% in 1960 to 76% in 2010, compared with a rise from 13% to 68% for South Korea (Ungor 2017).

Yet despite South Korea's greater success in expanding manufacturing output, the more market-sensitive strategy of Taiwan was more successful in boosting welfare. Taiwanese planners intervened more modestly than South Korea and were readier to retreat if problems emerged. Whereas South Korea evolved an oligopolistic firm structure (implying concentrated rent deployment) that stressed growth over financial returns and fed corruption, Taiwan built a flexible economy, characterized by small and medium-sized firms that deployed capital more diffusely and more efficiently. Boltho and Weber (2009) showed that during the first twenty-five years of outward orientation, investment peaked for Taiwan at around 25% of GDP, compared with 33% for South Korea. This implies that as development proceeded, Taiwanese citizens *consumed* a higher share of GDP than their South Korean counterparts. More-over, South Korea's ICOR of 4 compared with 3.6 for Taiwan suggests lower capital efficiency. Taiwan also achieved a more egalitarian outcome: the gini coefficient of Taiwan declined from 0.565 in 1953 to 0.277 by 1980, while that of South Korea rose to 0.389 (Auty 1997: 450).

Successive South Korean governments struggled to dismantle the complex conglomerate structures and focus them on fewer sectors so as to encourage small and medium-sized enterprises. The chaebol continue to dominate, how-ever, and to abuse their links to the highest level of government. They cap-tured many of the privatized banks and maintained the flow of cheap capital that subsidized their growth. Their rivalry periodically glutted regional prod-uct markets, squeezed financial returns, and undermined banking supervision (Noland and Pack 2003: 71). The 1997 financial crisis doubled the ICOR compared with its 1960s level of efficiency, lowered investment, and slowed GDP growth to 5.1% during 1999–2004. The wealth accumulated by the conglomerates through their preferential access to capital during the indus-trial big push remained resented by the broader electorate.

Nevertheless, four decades of rapid GDP growth and associated structural change and social diversification matured South Korea's political system. When the military leader retired in 1987, his hand-picked successor encoun-tered protests and submitted to elections. Subsequent elections saw power pass among the principal political parties, but economic policy remained stable, indicating that South Korea had become a consensual democracy (Auty 2007). Yet although elections disciplined governments against the abuse of power, rent-seeking inertia meant such abuse was not eliminated. Several administra-tions faced corruption charges and a president was imprisoned for extracting bribes worth over US$500 million. A generation after the heavy industry drive, the perception of corruption in Korea is higher than expected for its per capita income and it is deteriorating, which is the reverse of expectations, while its governance is less efficient than that of Taiwan (Table 3.1). Taiwan's more modest state intervention is associated with limited corruption and increasing control of graft with rising per capita income, as would be expected (Treisman 2002).

7.5 The Illusion of Premature Deindustrialization

Latin America pursued protected industrialization for longer than other major developing regions and slowly closed the gap in labour productivity with the US until the growth collapse of the 1980s. After the growth col-lapse, Chile was the only country to maintain its level of relative product-ivity out of nine Latin American countries for which complete data are available.[1] The rest regressed, notably Venezuela as productivity plummeted from 113% of the US level in 1960 to 38% in 2010. Argentina, Mexico, and Peru also declined sharply, almost halving their 1960–80 gain (Ungor 2017). GDP growth halved to 2.7% in Latin America through 1980–2008 from 5.4% in 1950–80, as lower investment slowed productivity growth (Palma 2011). In contrast, East Asia maintained its investment effort and GDP deceleration was modest, while South Korea and Taiwan continued to gain on US productivity.

Latin American governments pursued interventionist development strategies with soft financial constraints, using rents to cover deficits. They struggled to industrialize through import substitution in the face of failure to generate either sufficient foreign exchange to cover essential imported inputs or sufficient revenue to maintain investment and public consumption. Instead, recourse to frequent borrowing cumulated levels of debt that were increasingly difficult to service. With the exception of Chile, no Latin American government embraced competitive diversification under hard financial constraints until the growth collapses forced them to accept IFI reforms. Government attempts to grow out of the stop–start growth path such as the populist boom of Allende's Chile 1970–73 and of Chavez's Venezuela a generation later failed, as did the big push in the largest economies (Auty 1984b). Neither option closed the trade and fiscal gaps; rather, they exacerbated them.

Chile launched ambitious reforms to promote export-led growth under Pinochet, which succeeded after little more than a decade, during which policy errors hurt the poorest, however. Brazil reformed later than Chile, after the 1979–82 oil and interest rate shock, and took longer to stabilize its economy in the face of accelerating inflation. Rent from commodities, government manipulation of relative prices, and remittances fed Dutch disease effects that threatened to reverse gains in manufactured exports and stunt structural change. Moderate economic growth resumed in the late-1990s, but Brazilian governments struggled to maintain both capital inflows, even with high interest rates, and sufficient revenue to meet the copious rent-seeking demands on public expenditure. The accommodation of such demands squeezed domestic private investment despite ample investment opportunities.

In contrast, several governments in East Asia along with Mauritius embraced competitive diversification a generation earlier than in Latin America in the face of declining rents due to reduced foreign aid (Taiwan and South Korea), closure of the cropland frontier (Mauritius), or both (Singapore). Existential crises arising from the collapse of the US position in Vietnam

---

[1] The other countries are Argentina, Bolivia, Brazil, Colombia, Costa Rica, Mexico, Peru, and Venezuela.

and/or acute land scarcity strengthened elite incentives to grow the economy. The cautious and measured approach of pioneering Taiwan conferred higher welfare on its citizens than the aggressive growth-maximizing approach of South Korea.[2] Basically, greater investment efficiency allowed Taiwanese citizens to consume a higher share of GDP as development proceeded. The critical element in East Asian success was the retention of hard budget constraints, which encouraged pursuit of the region's initial comparative advantage in labour-intensive manufactured exports that drove rapid and beneficial structural change. Industrial policy at best accommodated such an outcome and at worst risked destabilizing the economy and entrenching rent-seeking and corruption.

Although Chile drew favourable comparison with the East Asian Dragons from the late-1980s, its diversification eventually encountered limited investment opportunities, whereas Brazil had investment options but limited funds with which to pursue them. The disappointing industrial trends in Latin America, like those in sub-Saharan Africa, prompted Rodrik (2015) to describe structural change outside Asia since 1980 as 'premature deindustrialization'. This seems an inappropriate characterization for three main reasons. First, the benchmarks for sector shares against which to measure premature shrinkage reflect the overdominant role assigned to manufacturing by fashionable interventionist policies in the early post-war decades (Syrquin and Chenery 1989). Some correction of the policy-induced structural distortions was inevitable as reforms realigned economies with their comparative advantage, but that is not premature deindustrialization. Chile provides a clear example of such restructuring, whereas the larger Brazilian economy experienced a more nuanced process because despite the efforts of leading companies to export, its manufacturing was mainly oriented to the domestic market, which afforded some protection.

Second, the unexpectedly rapid rise of China is considered by some to drive deindustrialization elsewhere within the global economy. Castro (2009) argued that China impacted mid-income resource-rich economies like Brazil through a pincer movement. China's booming market strengthened demand for commodities, which boosted the real exchange rates of commodity-exporting economies, weakening manufacturing, while the simultaneous expansion of export-oriented Chinese manufacturing intensified global competition. Yet, Petreski and Wong (2014: 29) found that although Chinese exports tripled to just over 13% of the total during 1990–2010, the impact on Latin America was concentrated on Mexico, minimal elsewhere in Latin

---

[2] Almost four decades after launching reform of the chaebol, South Korean governments still struggle against corruption and repression of the small and medium-sized enterprise sector (Economist 2018).

America, and mainly affected clothing and footwear. Moreover, the negative impact of imports from China seems likely to be a one-off, as continued rapid per capita GDP growth reorients China to consumer-driven growth and prices it out of early manufacturing (Harding 2017).

The third, and most important, factor shrinking developing countries' share of manufacturing in GDP is the rapid growth of service activity, driven by evolving demand in advanced economies. Service activity functions increasingly as a facilitator of production processes and confers value added on them. This process accelerates a practice that is at least two centuries old whereby manufacturing firms concentrate on what they do best and contract out other tasks, often services, to specialist providers. Accounting convention attributes extra value added to services at the expense of production. The service sector therefore grows relative to manufacturing but is supportive of it: the two activities increasingly function within global value chains and are mutually dependent.

Although process automation and global value chains may restore competitive advantage in advanced economies for some labour-intensive manufacturing, other basic goods like textiles and commodity processing are likely to remain attracted to low-income countries with cheap labour (Hallward-Driemeier and Nayyar 2017), as Bangladesh, Vietnam, and the Philippines suggest (Harding 2017). The latter countries can expect to reap the developmental advantages of at least the first stage of the competitive diversification model. However, the contraction of manufacturing in middle-income Latin American countries like Chile and Brazil appears to be a reversion to 'normal' long-term structural change through the espousal of market-oriented reforms. Reversing the contraction in manufacturing may not be desirable, especially if export services can match manufacturing in driving gains in economic growth and productivity. Chapter 8 explores this prospect with reference to the labour-surplus economies of South Asia and the Persian Gulf.

8

Prospective Growth Impacts
of Export Services

This chapter applies the rent-driven models to explain how the labour-surplus economies of South Asia and the Gulf states can benefit from participation in global value chains and export services. Both regions omitted the stage of labour-intensive export growth, albeit for very different reasons, and now struggle to absorb workers in productivity-enhancing employment. We argue that economies in both regions can generate from the service sector the competitive private sector employment that they need in order to reach their labour market turning point and harness structural change to propel productivity-driven economic growth.

India is selected as a case study because it has a dynamic service sector and is the dominant economy in South Asia. It embarked on independence in 1947 with favourable prospects for labour-intensive diversification (Lal 2005). However, post-colonial governments embraced command capitalism and autarkic development instead, and prioritized heavy industry (Auty 1994b). The strategy deployed large regulatory rents, which deflected the development trajectory towards a staple trap. The rent deployment initially benefited mainly bureaucrats until problems with the 1955–65 heavy industry big push strengthened the political influence of large industrialists and the larger farmers (Bardhan 1984). As elsewhere in other developing regions, autarkic development proved disappointing in India (Auty 1994b). However, the strategy perpetuated surplus labour that eventually elicited reform, albeit initially glacial, which unexpectedly sparked dynamic growth in export services. The vigour of the service sector owed much to escaping the stifling overregulation with which manufacturing had struggled.

In contrast, the capital-surplus Gulf governments deployed hydrocarbon rents to pursue resource-based industrialization, which as in Trinidad and Tobago generated limited downstream linkage and employment. Without a sizeable agricultural sector to absorb the labour surplus, Gulf governments

deployed their high natural resource rents to expand public sector employment for their nationals instead. The rent windfall from the 1973–78 and
1979–81 oil shocks facilitated that strategy, while an inflow of migrant labour
undertook work that was shunned by nationals, mainly in the private sector.
When plummeting oil prices triggered a prolonged growth collapse during
1985–2001, however, Gulf governments experimented with more radical
diversification options, including services, especially in Bahrain and Oman,
which faced the most pressure to diversify because they had the lowest oil
reserves per capita.

The chapter is structured as follows. Section 8.1 reviews the rise of export
services in the global economy over recent decades and the opportunities and
challenges it presents for global development. Section 8.2 explains how regulatory rents entrenched India's autarkic development, which slowed economic growth and impeded economic reform. Section 8.3 examines the
rapid expansion of Indian services since 1990, while Section 8.4 evaluates
the role of policy in promoting export services. Section 8.5 notes that South
Asia not only revealed the strong growth potential of export services, but also
showed that competitive diversification via labour-intensive manufactured
exports is still flourishing (in Bangladesh), contrary to the pessimism of
McMillan et al. (2016). Section 8.6 explains how export services may help
the Gulf governments to dismantle structural and labour market distortions
caused by heavy rent dependence. Section 8.7 summarizes.

8.1 The Dynamism of Global Export Services

The rise of the service economy was associated from the 1980s with deindustrialization in the advanced economies, initially evoking consternation,
which reflected the deeply ingrained pro-manufacturing bias of economic
policy. The policy consensus assumed that labour productivity within services
grows more slowly than manufacturing, mainly because services proved more
difficult to mechanize prior to the diffusion of ICT (World Bank 2004: 50–51).
In contrast, technology applied to industry continuously raised labour productivity but also economized on labour. Since these two trends resulted in
'unproductive' services dominating the advanced economies, the rise of the
service-driven economy was expected to lead inevitably to decelerating economic growth. Yet recent gains in the productivity of *productive* services (for
example, financial services and information and computer services, along
with the global expansion of sophisticated service exports) have eased the
initial apprehension. The share of service exports in total global exports of
goods and services has doubled, from around 9% in 1970 to over 20% by 2014
(Loungani et al. 2017).

8.1.1 *The Emergence of Global Service Exports*

The advanced economies led the shift from manufacturing to the service economy, but the nature of structural change in some developing countries suggests they have the possibility to leapfrog manufacturing and catch up on the advanced economies by embracing service activity. The service sector in developing countries has recently shown unusual vigour, with exports almost tripling in the decade 1997–2007, from about US$240 billion to US$692 billion, by which date service exports accounted for 5% of the US$14.3 trillion total global exports (World Bank 2009b).

Ghani et al. (2012) showed that over the three decades 1980–2009 services outperformed manufacturing in driving economic growth, accounting for four-fifths of growth in the advanced economies and just over half in the developing countries. These figures translate into a contribution by services to the rate of global economic growth of almost 3% per annum. The contribution to employment is even more striking: through 1991–2006 employment in the service sector of the global economy grew at around 3.5% annually, compared with a fall in employment in manufacturing of just over 1% annually and a fall in agricultural employment of 5% per annum.

The dynamism of services seems set to continue because trends in sector productivity suggest that gains by services will continue to outpace those of manufacturing. Through the 1990s and 2000s growth in the labour productivity of *manufacturing* in the developing countries began to slow and level out, reflecting a trend that is even more pronounced in the advanced economies. In contrast, the rate of productivity growth of services in the developing countries has accelerated sharply, rising above 5% annually. The productivity of services also continues to grow in the advanced economies, but at a more modest 1.5% annually (Ghani et al. 2012). Moreover, a promising trend for the developing countries is that they are building a stronger revealed comparative advantage in some more sophisticated service exports than that of the developed countries.

In fact, pioneering work on the productive services in the early-1980s by Noyelle (1986: 11) had already identified intermediate services (business services) as especially dynamic, whether in finance, professional services (accounting, legal, management consulting, and advertising), transportation, communication, or wholesaling. Noyelle estimated that by the early-1980s, the share of intermediate services in US GNP had risen above 40%, compared with less than 29% in 1947. Freed from the high logistical costs of most manufacturing, some of these services could be provided from remote locations, thereby allowing firms beset by underdeveloped transport systems to play a critical role in providing services to global value added chains undertaking component fabrication (McKinsey 2012). Within the service sector, telecommunications and ICT have proved most dynamic, expanding at 18% per annum through 1995–2014 (Loungani et al. 2017). Financial services are also dynamic and have rebounded from the global financial crisis.

Ghani et al. (2012) concluded that unlike manufacturing, service exports remain in the youthful stage of their product cycle and therefore retain scope to sustain expansion over many years. Meanwhile, the advanced economies have achieved faster rates of growth in service exports than in their manufactured exports (Flaaen et al. 2013). Some developing countries have also achieved substantial growth in exports of productive services in recent years as a consequence of the outsourcing of business processes from the advanced economies. Moreover, compared with manufacturing, services confer additional welfare advantages because: they provide employment across the entire skill range; achieve high rates of female participation in the workforce; and consume far fewer natural resources with less pollution than industry does.

In an in-depth investigation of the internal dynamics of export-led growth, Hausmann et al. (2007) determined, with reference initially to manufacturing, that it is not just exports that drive growth, but rather the increasing sophistication of exports. Building on this work, Mishra et al. (2012) developed an index of export sophistication for *services*. The index is constructed by first establishing the relationship between income and productivity for ten categories of service, spanning low to high levels of sophistication. The degree of specialization of a specific economy in each of the service categories can then be calculated and tracked over time, indicating trends in both those economies reliant on relatively simple exports and those with an above-average share in sophisticated export services. Among the advanced economies, Switzerland and the UK emerge as outliers with highly sophisticated service exports, while India is a pronounced outlier for sophisticated service exports among the developing economies (Mishra et al. 2012).

Mishra et al. (2012) tested the extent to which gains in the sophistication of export services drive economic growth and find a positive relationship. This result holds after controlling for per capita income, skills, financial development, goods sophistication, the size of the domestic service sector, rule of law, and country time invariant factors. Global data indicate that for twenty-five years after 1980, service exports in the advanced economies fluctuated as a share of services output at round 8%, before rising rapidly above 10%. As a result, service exports now represent a larger proportion of total services output than manufactured exports do of total manufacturing output. Data for 2000–08 show that services began to account for more than half of the economic growth in developing countries, around 55% (Anand et al. 2012).

Within the global service sector, productive services are expanding fastest, although some traditional services are also capable of raising productivity by availing themselves of ICT. Tests show that if the advanced economies are removed from the sample, the basic outcome remains the same. This implies that developing countries can grow by exporting services that are increasingly sophisticated. Anand et al. (2012) confirmed that faster economic growth is associated in both the manufacturing and service sectors with a shift out of classical export items (defined as those exhibiting a stable comparative advantage) and into emerging exports with increasing sophistication. More specifically, Anand et al. (2012: 11) calculated that increased export sophistication has a pronounced positive impact on economic growth, so that a one standard deviation increase in the sophistication of goods or of services is associated with, respectively, a 0.6% and 0.4% increase in the average annual rate of economic growth.

8.1.2 *Determinants of Service Exports Growth*

Anand et al. (2012: 12) demonstrated that the policy environment is critical to the effective growth of export services. The risk of sophisticated exports becoming an enclave with limited economic spillovers is reduced in the presence of appropriate policies, not least the absence of an overvalued exchange rate, high levels of information flows (measured by per capita internet usage), and market liberalization. Eichengreen and Gupta (2013) confirmed the sensitivity of productive services in particular to shifts in the real exchange rate. Of critical importance to commodity-driven economies like Trinidad and Tobago and the Gulf states, productive services experience decelerations in growth when the real exchange rate strengthens. Also, the more distorted the economy by Dutch disease effects and other policy failures, the less scope there is for the efficient intersector and intrasector reallocation of resources, as well as for capturing knowledge and technology spillovers.

Improvements in human capital accumulation (higher education) and information flows also help strengthen the growth of sophisticated exports and lower the risk of forming an enclave economy. More specifically, a one standard deviation increase in tertiary human capital and in information flows is associated with, respectively, a 0.34 and 0.5 standard deviation increase in the sophistication of services exports. Goswami et al. (2012) confirmed the prime role of tertiary education in facilitating the expansion of productive services. They suggest, however, that government provision of electronic communication is less critical because foreign investors can invest in the technology to eliminate host country deficiencies in connectivity. Among the other secondary factors, English language and shared colonial institutions are positively associated with service export growth. Lastly, FDI also has mild positive effects on services expansion by promoting trade through the introduction of new technology and management systems, improving market information, accessing major markets, and stimulating domestic competition.

Somewhat surprisingly, Goswami et al. (2012: 25–79) found that distance is inversely correlated with growth in service exports. However, this effect appears to be attenuating over time and is less critical for productive services. Consequently, activities that might have been undertaken under one roof at one location in the nineteenth century can now be executed in diverse locations that best match the specific needs of each activity involved, even if they are widely separated. Unfortunately, the spread of computer technology also works to geographically concentrate some specialized activities in large urban agglomerations that smaller economies cannot sustain. Such concentration is favoured by the compacting of information storage and delayering of that part of the workforce involved in its production and dissemination.

Noyelle (1986) attributed concentration to the benefits arising from agglomeration economies in the largest cities, often in their central business districts (CBDs) where access to highly trained workers is maximized. This is especially true for very high-order business services. However, Noyelle's research precedes the impact of the internet in facilitating communication between far-flung locations, not least through data exchange. This interaction incurs negligible transport costs and thereby extends the scope for small remote economies to participate in global production chains. Firms in isolated locations can establish and exploit one or more niche service roles, as Mauritius has demonstrated by providing financial services to both Indian investors and a growing number of economies in sub-Saharan Africa (Chapter 5).

In fact, several trends in economic structural change favour remote and landlocked economies. First, the importance of high-volume standardized assembly-line products in manufacturing is shrinking, compared with customized goods and services which are often supplied in batch form. Some of these products command prices with low ratios of transport costs to production costs, thereby reducing the disadvantage of remoteness. In fact, the most dynamic subsectors of manufacturing are less sensitive to traditional location variables like access to bulk transport, raw materials, and cheap labour. Instead, other factors become more important in attracting economic activity, such as proximity to educational establishments, scope to share information, and environmental amenity (Bosker and Garretsen 2010).

Second, the evolution of the firm reinforces the impact of changing demand in transforming the relative pull of factors of location. Noyelle (1986) noted a shift from large firms to small and medium-sized firms and an increased orientation from regional and national markets to world markets. These shifts are reversing the initial post-war movement towards large vertically integrated companies typical of, for example, aluminium, hydrocarbons, and automobile assembly. The rationale for vertically integrated companies was to reduce the risk of supply disruption along the production chain by internalizing transactions through vertical integration (Rumult 1974). By comparison, the new pattern of many interlinked firms seeks to reduce business risk by securing high flexibility of response. Suppliers of goods and services gain greater flexibility as a consequence of subcontracting out various activities to small and nimble firms in specialized niches, each performing a specific task.

A word of caution is in order regarding value chains, however. Recent research on the impact of the post-2007 financial crisis suggests that global value chains may amplify the effects of trade shocks, due to the much higher fraction of traded inputs that this system entails (Ferrantino and Taglioni 2014). For example, the final firm within the value chain may respond to a market slow-down by running down its inventory, thereby amplifying negative effects on suppliers higher up the value chain. Moreover, the increasing importance of social networking to modern businesses favours their location in large urban areas so as to capture agglomeration economies. Nevertheless, Mauritius shows that remote economies still retain sufficient scope to compete in niche markets like banking and ICT as well as tourism. To achieve this global integration, Mauritius has built on critical advantages that were part of its colonial legacy, including its institutional inheritance, and also long-established cultural ties, notably with Hong Kong, India, and western Europe.

Third, a dynamic service sector is becoming more attractive to governments because it can help to resolve the growing global problem of increased demand for skilled workers at the expense of unskilled workers, which threatens social stability irrespective of whether the economy is large or small, rich or poor. Acemoglu (2002) argued that since the mid-twentieth century the development of technology has augmented the importance of skilled labour, whereas a century earlier the presence of a large pool of cheap unskilled labour encouraged the search for technologies to compensate for lack of skills. He attributed the current skill bias in global technology to a steady growth in the supply of trained workers through greater access to secondary and tertiary education. A critical consequence of the skill bias has been to widen income disparity within the workforce, a trend that has intensified since the 1970s. In this context, a dynamic service sector may help to relieve social tensions by absorbing labour across the entire spectrum of skills.

Buera and Kaboski (2012) challenged the supply side skill theory, however, and argued that the growth in services since 1950 is driven by the growing consumption of more skill-intensive output. The US service sector steadily increased its share of value added from 60% in 1950 to 80% in 2000, due to disproportionate growth in both the price and real quality of services. The 20% increase in value added share is explained wholly by the growth of skill-intensive services, however, which grew by more than 25% of value added, whereas the share of low-skill services fell. Over the same period, remuneration of college graduates rose from 125% of the remuneration of high-school graduates to twice the level, while the fraction of workers with college education expanded from 15% to over 60%. In fact, the growth rate of college-educated labour, the skill premium, and the relative size of skill-intensive services all accelerated from about 1950. Finally, the increase in both the share of services and the relative wage does not connote slower productivity gains in services. Rather, the rate of productivity growth of services may be understated, and in fact it may be similar or higher than in manufacturing, thereby reconciling substantial structural change and a modest gain in the relative price of services.

Summarizing, dynamic sophisticated services have the potential to drive rapid growth in productivity, output, and exports. They may also help to counter rising income inequality. Moreover, although the decline of traditional location factors in favour of new ones like abundant skills, vibrant social exchange, and physical amenity may favour large agglomerations, the fact that productive service firms are knowledge-based eases this constraint. This is because modern communications reduce the costs of overcoming distance. Developing regions that pursued industrialization strategies that created few jobs and limited linkage, such as a heavy industry big push, resource-based industry, and import substitution, can boost export services by participation in global value added chains to achieve competitive diversification. India illustrates how regulatory rent triggered an initial policy error (Section 8.2); demonstrates the emergence of a successful export service sector (Section 8.3); and shows how to encourage it (Section 8.4).

8.2 Indian Regulatory Rent, Autarkic Industrialization, and Tardy Economic Reform

At independence, India was a large, relatively land-rich, low-income economy whose comparative advantage lay in labour-intensive agriculture and manufacturing. Its democratic government might have been expected to pursue this comparative advantage and trace a competitive diversification trajectory that expanded manufacturing jobs as population pressure shrank per capita cropland. Instead, the initially dominant Congress Party espoused autarkic development through a heavy industry big push during 1955–65. The big push entailed state intervention, which created large regulatory rents and exhibited considerable inertia, sustaining autarkic policies for a further generation after the growth collapse of 1965–67. However, the effects of the growth collapse were mitigated by the insulation against external shocks conferred by a closed economy and by the timely diffusion of the green revolution.

8.2.1 *The Nature of Indian Rents*

In 1960, Indian per capita cropland was 0.36 hectares, two-thirds that of land-rich Thailand but four times land-scarce South Korea. Rent in the form of foreign aid, minerals, and oil rarely contributed more than 2% of GDP (Table 8.1), but regulatory rent was substantial. Based on conservative assumptions, Mohammad and Whalley (1984: 410) estimated that total regulatory rent was at least 30% of GNP and required a large civil service to deploy it. They traced the rent extraction to four sources, namely: domestic price controls (16% of GNP); capital controls (8%); trade (4%); and labour (2%). Price controls boosted the cost of both luxury goods and many basic household goods. Rents from capital controls intensified when the banks and insurance companies were nationalized in 1969 and 1972, respectively. The controls included production licensing to deter FDI from all but essential needs, and to favour domestic firms, especially small firms, through subsidized finance with capped interest rates. The reliance of Indian manufacturing on subsidized finance caused output to expand through capital accumulation rather than productivity growth (Bell and Rousseau 2001).

Rent from trade intervention flowed from import quotas that complemented import tariffs ranging up to 450%. Two-fifths of imports encountered tariffs of 75–120%, with more complex processes receiving higher import protection. Estimates of effective rates of protection suggest that during 1980–85 total transfers to manufacturing exceeded sector value added. Some of the cost of using protected domestic inputs was offset by complex export permits and duty drawbacks that incurred substantial administrative costs. However, not all the regulatory rent was cycled to manufacturing: after the 1965–67 food crisis the government raised food prices and farm input subsidies to boost agricultural returns above market levels (Mohammad and Whalley 1984: 399–400), in contrast to most developing economies.

Bardhan (1984) identified three major beneficiaries from India's rent-driven command capitalism, namely professionals (mostly civil servants), large industrial capitalists, and large farmers. The professionals initially dominated and directed educational investment to limit entry and maintain their skill premium, the income-earning potential of which they augmented by levying illicit margins on licensing controls (Bardhan 1984: 52). The second of the three benefiting groups comprised a small number of powerful families, mostly from western India, which dominated the capitalist group. Some twenty family conglomerates controlled almost two-thirds of private productive capacity in the formal sector. They initially welcomed increased state intervention because import protection reduced their investment risk. Finally, larger farmers (with holdings over 4 hectares) comprised one-fifth of farm owners but held three-fifths of the land and produced just over half the output (Bardhan 1984: 46).

Table 8.1 Selected economic indicators, India, 1960–2014 (% GDP, except where stated)

	1960–64	1965–69	1970–74	1975–79	1980–84	1985–89	1990–94	1995–99	2000–04	2005–09	2010–14
Rent proxies											
Total natural resource rent	n.a.	n.a.	0.9	3.1	3.7	2.6	2.7	2.1	2.6	4.8	4.1
Mineral rent	n.a.	n.a.	0.2	0.4	0.3	0.2	0.3	0.2	0.5	1.6	1.1
Net ODA received (% GNI)	1.9	2.2	1.2	1.2	0.9	0.7	0.7	0.4	0.2	0.2	0.1
Regulatory rent[1]	n.a.	n.a.	n.a.	n.a.	n.a.	n.a.	n.a.	n.a.	n.a.	n.a.	n.a.
Remittances	n.a.	n.a.	n.a.	0.7	1.3	0.9	1.2	2.0	3.2	3.3	3.5
Arable land per capita (ha)[2]	0.3	0.3	0.3	0.2	0.2	0.2	0.2	0.2	0.1	0.1	0.1
Economy openness											
Exports	4.2	3.9	4.2	6.4	6.1	5.9	8.9	11.0	14.7	21.5	24.0
FDI	n.a.	n.a.	n.a.	0.0	0.0	0.0	0.1	0.6	0.9	2.3	1.6
Net barter terms of trade[3]	n.a.	n.a.	n.a.	n.a.	75.9	91.4	101.9	108.7	94.9	86.3	92.2
REER[3]	n.a.	n.a.	n.a.	n.a.	n.a.	n.a.	n.a.	n.a.	n.a.	n.a.	n.a.
Absorption											
Gross fixed capital formation	13.9	15.6	15.7	18.3	20.6	23.5	24.3	25.6	27.0	34.3	32.6
Final government consumption	7.8	8.7	9.2	9.8	10.2	11.8	11.2	11.5	11.5	10.6	10.7
Household consumption	78.2	76.2	73.6	69.7	71.0	64.9	62.9	62.0	59.9	53.7	56.6
Structural change											
Agriculture	43.2	44.4	42.8	37.2	34.9	30.9	29.9	26.8	21.2	18.8	18.4
Industry	23.9	24.0	24.0	28.2	29.9	31.0	30.8	31.4	31.3	33.9	31.5
Manufacturing	16.9	15.7	17.1	18.9	19.0	18.8	18.5	18.8	17.7	18.4	17.0
Services	32.9	32.0	32.3	34.6	35.2	38.1	39.2	41.8	46.6	47.2	50.0
Growth											
Per capita GDP (US$, 2010)	321.7	335.0	357.6	384.1	412.9	481.5	553.9	679.2	820.5	1,108.1	1,486.8
GDP growth (%/year)	5.0	3.0	1.6	3.7	5.5	5.9	4.7	6.8	5.6	8.2	7.2
Population growth (%/year)	2.0	2.1	2.3	2.3	2.3	2.2	2.0	1.9	1.7	1.5	1.2
Per capita GDP growth (%/year)	2.9	0.9	−0.7	1.3	3.1	3.6	2.6	4.8	3.9	6.6	5.9
Crop output index[4]	35.5	36.8	42.5	48.9	55.4	64.2	77.0	88.8	92.5	110.3	136.1

[1] Early-1980s = 30% of GDP (Mohammad and Whalley 1984).
[2] Cropland share 2014 = 2.6% of GDP (Lange et al. 2018).
[3] 2000 = 100.
[4] 2005–06 = 100.

Source: World Bank (2017a).

Lipton (1968) argued that urban businesses and unions sought low-cost food, which large landowners conceded in exchange for loopholes in land reforms, lower taxation, and subsidized irrigation and fertilizer. In addition, administered food prices rose well above production costs (Bardhan 1984: 56–57). Yet agricultural growth decelerated from 3.2% per annum during 1980–92 to 1.3% in 2003–05, mainly through declining productivity (World Bank 2006c: 22). In aggregate, India's system of rent-seeking helped to double the share of public expenditure in GDP to one-third from the early-1960s to mid-1980s, mainly by increased public consumption rather than capital formation.

8.2.2 State-Led Rent-Driven Development

State-led rent-driven development modestly expanded the share of manufacturing in GDP (Table 8.1), but to only one-third to one-half that of East Asian comparators. The heavy industry big push boosted public investment from 4.8% of GDP through the 1950s to 10.1% in the 1980s (Singh and Berry 2005: 29). Like big pushes elsewhere, the Indian push outstripped domestic implementation capacity and triggered inflation that caused the real exchange rate to appreciate by more than half through the 1960s (Auty 1994b). The prioritization of heavy industry neglected labour-intensive textile manufacturing, which lost competitiveness and declined in relative terms. Agriculture was also neglected. Farm output shrank drastically during the 1965–67 droughts, destabilizing the economy. It reduced rural purchasing power, which deprived manufacturing of markets, triggering a recession and financial crisis (Mellor 1976) that pushed rural poverty up from 38% to 56%. This led the government to boost both food prices and farm input subsidies (Dev 1993).

Indian economic growth was driven mainly by capital accumulation and the big push strategy eroded capital efficiency: the average ICOR deteriorated from 2.5 in the 1950s to 5.5 in the 1970s, before initial reforms improved it to 3.4 through the 1980s (Lal 1988). The ICORs of Taiwan and South Korea at similar levels of per capita income were around 3 (Auty 1997). By the late-1970s, the public sector held three-quarters of the investment in formal manufacturing, but produced only one-third of the output and none of the profits (Economist 1980). The state-owned steel plants required twice the investment per ton of capacity of South Korea, and Indian production costs were double those of an efficient world producer (Auty 1994a: 193). Even in the early-2000s the public sector generated 26% of NDP (net domestic product (GDP minus depreciation on a country's capital goods)) compared with 14% for the formal private sector and 60% for the informal sector, which dominated agriculture, construction, and trade and hospitality (Singh and Berry 2005).

As with autarkic industrial policies elsewhere, recurrent fiscal gaps increased the share of public debt in GDP: Indian public debt rose from one-quarter of GDP in the early-1950s to two-thirds by the mid-1980s, when debt service absorbed one-sixth of public expenditure. Partial economic reform in the 1980s improved total factor productivity, reflecting more efficient use of both sunk capital and workers in overmanned factories (Ahluwalia 1991: 194). An acute balance of payments and fiscal crisis in 1991 pushed the combined central and state budget deficits to 10% of GDP, however, and debt service to one-quarter of export earnings, rendering foreign borrowing unsustainable (Panagariya 2005). The 1991 crisis finally ended government dominance of investment in favour of the private sector and markets. This switch created propitious conditions for the expansion of India's export services.

Reform quickened in the 1990s, compressing tariff bands to confer a mean tariff of 25%, while the average rate of effective protection fell from 115% in 1980–84 to 40% by 2000–04. These measures were accompanied by the shift to a floating exchange rate and depreciations to maintain export competitiveness. Exports more than doubled to 16% of GDP (Table 8.1), yet the Indian economy remained relatively closed, with a mean tariff in the early-2000s twice that of Thailand and sub-Saharan Africa and four times that of South Korea and Malaysia (IMF 2003: 61). Nontariff barriers also impeded trade. The reformed trade regime conferred the highest protection on agriculture, paper and printing, textiles and clothing, beverages, food, and tobacco, in which India might be expected to hold a competitive advantage.

Further reform was required. The fraction of the population surviving on less than 1,890 calories per day increased fourfold during 1970–2000, partly because policy capture by large farmers slowed grain expansion, which merely doubled during those decades. Of the grain stocks purchased to alleviate poverty, one-third rotted, one-third was corruptly diverted, and one-third reached poor consumers at a price 60% above the purchase price, rather than half of it as was intended (Ungar 2001). As in low-income sub-Saharan Africa, prolonged agricultural neglect and discrimination against light manufacturing failed to pull workers off the land, perpetuating the dependence of India's rural majority (55% of the population) on off-farm incomes. In this context, the rapid growth of export services since 1990 widens scope for labour absorption.

8.3 The Rise of India's Service Sector

The dynamic contribution of the service sector to Indian economic development since the 1990s has surprised many development economists on account of not only the rapid rate of growth, but also gains in productivity and the expansion of service exports. The paradox of impressive growth of services within an economy plagued by inefficiencies can be attributed to aspects of a dual economy. As Section 8.2 explained, the early Indian focus on manufacturing within a command economy spawned burdensome regulation along with corruption and the inefficient accumulation of capital. In contrast, India's services expanded within a competitive environment that also included lighter regulation as well as the availability of excellent management and engineering skills[1] and timely broadband provision.

8.3.1 *The Dynamism of India's Service Sector*

Since 1990 India has expanded its total exports of goods and services to 24.5% of GDP (Syed and Walsh 2012: 37), while within those figures service exports expanded from 1.7% of GDP in 1990 to 8.6% by 2009 (Goswami et al. 2012) to reach around one-third of total exports. Anand et al. (2012: 10) found that a shift to more than 50% *sophisticated* service exports lay behind the rapid growth of the Indian service sector. Moreover, export services have boosted national economic growth even though barely 1% of the workforce is engaged in their supply (Mishra et al. 2012).

Prior to 1990, however, the pattern of structural change in India conformed to the Syrquin and Chenery norms (Figure 2.1). From 1950 to 1990 the share of agriculture in GDP contracted by 25%, whereas industry and services each expanded their share of GDP by around 12% in compensation. Since 1990 the share of manufacturing in GDP has stabilized at around 18% (Table 8.1) rather than rising further, as Syrquin and Chenery predict for a country of its per capita income. Yet agriculture continued to shrink, so the service sector expanded to fill the gap, generating 50% of GDP by 2010–14 (World Bank 2017a).

Interestingly, however, Indian services employed only 27% of the workforce in 2010 (the latest figure available), indicating above-average productivity within the sector. Moreover, the surge in the share of services in India's GDP was accompanied by a less than proportionate increase in the sector's share of employment, indicating that productivity growth has played a role in the service sector's expansion. By comparison, industry generated 18% of India's employment while producing 32% of output, implying a slightly inferior level of productivity to that of services. Meanwhile, agriculture performed well below its potential, employing 56% of the population but generating only 18% of GDP, reflecting much lower productivity (World Bank 2009b).

---

[1] Achieved through, as elaborated in Section 8.4, institutions originally modelled on the US and established soon after independence to promote India's heavy industry big push.

It is India's more dynamic private services, rather than services as a whole, that drove the faster rate of economic growth following economic reform (Goswami et al. 2012). The dynamism of this subsector finally reversed India's prolonged loss in global export share. During 1988–2005 total Indian exports grew fourfold to 16% of GDP and doubled the country's share of total global exports (IMF 2008). More recent data for 2000–13 show that the share of services export in India tripled to over 3% of world service exports. Even so, the Indian economy remained relatively closed and the degree of closure helps sustain regulatory rent extraction within manufacturing. The less-regulated Indian service sector is less susceptible to corruption.

India demonstrates that the service sector can not only generate exports but also drive rapid economy-wide productivity growth. Whereas productivity in Indian manufacturing grew twice as fast as that of agriculture, the productivity of the service sector grew four times faster (Bosworth and Collins 2008). Eichengreen and Gupta (2011) attributed this to a catch-up effect, but nevertheless expected the pace to be sustained. The service sector achieved faster growth in total factor productivity than the Indian economy as a whole, with the annual rate accelerating through the 2000s to an average of 3.3%. This is faster than the US and Japan, albeit slower than some estimates for China.

The rapid growth in services appears sustainable because even as India takes advantage of its low labour costs (80% below the US) to expand its share of service provision, the leading global service economies like the US and UK extend the global services productivity frontier and vacate lower-order service activity where their competitive advantage is diminishing. For instance, the growth of productive impersonal service exports in India averaged more than 25% annually through 1995–2005 (World Bank 2009b). Das et al. (2013) confirmed the strong contribution of services to Indian GDP growth, especially the ICT sector. They showed that the reallocation of labour to services had a positive effect on growth throughout 1980–2009, an effect that strengthened during the 2000s, indicating growth-enhancing structural transformation. Labour productivity has risen, largely due to capital deepening, with the contributions from market sector services such as ICT, finance, and telecommunications especially strong (Loungani et al. 2017).

8.3.2 Factors Driving India's Service Sector Growth

The dynamism of India's service exports has been facilitated by: advances in telecommunications technology; sharply falling communication costs; low trade barriers for services compared with physical goods; and the growth in global demand for impersonal standardized services. By the mid-2000s, the contribution of services to Indian GDP was already above the average expected for countries at a similar income level (Winters and Yusuf 2007). Business services and software spearheaded the growth and the firms responsible became the largest in the world for these sectors. By the mid-2000s, IT services already accounted for 6% of Indian services output but generated US$12 billion in exports and employed 3 million workers in five large agglomerations. One-third of IT and professional service exports emanated from Bangalore alone (D'Costa 2006). By the late-2000s, the service sector had reached a sufficient size relative to GDP that it had begun to significantly impact total GDP growth and economy-wide productivity.

An additional factor driving growth in services has been a spillover from trade liberalization, although the trade reforms were aimed primarily at boosting the resilience of manufacturing. Dehejia and Panagariya (2014) showed that in India the annual rate of growth for industry accelerated from 5.6% to 8% between the periods 1992–2003 and 2003–12, while that for services increased from 7.1% to 9.6%, with the second period being strongly affected by trade reforms. Dehejia and Panagariya (2014) drew upon firm-level data to show that the beneficial impacts of trade reform, which were aimed at stimulating manufacturing, also stimulated the services sector's gross value added, wages, employment, and worker productivity. The gains have been most pronounced for the larger urban service firms and for those services whose output is used by the manufacturing sector as an input. More specifically, improved access to inputs as a consequence of trade liberalization boosts gross value added and worker productivity in the more capital-intensive services as well.

Although early Indian trade reforms did directly target key services like finance, telecommunications, and civil aviation, the rapid growth of these services cannot explain why several nontraded services such as education, health, catering, and transport also accelerated. Dehejia and Panagariya (2014) suggested two possible channels for their buoyancy. First, although some service activity may be nontraded, it draws upon inputs that are traded, so to the extent that trade liberalization improves access to such superior inputs, this makes all service provision more efficient. The second pathway for growth transmission derives from a dual mechanism that comprises, first, a direct channel by which services are deployed as inputs by manufacturers; and second, an indirect channel via increased expenditure on services by a more efficient manufacturing sector. Both these channels encourage faster growth in the services.

An additional boost to service-driven growth in India arose from the sector's resilience and resistance to cyclical economic downturns compared with manufacturing. Borchert and Mattoo (2009) found that whereas manufacturing trade was strongly negatively affected by the 2007–09 global financial shock, as was trade in goods-related transport services, trade expanded in financial services, overseas tourism, professional and business services, and technical services. A greater reliance on exports of business and IT services therefore helped limit the fall in India's total exports to the US compared with, for example, Brazil, China, and African countries, which export goods, transport services, and tourism services. By the late-2000s, services provided 38% of Indian exports, compared with 15% for Africa, 12% for Brazil, and 9% for China (Borchert and Mattoo 2009: 3).

The productivity-driven growth in Indian services and exports has been a modest consumer of capital, being driven less by investment and more by deploying skilled labour. The frugally funded growth of India's services contrasts with the sharp rise in the investment rate of China following its post-1978 reforms. Investment in manufacturing in China absorbed a much higher share of GDP, typically above 40% of GDP. This has resulted in China not only exhibiting low capital efficiency but also foregoing substantial consumption during the growth process. Manufacturing dominated policy in China and the principal role of services was to provide employment. In contrast, in India dynamic service-providing firms are much more prominent than manufacturing firms in generating total economic output due to the boost to productivity that services confer.

Nevertheless, there remains more scope for restructuring the Indian economy towards services because in the early-2000s India's cumbersome public sector still generated more than half of all service output in the formal sector, with the remainder emanating from the formal private sector. However, overall, an estimated 60% of total economic production was generated by the informal sector, which was particularly dominant not only in agriculture and construction but also in trade and hospitality within the service sector (Singh and Berry 2005).

Summarizing, productive services have grown fastest among Indian services and they have reached a scale where they are now large enough to significantly impact total GDP growth. Moreover, as the ratios of skilled to unskilled labour in the manufacturing and service sectors are converging, so manufacturing becomes less important as a leading source of employment growth. In addition, the service sector as a whole generates jobs requiring a wide range of skills and not just those of the most educated, which can help assuage income inequality. With regard to higher-income developing economies like those in Latin America, let alone the Gulf, productive services appear to offer the most scope for service-driven growth because they can more easily absorb the relatively high labour costs of such countries, which are the legacy of decades of Dutch disease effects.

8.4 How India Stimulated Service Sector Expansion

8.4.1 *Positive Aspects of India's Service-Driven Development*

Indian export services developed in three stages (Economist 2005). The first stage saw domestic firms like Tata Consultancy Services (TCS) develop in the 1980s and acquire world-class expertise in the application, development, and maintenance of low-cost software, which attracted western IT partner firms. The second stage involved domestic firms combining with the local captive operations of multinationals to offer low-end back-office services to global markets via telephone call centres that involved, for example, transcribing medical records and processing insurance claims. The third stage saw a shift in both IT and other business process services towards increasingly sophisticated activity.

Looking towards the next stage, India expects to progress by capturing an increased share of whole system service management in IT, an area of expertise that is currently dominated by multinational corporations (MNCs), together with a major extension in legal services such as drafting contracts and patent applications, research, and negotiation. Cost has been the key Indian advantage: for example, it is estimated that within the legal sector, outsourcing to India can cut costs by three-quarters. The scale of the projected expansion in India implies a more than threefold increase in the number of workers in IT and business-process exports every five years.

Currently, most of India's export services comprise software development and maintenance, along with business services (financial, legal, medical, and accounting). Call centres dominate, but large domestic firms like TCS and Infosys are being joined by multinationals including IBM, Cisco Systems, and Texas Instruments. India has the benefit of a head start that confers cost-constraining Verdoorn effects that arise when the phenomenon of rapid growth expands the economies of scale to encourage sustained reinvestment that constantly hones competitiveness. Although Brazil, Mexico, eastern Europe, and Russia are potential competitors for India, they struggle with higher costs and inferior institutions, which have caused them to underperform to date. Apart from movie-making, however, India appears unlikely to develop an export presence in additional services through the medium term. This is due to deficiencies in the country's telecommunications and finance sectors, which in the past has provided scope for countries like Mauritius to fill the financing gap.

A critical factor in India's rapid export service expansion has been the interaction with overseas nationals who have thrived to the extent that they run one-tenth of recent IT start-up firms in Silicon Valley (Goswami et al. 2012: 114). They play a key role in forging business contacts and supplying capital to the software sector. The overseas contacts helped to overcome initial shortages of domestic computers in the 1980s that were caused by the high import taxes imposed by the discredited prereform Licence Raj. Three-quarters of India's twenty largest IT service firms are local firms that trace their roots to the 1980s, but they also forged links to Indian professionals who had migrated to the US. This contact network encouraged Indian IT operators to establish links to innovative foreign companies, notably in California and Greater Boston. From the 1990s, the networks provided further advantages when the expansion of the internet created scope for outsourcing. US companies took the lead to tap India's plentiful, inexpensive, but fairly well-educated English-speaking workforce.

In addition to astute well-connected firms, the second factor behind Indian success is human capital accumulation. Seven higher education institutions modelled on Massachusetts Institute of Technology (MIT) were established by the Indian government in the 1950s and by 2004 they enrolled 30,000 engineering students annually, which along with six Indian management schools and several more IT centres provide exceptionally well-trained graduates in engineering, management, and IT (Winters and Yusuf 2007: 46). Amin and Mattoo (2008) examined the link between sector growth and educational endowment at the regional level for the fourteen largest Indian states. They demonstrated that the relationship between education and the growth in services is strongly positive, whereas they find no link between education and the rate of growth in either agriculture or manufacturing.

A third factor explaining the rise of Indian services is the development of geographical clusters to capture localization economies, whereby once a region is established as a successful service exporter, cumulative-causation then attracts skilled people (Bosker and Garretsen 2010). As an example, the critical attractions of one prominent service exporting centre, Bangalore, are rooted in the availability of innovative broadband, cheap land, and reliable electricity supply. The knowledge of skilled people, once assembled, becomes a resource in itself, attracting foreign investment that brings technology as well as international market access.

A fourth positive factor for India has been government assistance to the service sector, especially the control of telecommunication charges and relaxation of labour market rigidity for exporters of services. This more light touch approach to the service sector contrasts with the heavy regulation of manufacturing and the associated corruption that the licence regime engendered. More specifically, Goswami et al. (2012) identified the industry association the National Association of Software and Services Companies (NASSCOM), established in 1988, as a positive factor through its liaising with entrepreneurs and government to coordinate sector cooperation and limit negative externalities. As an example of the scale of the potential demand and also of the associated economic infrastructure required, the growth of export services is projected to need an extra 150 million square feet of office space every five years.

Continued growth will also require further substantial government expenditure on education to achieve a sizeable expansion of qualified graduates.

8.4.2 Negative Aspects of India's Service-Driven Development

There are some shortcomings in Indian service promotion that late-comers can avoid. First, the potential benefits from localization economies have not been maximized within the dominant Indian IT and business-processing centres of Bangalore, Mumbai, and Delhi region, as well as in the second tier clusters emerging such as Pune, Hyderabad, and Chennai. D'Costa (2006) argued with reference to Bangalore that Indian IT has retained a rigid linear structure from the second stage of its three-stage development cycle, so that it relies heavily on the US market to the detriment of alternatives. In particular, Indian IT often has stronger links to overseas firms and individuals than to adjacent Indian universities and businesses.

D'Costa attributes the weak local interaction partly to the manner in which the industry has evolved, with its strong links to Indian agents in the US. But D'Costa also notes that ease of entry fosters intense competition that impedes local cooperation through the exchange of ideas, despite the fact that in the case of Bangalore several hundred IT firms are clustered in close proximity to universities and to each other. Indian firms may therefore be forced to abandon their favoured linear US–local model of interfirm relationships in the face of anticipated competition from eastern Europe and elsewhere. Such extended competition may force Indian firms to widen their spatial horizons by deploying more skilled workers to develop more sophisticated services in order to diversify markets, including building a greater presence in those parts of the domestic market that remain dominated by multinational firms.

A second undesirable outcome for late-followers to avoid is the uneven distribution of the welfare benefits generated by services. Although the dynamism of the Indian service sector has helped reduce the incidence of poverty, not least by increasing employment opportunities at a faster rate for women than either manufacturing or agriculture, the overall pattern of structural change within the Indian economy since the economic reform of the early-1990s is associated with some regression in income distribution, for which service-led growth may bear some responsibility. When economic reforms first began to accelerate in the 1980s, the poorest groups in India were experiencing a faster rate of consumption growth than the higher-income groups. However, through the 1990s the richer section of the population achieved substantially higher gains in consumption than those on the lowest incomes. Consequently, income inequality grew within states, between states, and between rural and urban areas. This may partly reflect the tendency for service employment to cluster in relatively few emerging agglomerations (World

Bank 2009b). The remedy is not to raise lagging incomes by decentralizing service activity, however, but rather to facilitate labour migration from lagging regions to the centres that generate service sector employment (World Bank 2009b).

For India and other larger federal states, service sector policy may benefit by harnessing the fierce intergovernmental competition that arises from a federal structure of government. India shows how local and regional governments can play a role in promoting more equitable service-driven growth. Variations in state-level policy interventions suggest how benefits may be more equally distributed. The IMF (2008) found that the ability of the poor to gain from economic growth is strongest in those Indian states with: higher levels of financial development (which improves access to finance by the poor); more flexible labour markets (which encourage hiring); and higher human capital investment (through secondary education that extends employment opportunities). In addition, improvements to infrastructure (electricity, surfaced roads, and drinking water access) can help the poor, whereas more general regional social expenditure on health and education shows little correlation with reduced poverty.

Finally, India harbours fears that its success with export services may invoke protectionism in its export markets. These fears emanate from the potential of policy-makers located in India's overseas markets to seek to limit the outsourcing of service activity 'in the national interest'. This could deflect service activity away from competitive suppliers like India and hamper progress by lagging service economies. Such trade discrimination might take the form of the governments of service-importing economies providing politically sensitive assistance during periods of economic hardship.

8.5 A Role for the Competitive Diversification Model in Low-Income South Asia

McMillan et al. (2016) are pessimistic about growth in the developing countries due to the diminished prospects for labour-intensive export manufacturing and the associated deceleration since 1980 in the rate of productivity growth arising from intersectoral structural change. South Asia provides an antidote, however, despite a lagged start. First, as just established, the Indian economy exhibits rapid growth, driven by a dynamic service sector, while retaining strong manufacturing potential, provided that deregulation persists. Second, and the main focus of this section, Bangladesh has been belatedly expanding labour-intensive manufactured exports.

In newly independent Pakistan, the West wing initially dominated the country and pursued industrialization by import substitution. It treated the East as a colony, which until the mid-1960s surrendered to West Pakistan the foreign exchange from its sizeable trade surpluses at an unfavourable exchange rate. Khan (1972) estimated that the closure of trade policy transferred annually 10% of GDP from East to West Pakistan through 1949–69, which depressed jute farmer incomes in East Pakistan and curbed rural demand for domestically produced manufactured goods. Maddison (1995) estimated that annual growth of per capita GDP in East Pakistan averaged only 0.27% during 1950–70, far below Baldwin or Mellor's expectations for crop-driven growth, on top of which the dislocation arising from political secession caused the economy to contract by 18% between 1970 and 1973.

After secession Bangladesh did not immediately embrace the developmental political state or labour-intensive export manufacturing, perhaps because geopolitical rent averaging over 6% of GDP annually through 1970–90 sustained rent-seeking behaviour and thereby eased incentives for reform, despite shrinking per capita cropland (Rahman 1992). However, the government did follow IFI-backed reform from 1988, which lifted investment to one-quarter of GDP by 2016 and expanded the share of manufacturing in GDP from 6% to 17% through 1988–2016 (World Bank 2017a).

By 2016, Bangladesh garment exports were 60% higher than those of India, which had eight times as many people. Bangladeshi GDP grew at 6–7% per annum and population growth decelerated (World Bank 2017b). Services increased their contribution to economic growth and generated 55% of GDP, compared with 17% for manufacturing and barely 15% for agriculture. Moreover, the marginal product of services is seven times higher than that of agriculture, whereas that of manufacturing is four times higher. Contrary to McMillan et al. (2016), the competitive diversification model still functions, and it does so in Vietnam and the Philippines (Harding 2017) as well as in Bangladesh.

8.6 Export Services in the Capital-Surplus Gulf Economies

This section applies the staple trap model to the Gulf economies, with particular reference to Saudi Arabia, the region's largest economy. We identify slow progress with diversification and strong distortions of the economy and labour market, and suggest that the expansion of service exports may provide a more satisfactory solution than industrialization has achieved so far.

8.6.1 *Tardy Economic Diversification*

Gulf governments prudently deployed their large oil windfalls through the 1973–81 oil booms (Table 8.2) by sterilizing some revenue in stabilization funds and investing domestically in economic capital and human capital to

Table 8.2 Hydrocarbon rent, capital-surplus Gulf economies, 1970–2014 (% GDP)

	1970–74	1975–79	1980–84	1985–89	1990–94	1995–99	2000–04	2005–09	2010–14
Kuwait	69.1	67.7	48.9	31.0	29.2	35.8	46.5	34.6	55.9
Qatar	71.5	73.9	60.2	35.1	39.1	22.8	27.7	26.5	19.6
Saudi Arabia	52.3	63.1	54.3	29.0	39.4	32.5	44.7	36.4	44.7
UAE	n.a.	62.6	50.3	30.7	36.0	26.8	30.1	22.0	24.1
Oman	7.9	44.4	37.7	31.1	30.4	26.9	36.1	39.9	42.8
Bahrain	n.a.	n.a.	12.1	7.0	5.5	3.8	4.2	6.0	7.6

Source: World Bank (2017a).

expand domestic absorptive capacity. Less wisely, they also boosted consumption by lowering taxes, expanding subsidies, and providing public sector employment to nationals. Saudi expansion of entitlements helped to triple the share of government consumption to one-third of GDP through 1973–89, which proved difficult to both sustain and cut (Table 8.3). Gulf governments operated with soft budget constraints and struggled to rebalance public finances when oil prices first softened and then fell through 1981–99. They thereby heightened their dependence on oil rents rather than containing it. The Saudi government first sought to adjust to lower oil prices by depleting its US$170 billion of accumulated reserves and then expanding domestic debt to 85% of GDP. Modest cutbacks in entitlements finally stabilized government consumption at one-quarter of GDP in the 1990s, within which subsidies on fuel, water, and electricity still absorbed 13% of GDP (Askari et al. 1998).

The Gulf states initially focused their diversification efforts on resource-based industry, sensibly undertaken as joint ventures between state-owned enterprises and multinational partners that efficiently supplied technology, managers, and market access (Auty 1990). The smelters were world scale and capital intensive, but employed relatively few workers directly. As in Trinidad and Tobago, the anticipated proliferation of labour-intensive downstream linkages proved elusive. Moreover, the domestic private sector remained weak because high real exchange rates encouraged investment either overseas or in basic domestic services and agriculture that were protected against imports. Such activity was often a source of rents since entry was restricted and relied on political connections rather than efficiency.

Gulf governments with fast-depleting oil reserves like Bahrain, Oman, and oil-poor Dubai within the UAE diversified sooner and increasingly into services. Bahrain expanded into regional banking (one-sixth of GDP) in competition with Dubai, which also stressed international travel and tourism. Dubai's Jebel Ali free trade zone attracted one-third of all FDI into the UAE, involving over 7,000 global companies, 144,000 workers, one-fifth of Dubai's GDP, and US$87.6 billion of trade. At the other extreme, Kuwait is the most

Table 8.3 Selected economic indicators, Saudi Arabia, 1960–2014 (% GDP, except where stated)

	1960–64	1965–69	1970–74	1975–79	1980–84	1985–89	1990–94	1995–99	2000–04	2005–09	2010–14
Rent proxies											
Total natural resource rent	n.a.	n.a.	9.0	43.8	39.8	23.0	29.1	24.7	35.9	48.7	44.8
Oil rent	n.a.	n.a.	9.0	43.8	39.6	22.7	28.8	24.5	35.4	47.9	43.7
Net ODA received (% GNI)	-0.1	0.0	0.0	n.a.	n.a.	0.0	0.0	0.0	0.0	0.0	n.a.
Regulatory rent	n.a.	n.a.	n.a.	n.a.	n.a.	n.a.	n.a.	n.a.	n.a.	n.a.	n.a.
Remittances	n.a.	n.a.	n.a.	n.a.	n.a.	n.a.	n.a.	n.a.	n.a.	0.0	0.0
Arable land per capita (ha)[1]	0.3	0.2	0.2	0.2	0.2	0.2	0.2	0.2	0.2	0.1	0.1
Crop output index[2]	11.4	14.1	19.2	25.0	34.1	70.1	90.7	80.8	87.2	97.7	81.4
Economy openness											
Exports	n.a.	48.0	65.8	58.9	50.0	30.5	37.2	36.2	44.2	57.2	51.7
FDI	n.a.	n.a.	-2.7	0.8	3.4	-0.9	0.6	0.4	-0.3	6.1	2.4
Net barter terms of trade[3]	n.a.	n.a.	n.a.	n.a.	n.a.	n.a.	n.a.	n.a.	100.2	168.5	202.9
REER[4]	n.a.	n.a.	n.a.	n.a.	211.4	161.4	122.5	120.3	117.0	97.2	100.8
Absorption											
Fixed capital	n.a.	14.8	65.8	58.9	32.3	20.9	19.9	18.8	18.2	22.4	23.6
Final government consumption	n.a.	16.4	12.9	19.1	24.3	33.3	28.7	25.5	25.3	20.8	21.6
Household consumption	n.a.	34.3	24.0	24.6	27.5	42.6	45.9	43.9	35.0	27.6	30.0
Structural change											
Agriculture	n.a.	4.9	3.2	1.1	1.7	5.4	5.8	5.7	4.7	2.8	2.3
Industry	n.a.	62.0	68.9	68.9	59.4	40.2	49.0	48.7	53.8	62.0	60.4
Manufacturing	n.a.	7.7	6.3	4.7	5.6	8.6	8.9	10.1	10.2	9.8	10.3
Services	n.a.	33.5	28.5	32.0	38.8	54.6	45.1	45.5	41.1	35.2	37.4
Growth											
Per capita GDP (US$, 2000)	n.a.	14,398	30,420	36,331	27,291	16,394	19,345	18,4487	17,849	19,281	20,616
GDP growth (%/year)	n.a.	n.a.	28.5	4.5	-6.8	2.6	6.7	0.6	4.2	2.5	5.4
Population growth (%/year)	3.4	3.6	4.6	5.2	6.1	4.6	3.0	2.1	2.7	2.8	2.9
Per capita GDP growth (%/year)	n.a.	n.a.	22.7	0.8	-12.3	-2.0	3.5	-1.4	1.4	0.5	2.4

[1] Cropland share of GDP 2014 = 0.2% (Lange et al. 2018).
[2] 2004–06 = 100.
[3] 2000 = 100.
[4] 2010 = 100.

Source: World Bank (2017a)

Table 8.4 Hydrocarbon rent dependence, capital-surplus Gulf economies, 2012

	Rents/head (US$)	Rents/national (US$)	Rents (% GDP)	Rents (% government revenue)	Fiscal breakeven oil price 2015 (US$/bl)
Kuwait	31,007	103,517	55	83	49
Qatar	22,447	153,398	24	62	52
Saudi Arabia	12,896	18,857	50	90	95
UAE	9,938	86,628	24	89	69
Oman	9,904	14,033	42	88	96
Bahrain	5,469	11,549	24	87	108

Source: World Bank (2017a); IMF (2017).

oil-dependent Gulf state, having approached the status of a true rentier state prior to the 1991 Iraqi invasion when revenue from the country's external investments exceeded that from oil production (Chalk et al. 1997). The sophistication of the goods and services produced can be measured by the economic complexity index, which accords the UAE and Saudi Arabia a lowly 0.45, slightly above Indonesia but lagging scores of 0.6–0.7 for Canada, Malaysia, and Mexico. Bahrain and Qatar, however, match the latter trio for export sophistication (IMF 2016: 10).

Nevertheless, the Gulf economies have diversified less than countries with similar per capita incomes (Table 8.4), so that their prosperity remains heavily dependent on resource rents (IMF 2016: 31). In 2014 oil still supplied 24–63% of GDP; some 65% of government revenue (UAE) to 85% (Qatar, Bahrain, Oman); and 60–85% of exports, except for the UAE with 31% (IMF 2016: 8). Their economic growth rates reflected fluctuations in oil prices: the Gulf economies averaged growth of 5.8% per annum during 2000–11, but the rate halved in 2015–16 when oil revenues shrank. At the same time, Gulf fiscal deficits expanded and ranged between 3.6% and 7.9% of GDP, compared with an aggregate mean surplus in 2000–11 of 12.4% (El-Katiri 2016).

Alsweilem (2015) argued that policy lessons still need to be learned. For example, the Saudi government strengthened its oil dependence during the commodity super-cycle. Whereas the collapse of oil prices to US$50/bl in 2015 still left Qatar and Kuwait with sufficient revenue to cover public expenditure without drawing on reserves, the UAE required a price of US$69/bl, Saudi Arabia US$95/bl, Oman US$96/bl, and Bahrain US$105/bl (IMF 2017). Saudi Arabia illustrates the scale of the upward expenditure drift through the commodity super-cycle: the price of oil required to balance the budget was US$40/bl in 2004, just two-fifths of the level required in 2014.

The greater progress with competitive diversification in oil-rich economies like Indonesia, Malaysia, and Mexico suggests that Gulf governments need to provide not only an enabling business environment embracing prudent macro management, institutional strengthening (Table 3.1), and more competitive markets (Table 7.4), but also incentives for private firms to constantly upgrade export sophistication. Cherif and Hasanov (2016) favoured diversification into manufacturing and dismissed export services as either low-wage, low-productivity activity like tourism and catering or, if they are high productivity, too small to significantly impact the economy. They cite Bahrain's financial services as an example, which generate 17% of GDP and less than 10% of employment (Cherif and Hasanov 2016: 13). In fact, export services in the Gulf to date remain dominated by unsophisticated travel services (tourism), which comprised 55% of service activity in 2008, in contrast to South Asia where productive services like ICT and finance generated 55% of service exports and transport just 24% (Diop and de Melo 2016: 85).

The Gulf region, like sub-Saharan Africa and Latin America, lags East and South Asia in expanding the share of GDP in dynamic export services like ICT and finance. Diop and de Melo (2016: 85) attributed this to Dutch disease effects in high-rent Gulf economies, which encourage imports of tradeable services. For example, the share of services in the nonmining GDP in Saudi Arabia and Kuwait, two countries for which mining sector data are available, has declined with rising per capita income, while that in low-rent Jordan and Tunisia has expanded. The resource-poor economies export services to the high-rent economies, which have become large importers of services. The adverse impact of Dutch disease effects on Gulf export services from the high-rent economies is reinforced by the proliferation of regulations that raise barriers to entry in services. The barriers also create regulatory rents that increase the domestic price of services and undermine their competitiveness.

8.6.2 *Persistent Distortion of Labour Markets*

The labour markets of Gulf states are also distorted because the oil booms were associated with population growth that outstripped job creation (Table 8.3), prompting Gulf governments to expand public sector jobs for nationals. The Saudi public sector initially expanded employment very rapidly during 1973–81 (Chalk et al. 1997) to cover 90% of nationals (Sirageldin and Al-Ebraheem 1999). The expenditure of public sector wages created demand for private sector services that remain supplied almost wholly by expatriate labour, whose basic living expenditure in turn provides additional demand. Little progress has been made in shrinking the public sector workforce, which in 2014 employed more than 80% of the national workforce in Qatar, Kuwait, and the UAE, 65% in Saudi Arabia, and 40–50% in Bahrain and Oman (IMF 2016: 9). The global average, excluding China, is 18%.

Migrant labour was initially perceived as a buffer against fluctuating oil rents, expanding during booms and repatriating when oil revenues fell. But Saudi employers prefer immigrant workers to nationals because they are cheaper to employ (30% below Saudi nationals), better educated (with market skills rather than theocratic knowledge), and more pliable (Saudi culture sees loss of face in taking orders). Compared to developing economies with a similar per capita income, Gulf nationals lag in secondary education and shun technical and business skills, whereas their salary expectations outstrip productivity, reflecting job security that constrains hiring and firing (Al-Sheikh and Erbas 2016). Although the public sector deploys labour less efficiently than the private sector, public sector wages are 1.3 times private sector levels, compared with the global regional average ratio of 0.8 (Pissarides and Véganzonès–Varoudakis 2007: 150).

Saudi economic growth has been extensive, relying on factor accumulation rather than productivity growth, because much labour and capital is deployed outside the market. For example, Bisat et al. (1997) estimated that total factor productivity declined by –4.6% per annum during 1974–85 and by –0.1% per annum through 1986–96. Data for total factor productivity for 1960–2000 (Bisat et al. 1997: 146) indicate that the Middle East and North Africa region fell further behind the advanced economies, whereas East Asia kept pace and South Asia lagged slightly. Only Oman among the Gulf economies held total factor productivity steady during 1970–2010; elsewhere it fell by 50% or more (Cherif and Hasanov 2016: 9).

Cherif and Hasanov (2016) urged Gulf governments to shrink public sector employment and encourage clusters of supply firms around established heavy industry. They suggested that governments should provide cheap capital and other subsidies to encourage entry into new export products; and motivate universities to interact with businesses to upgrade products and join global networks, specializing in specific stages of the production of complex economic goods and services. However, most such industry developments have struggled to emerge. Consequently, productive services may offer more promising opportunities for populous labour-surplus economies like Saudi Arabia to boost market employment of nationals.

Two options for enticing nationals out of the overexpanded public sector are: an expansion of export services such as Islamic finance to the broader Middle East region, via both local business banking and sharia-complicit small-scale banking; and cultural tourism in Saudi Arabia. To succeed, the high-rent Gulf economies require reforms to curb growth in public sector employment, lower the public/private wage differential, equalize fringe benefits between public and private employment, improve skills, and facilitate worker dismissal. Henry (2016) added more fundamental reform, beginning with raising the employment aspirations of primary school children and strengthening their skills, notably in mathematics.

As noted earlier in this section, additional reforms that are required include stronger institutions, removal of barriers to entry in services, and muting Dutch disease effects. Elbadawi and Kaltani (2016) found that maintaining the real exchange rate close to equilibrium is a necessary condition for sustained economic growth. Economies that avoid overvaluation are associated with sustained export-led growth and significant export diversification. However, since Saudi Arabia shows limited success through the commodity super-cycle in this regard (Table 8.3), a mild undervaluation may be required, especially in the face of deficient institutions and underdeveloped financial markets.

8.6.3 *Achieving Rules-Based Hard Budget Constraints*

As the case study of Trinidad and Tobago shows, control of rents lies at the root of sustained growth and the competitive diversification of mineral economies. Alsweilem (2015) advocated a rules-based system to manage the competing claims of current and future generations on the depleting oil reserves. The system that he recommends for Saudi Arabia allocates cumulated revenues among three funds, namely a Savings Fund, a Stabilization Fund, and a Development Fund. Alsweilem (2015) suggested that US$500 billion of the US $800 billion in assets accumulated by the Saudi government prior to 2014 should be assigned to the Savings Fund to preserve for future generations the value of the natural capital that has already been converted into alternative wealth-generating assets. The bulk of the residual goes to the Stabilization Fund to cushion the economy against macroeconomic shocks, leaving a much smaller amount for the Development Fund.

The rules-based system adds annual oil revenue to the Stabilization Fund, from which the first rule assigns 10–20% to the Savings Fund to augment long-term capital accumulation. The second rule allots 80% of the Stabilization Fund to the annual budget according to the previous year's allocation to maintain continuity, but with adjustments to reflect market trends. Rule three allows the annual budget revenue to be increased from the Savings Fund by a set amount that is no more in any year than the sum generated by the invested assets of the Savings Fund. This ensures that the Saving Funds steadily expands to avoid dependence on the depleting oil reserves. Finally, a modest residual from the Savings Fund is allocated to the Development Fund, augmented by private investment, to diversify the economy by producing more varied goods and ever more sophisticated services, which steadily increase the complexity of economic activity.

8.7 Conclusions

Despite substantial differences in resource endowments and welfare between South Asia and the Gulf states, the two regions share a lag in development that has created a large labour surplus. McMillan et al. (2016: 30–31) argued that scope for low-income countries such as those in South Asia to benefit from labour-intensive export growth has been greatly reduced since the 1980s. ?However, they are overly pessimistic on two counts. First, low-income countries like Bangladesh, Cambodia, and Vietnam exhibit dynamic manufacturing sectors that can be emulated by economies in South Asia and also parts of sub-Saharan Africa. Moreover, the staple of labour-intensive manufacturing is garment making, which is difficult to automate due to the physical properties of cloth, and so is likely to resist reshoring (Economist 2017). Second, services can rival manufacturing in boosting productivity and economic growth in labour-surplus economies, notably in low-income South Asia but also in the high-income Gulf states. Research by Ghani et al. (2012) and Loungani et al. (2017) has identified a comparative advantage for developing countries in an increasing range of sophisticated export services, which confer high productivity and high salaries upon those qualified to undertake them. In addition, service activity can employ workers with a wide range of skills, enhancing scope to upgrade employee skills and reducing the risk of some workers being left behind.

India provides a classic illustration of the rent curse, despite the fact that its comparative advantage at independence already lay in labour-intensive growth based on raising agricultural productivity (subsequently augmented by the green revolution) and textile manufacture and export. The first independent government opted instead for autarchic development and created large regulatory rents with which to pursue it. The rents were deployed by a cumbersome bureaucracy to launch a heavy industry big push to close the gaps in the structure of the colonial economy. The big push led to a growth collapse and recovery to the Hindu rate of economic growth, around 3% per annum, deemed by some to be the limit that Indian society could tolerate (Datt 2016). One result was a growing labour surplus in the neglected agricultural sector and the informal economy, until mounting debt finally encouraged fundamental economic reforms.

Unlike Bangladesh, faster economic growth in India was not driven by labour-intensive manufactured exports, but by the rapid expansion of services, spearheaded by export services and dominated by ICT and financial activity. The service sector benefited from less intrusive government regulation than the industrial sector, which allowed Indian nationals running companies in Silicon Valley and Greater Boston to deploy their skills in India to establish export service clusters. The service sector also benefited from the expansion of skills and infrastructure by both the national and federal governments. In fact, the experience of India underpins much of the recent research by IFIs (Ghani et al. 2012; Loungani et al. 2017), which identifies rapid growth in both the productivity and output of services that match or outstrip those of manufacturing. It is increasingly likely that lagging developing countries can leapfrog manufacturing-led development and expand via increasingly sophisticated service exports instead.

Governments in the Gulf states absorbed their natural resource rents too rapidly, diversifying into resource-based industry, which, as in Trinidad and Tobago, proved capital intensive and created insufficient employment to absorb the rapidly expanding workforce. Governments responded by increasing public expenditure to limit unemployment by subsidizing public sector jobs, housing, and basic goods and services for nationals. The policy created dualistic labour markets, with well-remunerated but unproductive public sector employment for nationals and lower wages for large immigrant workforces that provide private sector goods and services. Dutch disease effects retard the growth of productive export services in the Gulf states, if not of basic services like tourism and tourist travel. Reform therefore needs not just to narrow the discrepancy in remuneration between the public and private sectors but also to depreciate the real exchange rate to generate unsubsidized employment for nationals displaced from a shrinking public sector in productive private sector services (Elbadawi and Kaltani 2016).

Section 4
Analysing the Role of Rent in Economic Development

9

The Principal Findings and some Policy Implications

9.1 Reconceptualizing the Resource Curse

Stiglitz and Kanbur (2015) suggested that critical development issues, such as rising global income inequality, require a more subtle analytical approach than economists have deployed hitherto. They see this as involving the construction of a theory of rent in order to better incorporate the political dimension of economic development. However, the standards of proof required by mainstream economics to test such a theory require robust time series data, which has so far proved elusive in the case of regulatory rent and crop rent, for example. We concur with Stiglitz and Kanbur regarding the importance of focusing upon rent. We adopt an approach based on rent cycling theory (Auty 2010), which trades some analytical rigour to gain flexibility of data coverage. We rely on case studies for estimates of regulatory rent and cropland rent, along with proxy indices, such as trade policy closure and export share, respectively.

Our approach makes four significant modifications to the conceptualization of the resource curse. First, we argue that the resource curse is part of the broader rent curse that can be triggered by other streams of rent, notably regulatory rent, geopolitical rent, and to a lesser degree worker remittances. Each rent stream can match resource rent in terms of size and impact on structural change (Table 2.1). One consequence of this approach is that resource-poor economies like those of the Sahel and South Asia can exhibit 'resource curse' symptoms. A second consequence is that most developing countries in the 1960s had high-rent economies (Auty 2001: 4), and many subsequently experienced protracted growth collapses, an outcome that piqued interest in the resource curse.

Second, we find that the rent curse is not a deterministic phenomenon, and its global incidence fluctuates through time in response to fashions in development strategy. Its incidence intensified through 1970–95 and then eased. This implies that the results from tests of the impact of rent are sensitive to the period studied.

Third, we distinguish two basic types of rent stream. Diffuse rents are associated with rent cycled by numerous economic agents, as, for example, in peasant agriculture. They tend to be deployed more efficiently than the concentrated or point source linkages associated with, for example, rent from large-scale mining, which, as in Trinidad and Tobago, relies heavily on government deployment.

Fourth, the rent curse has not only economic causes but also institutional and political ones, including policy failure, notably the closure of trade policy to promote industrialization by import substitution. The consequent expansion of rent-seeking opportunities invariably caused the policy to degenerate into a source of political patronage, with adverse impacts on structural change.

The pioneering work on economic development of Kuznets (1971) and Chenery and Syrquin (1975) suggests that most developing countries will follow a similar sequence of structural change to that of the advanced economies as their per capita incomes rise. They predict the expansion of first manufacturing and then services, which each draw labour out of initially low-productivity agriculture and into increasingly productive and well-remunerated urban employment (Table 2.3). Yet four of the five major global developing regions diverged from the predicted pattern, albeit in different ways. In the process, the Latin American economies surrendered their head start on economic development to East Asia, while South Asia made a lagged start, sub-Saharan Africa made a false start, and the Gulf governments boosted their nationals' income without them acquiring the skills required to maintain it.

There are potentially numerous rent-driven stylized facts models, but we find that just two explain much of the divergent development of the five principal developing country regions. They are the low-rent competitive diversification model, which rapidly achieves self-sustaining structural change, and the high-rent staple trap model, which is vulnerable to growth collapses that are protracted. The competitive diversification model is associated with the East Asian Dragon economies plus Mauritius, an Indian Ocean outlier. The staple trap model captures key features of the resource-rich economies of most of Latin America, sub-Saharan Africa, and the Gulf states. It can also be applied to densely settled South Asia during its early post-war development when governments deployed copious amounts of regulatory rent.

The predominance of the staple trap development trajectory lies behind the gloomy ruminations of Rodrik (2018) regarding the growth prospects of most developing countries, and those of sub-Saharan Africa in particular. Rodrik cites the failure of most African countries to industrialize; queries prospects for crop-driven development; doubts that the productivity gains conferred by export services will extend beyond the highly skilled; and dismisses mineral-driven development as creating capital-intensive enclaves. However, few economies depend for their development upon a single sector, and they are wise to diversify rapidly if they do. Given that most economies rely on several sectors that are complementary, we are more optimistic than Rodrik about development prospects, especially given: the spread of global value chains; continuing scope for low-income competitive diversification; and emerging opportunities for export services.

In retrospect, some Latin American economies and most in sub-Saharan Africa might have fared better by pursuing a third rent-driven model that is identified by Baldwin (1956) and elaborated by Mellor (1976). Baldwin's diffuse competitive diversification model assumes that family farms accommodate modest increments in investment to confer steady gains in productivity and income. In the early stages of development these gains stimulate a rural multiplier that expands unsubsidized manufacturing that makes some products for local demand and eventually others for export, along with supportive services. Examples of this trajectory are provided by Denmark in the nineteenth century (Johnson 1970: 21–27) and by some land-rich tropical economies like Thailand during Lewis's (1978) first golden age of economic growth 1870–1913.

Baldwin's model could have been widely pursued during the second golden age of economic growth commencing in 1950, and should have been according to a handful of scholars like Bauer and Yamey (1957). Instead, the near universal prioritization of industrialization by import substitution by developing country governments precluded that option. We concur with Mellor (1976) and Lipton (1977) that the neglect of agriculture in favour of industrialization in the early stages of development proved a policy error. It retarded structural change and delayed the demographic transition, which fed agricultural involution, creating a rural reservoir of low-productivity labour that constrains economic development. Correction of the policy error challenges reforming governments to build a pro-growth political coalition as Mauritius did.

The rest of this chapter is structured as follows. Section 9.2 summarizes the strengths of the competitive diversification model with reference to Mauritius, and then identifies the weaknesses in the staple tarp model with respect to Trinidad and Tobago. Section 9.3 critiques the prioritization of industrialization; queries the existence of premature deindustrialization; and argues that the process of self-sustaining structural change drove successful East Asian development, rather than industrial policy. Section 9.4 makes the case for a sector neutral development policy and specifies its principal requirements. Section 9.5 considers further research.

9.2 The Political Economy of Structural Change

The basic motivation of rent cycling theory is that low rent incentivizes the elite to enrich itself by growing the economy through the efficient deployment of resources; whereas high rent encourages the elite to prioritize immediate enrichment at the expense of long-term economic growth. From this premise, rent cycling theory generates two stylized facts development trajectories, namely the low-rent competitive diversification model and the high-rent staple trap model (Table 2.2). The low-rent model is associated with: rapid self-sustaining and relatively egalitarian economic growth; the accumulation of a self-reliant form of social capital; and incremental democratization. The high-rent model is characterized by growth spurts and structural distortion leading to: a protracted growth collapse; the emergence of a dependent social capital; and a brittle polity. We have shown that between them the two models capture the experience of most developing economies through the second half of the twentieth century when most were high-rent economies and many experienced protracted growth collapses (Auty 2001). Our study has focused on the interaction of the political state and structural change, leaving the evolution of the political state for subsequent study.

Mauritius and Trinidad and Tobago were selected as case studies of the low-rent and high-rent economies, respectively, because they shared remarkably similar initial conditions, apart from their mineral endowments. Although their small size conferred extra development challenges, they proved surmountable (Demas 1965). Critically, their small size does not render their basic patterns of structural change unrepresentative of the developing countries as a whole, as Chapters 6–8 illustrate. Moreover, Mauritius provides an instructive counterfactual to explain why high-rent economies like Trinidad and Tobago have tended to underperform. It identifies the omission of the phase of rapid labour absorption as the critical weakness of the high-rent trajectory. The staple trap model captures the essence of the post-1960 trajectory of the majority of developing economies, covering all four of the five principal global developing regions that initially had relatively high ratios of rent to GDP.

9.2.1 *Critical Elements of Low-Rent Competitive Diversification in Mauritius*

Based upon Mauritius's experience, we identify five elements in the competitive diversification model as critical. First, the Mauritius elite were incentivized to form a pro-growth coalition government at independence by an existential crisis caused by an expanding population amid looming land shortages. The Malthusian prospect was exacerbated by tapering geopolitical and natural resource rent. Consistent with rent cycling theory, these conditions incentivized Mauritius's first independent government to function as a developmental political state, which Lal (1995) defined as a state with both the goal of long-term development and the capacity to pursue the policies to achieve it. The East Asian elite also experienced this motivation as increasing land scarcity and the existential crisis posed by the deterioration of the US position in Vietnam incentivized developmental states in Taiwan, South Korea, Singapore, and Hong Kong.

Second, Mauritius's first independent government shifted policy away from an inherited failing policy of industrialization by import substitution in favour of labour-intensive manufactured exports in line with its emerging comparative advantage. Mauritian export incentives attracted both overseas and domestic investment into manufacturing labour-intensive exports under hard budget constraints. Yet Mauritius's rent-distorted residual manufacturing sector retained high rates of effective protection into the 1980s, for reasons explained below.

Third, in contrast to Mauritius's limited domestic market, dynamic global demand accommodated a rapid expansion of textiles and garments exports at a rate that absorbed Mauritius's surplus labour within two decades. This permitted export manufacturing to trigger a singular pattern of structural change whereby the rapid arrival of the Lewis (1954) labour market turning point strengthened real wages that drove self-sustaining diversification into increasingly productive manufacturing and services, including both basic export services like tourism and sophisticated export services like finance. The economic growth was also relatively egalitarian because the elimination of surplus labour put a floor under the wages of the poorest, while proliferating skills capped the skill premium (Londono 1996).

Fourth, Mauritius pursued a dual track reform strategy (as did China later), which postponed reform of the rent-distorted economy (Track 2) until the dynamic market economy (Track 1) achieved sufficient size and political strength to neutralize and absorb Track 2. The policy aimed to limit the risk of the reforming government being unseated by the losers from reform within Track 2 before the reforms were complete (Lau et al. 2000). However, we note that the deployment of some rent from the 1970s sugar boom to undercut political opposition from the rent-distorted sector bred staple trap symptoms that triggered a brief growth collapse in the early-1980s.

Fifth, the reforming government took advantage of the negative shock of the growth collapse to justify speeding the integration of Track 2 into Track 1 by reducing protection and extending hard budget constraints across the entire economy. Meanwhile, rising incomes accelerated Mauritius's passage through the demographic transition as the annual rate of population growth slowed from 2.8% in 1960–64 to 0.6% in 2010–14 (World Bank 2017a). Overall, Mauritius's sustained rapid GDP growth that narrowed the per capita income gap with Trinidad and Tobago. The latter experienced economic growth that was both more erratic and slower. From a global perspective, low-rent East Asia is the only developing region to have effectively pursued a competitive diversification trajectory. However, low-rent Vietnam and Bangladesh are endeavouring to do so.

9.2.2 Critical Elements of the High-Rent Staple Trap in Trinidad and Tobago

Trinidad and Tobago demonstrates five critical elements of the staple trap trajectory. First, the initially modest size of Trinidad and Tobago's oil reserves encouraged the first independent government to function as a developmental political state. Yet, as hydrocarbon reserves were expanded, the government complemented the import substitution strategy inherited from the colonial regime with export-oriented oil- and gas-based industrialization. Thereafter, a combination of extra-parliamentary protests about unemployment and the sudden receipt of large windfall rents after the 1973–74 positive oil shock destabilized the government and motivated it to scale up industrial expansion and subsidize consumption (Auty and Gelb 1986), launching a staple trap trajectory.

Second, accelerated domestic rent absorption through 1974–81 exceeded the absorptive capacity of the domestic economy, strengthening Dutch disease effects. Gas-based industry proved capital intensive and failed to generate labour-intensive downstream manufacturing on the scale expected. Trinidad and Tobago therefore leapfrogged the phase of labour-intensive export manufacturing, forgoing the associated benefits of rapid and self-sustaining structural change, including speedy elimination of surplus labour. As the staple trap model predicts, instead of achieving full employment and self-sustaining competitive diversification, unemployment persisted and the government deployed rent to subsidize jobs in protected industry, an overexpanded bureaucracy, and make-work schemes for low-skilled workers.

Third, far from strengthening *competitive* diversification of the nonenergy economy, the share of tradeables in nonmining GDP contracted, while dependence on gas-based exports increased. This is the essence of the staple trap trajectory: the expanding demands of the rent-subsidized urban sector outstrip the rent supply. In Trinidad and Tobago this occurred when oil prices faltered in 1981, locking the economy into a staple trap that triggered a protracted growth collapse (Table 3.1). The 1981–93 growth collapse cut incomes by one-third and boosted unemployment to 20% in 1990, just as Mauritius reached its labour market turning point.

Fourth, rent cycling exhibits strong inertia, which resists market reform because reform towards competitive markets shrinks the scope for rent extraction. Rent-seeking in Trinidad and Tobago has persisted ever since the sugar plantations were established in the nineteenth century. The inertia of rent-seeking explains why a severe growth collapse failed to motivate the formation of a growth-oriented government in Trinidad and Tobago. When economic growth resumed in 1993 it was driven not by investment in nonoil activity, but by a massive expansion of LNG exports and gas-based industry. Once again, rent was absorbed overrapidly after a cautious start and dependence on gas-based industry intensified, despite its minimal diversification from hydrocarbon dependence. The 2004–08 economic rebound during the commodity super-cycle restored incomes in Trinidad and Tobago, but not on a sustainable basis.

Fifth, Trinidad and Tobago supports the evidence provided by Warner (2015) regarding the widespread failure of mineral booms to stimulate investment in nonmining activity. The economy of Trinidad and Tobago has experienced negligible investment in the nonenergy tradeables sector for more than three consecutive decades. While Mauritius consolidates a competitive and sustainable economy, including export services, Trinidad and Tobago's heavy dependence on gas rents risks a second growth collapse. This may well occur if US fracking technology and new oil and gas provinces within the region deter exploration for the hydrocarbon reserves that are required to maintain Trinidad and Tobago's gas-dependent economy.

Gas-based industry rarely generates the downstream multipliers expected (Auty 1990), partly because the processing plants are scale-sensitive and supply chains serving overseas markets for downstream derivatives are uncompetitive. Additional problems arise from inexperience and overambitious investments, which result in cost overruns that hamper capital recovery. The IADB (2007) confirmed the disappointing outcome in Trinidad and Tobago, which demonstrates that gas-based industry is a minimal diversification from rent-dependence.

9.3 Some Developmental Implications of Prioritizing Industrialization

9.3.1 *Dethroning Manufacturing as the Growth Motor of Economic Development*

The prosperity of the advanced economies was widely attributed to industrialization. However, prominent development economists such as Prebisch (1950) and Singer (1950) concluded that developing country governments needed to build up their manufacturing behind protective trade barriers because international trade favoured the accumulation of capital by the industrial countries. Once competitive industries were established, trade barriers would fall and countries would compete on equal terms. A further reason for initially promoting protected manufacturing lay in the acquisition of technological knowledge. Although developing countries could tap advanced country technology, they might struggle to close the technology gap because established producers could use their head start to resort to predatory pricing to force new competitors out of business. Developing country entrants into manufacturing therefore required assistance in bearing the risks of closing the technology gap.

Whatever its theoretical merits, industrialization by import substitution proved acutely vulnerable to policy capture and rent-seeking. Moreover, the prioritization of industry creates other practical difficulties. Some initial deterioration occurs in the balance of payments as capital goods are imported to build new plants. In addition, import content may remain high because manufacturing assembles components that are unavailable in a developing economy. Customs revenue is also lost when trade barriers curb imports because they effectively transfer resources from the government to the new entrants. Taxpayers must make up the loss of potential government revenue, and they lose out further as consumers because new local products typically cost significantly more than imports and are of inferior quality. Finally, the promotion of industry distorts the economy, favouring production for (protected) domestic markets over production for exports, which is riskier. Effective rates of protection on manufacturing may exceed 100%.

The creation of rents by placing restrictions on foreign and domestic competition lies at the root of the problem with policies that prioritize forced manufacturing. Research suggests that regulatory rents may have been 20–30% or more of GDP in Brazil (Bergsman 1970), India (Mohammad and Whalley 1984: 410), and Iran (Esfahani and Taheripour 2002), for example. This makes it more remunerative for firms and workers to compete for rent rather than seeking to improve competitiveness. There is also scope for corruption as the rents are shared with the politicians who create them and the civil servants who administer them. All too frequently, industrial policies have been captured by the vested interest groups which benefit most from them. Such groups then pose a formidable obstacle to reform no matter what the political system. For example, the South Korean chaebol have stalled reforms for over four decades despite the fact that their access to regulatory rent heightened income inequality and imposed significant costs on domestic consumers (Holcombe 2013).

Rent inflicts other distortions on the economy. Rent-seeking interest groups favour overvalued exchange rates because they are insulated from any loss of competitiveness that this confers, while the prices of their imported inputs are reduced in local money terms. Yet a strengthening exchange rate erodes the competitiveness of unprotected tradeables such as agriculture, mining, and export services. Critically, once allocated, protection and subsidies tend to persist, so that industry fails to mature. Typical maturation rates of several decades rather than a maximum of five to seven years (Krueger and Tuncer 1982) place a substantial economic burden on the rest of the economy, squeezing profitability and expanding fiscal gaps. They also expand trade deficits because protected activity fails to earn the foreign exchange it requires to purchase imported components. The fiscal and trade gaps engender stop–go macroeconomic policies, causing economic growth to become both more erratic and slower (Lal 1983; Greenaway and Chong 1988).

Developing country farmers in particular have tended to bear the brunt of discrimination in favour of manufacturing, which sets the internal terms of trade against them (Krueger 1992). A corollary of manufacturing support is the neglect of agriculture as a potential growth motor in the early stages of development, despite farmers dominating both the economy and employment at that time. In fact, farmer expenditure is a potentially important source of domestic demand, especially when gains in productivity boost farm incomes. Farming can also provide a source of foreign exchange, taxes, food, and raw material supplies and a reservoir for surplus labour. Significantly, agriculture did play a dynamic role during the early stages of economic development in Taiwan and South Korea. Recent gains in the productivity of both agriculture (Fuglie and Wang 2012) and services (Ghani et al. 2012; Loungani et al. 2017) further undermine the case for prioritizing manufacturing.

9.3.2 Premature Deindustrialization in Latin America and Sub-Saharan Africa?

After the disruption of two World Wars and the Great Depression, most Latin American countries reintegrated into the global economy with their structural change at least one generation, if not two, ahead of developing countries in sub-Saharan Africa and most of Asia. However, Latin American governments retained protectionist policies of industrialization by import substitution in preference to lowering tariff protection to compel manufacturers to compete in the re-emerging global economy. The policy caused recurring current account and fiscal gaps that led to stop–go economic policies as the demands of subsidized urban sectors outstripped the resources available to fund the trade and fiscal gaps. This motivated Latin American governments to borrow recycled petro-dollars through the late-1970s at favourably low interest rates to bridge the gaps. However, the combined negative shocks of both higher oil prices and interest rates through 1979–82 precipitated growth collapses that engendered requests for IFI assistance with stabilization and structural adjustment.

The widespread espousal of orthodox economic policies eventually achieved stabilization (Palma 2011), but it also honed a comparative advantage in commodity exports that was associated with a contraction of the share of manufacturing in GDP. It also ushered in slower growth rates for both productivity and the economy. This raised concerns about premature deindustrialization (Rodrik 2018), which can, however, be queried. First, at its peak in the early-1980s the share of manufacturing in GDP reflected the bias towards industrialization in post-war policy, so some contraction was to be expected to match the outcome under sector neutral policies. Much manufacturing has functioned as a vehicle for rent-seeking that has misallocated resources and inflated output, compared with the outcome under more rational economic policies, which do not discriminate against agriculture and services as the pro-industrial policy bias did. Second, the contraction in manufacturing during the commodity super-cycle was heightened temporarily by the inflation of commodity prices. As the boom subsided, the commodity share of GDP contracted and that of other sectors like manufacturing expanded.

Nevertheless, the dismantling of import substitution policies in Latin America appears to diminish industrial prospects. For example, the early reformer Chile was hailed in the 1990s as best practice in Latin America and a possible rival to East Asia but subsequently experienced decelerating GDP growth amid rising public expenditure, while diversification prospects appear disappointing aside from service exports. Yet Brazil remains a potential major exporter of manufactures, some quite sophisticated. Its manufacturing weathered repeated stabilization programmes in the 1980s and 1990s and yet prior to the commodity super-cycle established a global presence. It has subsequently struggled with a strong real appreciation of the exchange rate, which together with expanded social entitlements constrains public and private investment amid revelations of significant corruption.

Prior to reform, the net effect of industrial policy was often to turn the internal terms of trade against agriculture. Such policies had especially adverse effects in sub-Saharan Africa, where they extracted almost twice the revenue from world crop prices (around 50%) compared with policies in Latin America and Asia (Krueger 1992: 61; Anderson and Masters 2009). The resulting staple trap growth collapses caused most countries in sub-Saharan Africa to evolve from being land-rich to land-poor without achieving either sustained gains in income or accelerated passage through the demographic cycle. Without labour-intensive diversification, the neglected agricultural sector, and the urban informal sector acted as reservoirs of the underemployed at remarkably low levels of productivity. The depressed incomes of the majority of the population reflect a substantial loss of both welfare and purchasing power that indefinitely retards the labour market turning point.

Mellor (1995) gives some idea of the magnitude of the losses. Based upon East Asian experience he suggested that small-scale farming can expand at 4–6% annually in low-income economies, which can drive total GDP growth at 7.5% annually. Instead, thin food markets characterized by predominantly inelastic subsistence agriculture in sub-Saharan Africa risk sharp price increases from higher demand that may erode any potential competitive advantage in labour-intensive manufacturing. The share of manufacturing in GDP in sub-Saharan Africa has shrunk to 10–14% and sustained development rests on commodity exports and export services, although Ethiopia exhibits keener competitiveness.

9.3.3 The Contribution of Industrial Policy to Structural Change in East Asia

The role of industrial policy in East Asian success is disputed. The extent of government intervention has ranged upwards—from Hong Kong's basic focus on expanding human and physical capital to facilitate private investment; through Taiwan's cautious mix of state-owned firms and flexible small and medium private businesses; into the funnelling of subsidized capital to create large conglomerates in South Korea; and to heavy dependence on FDI and micromanagement in Singapore. Such a range of strategic intervention across four successful economies suggests that, contrary to Amsden (1989) and Wade (1990), industrial policy has not been critical to structural change. This conclusion is consistent with the detailed empirical studies summarized in Chapter 7 (Stern 1990; Stern et al. 1995; Auty 1997; Noland and Pack 2003), which suggest that at best, industrial policy was neutral in its effects. Rather the critical factor in East Asia was investment under hard budget constraints that encouraged a singular pattern of rapid and self-sustaining structural change in line with emerging comparative advantage as tracked by the competitive diversification model.

Hong Kong has been criticized for allowing the hollowing out of its manufacturing, but its sector neutral stance led to heightened specialization in services, which is prudent given shortages of land and integration into the mainland economy. In contrast, the Singapore government made mistakes through counter-productive micromanagement. For example, in response to the labour market turning point in 1973, it first repressed wages, only to reverse policy in the early-1980s. From the late-1980s Singapore channelled surplus regulatory rent into investment overseas to mute appreciation of the real exchange rate and to diversify against economic shocks. Pang and Lim (2015) criticized Singapore's overemphasis on manufacturing, given that services, especially financial services (25% of GDP), exhibit higher productivity. They argued that a more sector neutral approach would rebalance the economy away from global manufacturing towards regional services, which would shrink the investment share in GDP, boost consumption, and deploy a rising share of labour in export services.

South Korea's overambitious heavy industry big push triggered a growth collapse in 1979–81, which discredited the policy and ushered in liberal economic reform (Park 1986). The chaebol continue to resist the reforms four decades later, however, and with some success. The struggling reforms aimed to: limit chaebol access to cheap capital derived from their ownership of privatized banks; narrow their product ranges; raise investment efficiency; and strengthen small and intermediate firms. Corruption is a further unwelcome legacy of South Korean cycling of regulatory rent in the 1970s, which periodically embroils the highest tier of government. In contrast, the cautious interventions of Taiwan and Hong Kong deployed investment efficiently, which enabled their citizens to consume a larger share of GDP as development proceeded.

9.4 Implications of the Models for Development Policy

In this section we argue for a sector neutral development policy, which requires governments to build an effective political coalition to support pro-growth policies rooted in sound macroeconomic management to support an enabling environment for investors.

9.4.1 Building a Pro-Growth Political Coalition: The Example of Trinidad and Tobago

Like many high-rent economies, Trinidad and Tobago requires a radical change of development strategy because in its case a long-established gas-based industrialization policy has conferred a minimal diversification away from rent-driven growth. Rather, gas-based industrialization rapidly monetized the gas, with the ostensible objective of boosting investment in the infrastructure of a modern economy. The availability of relatively cheap gas was used to attract new manufacturing enterprises, but these have been concentrated on steel, methanol, and fertilizer. Research by Massol and Banal-Estanol (2014) concluded that diversification into metals like aluminium and steel is not an optimal use of gas for Trinidad and Tobago, compared with a production mix embracing LNG and methanol with a ratio of 3:1.

The alternative mix of petrochemicals still depends upon a finite resource, namely low-cost gas that faces uncertain prospects regarding available reserves and is subject to fluctuating prices, as the netback calculations in Table 4.2 reveal. Moreover, the gas-based plants are capital-intensive and employ few workers, whose wages nevertheless exert a demonstration effect that inflates wages in the nonenergy sectors, which are insufficiently productive to merit such rates (Seers 1964). It seems likely that four decades of pursuing gas-based industry has encouraged complacency with respect to the achievement of the critical long-term goal of *sustainable* economic diversification. At this stage therefore, Trinidad and Tobago needs to follow a sequenced diversification away from gas-driven growth and into activity that is skill-based and increasingly innovative. Wake-up calls for development strategists in Trinidad and Tobago have been provided by the economic downswing of 2009–15, along with rising concern over both the scale of domestic gas reserves and future gas markets for Trinidad and Tobago, given the expansion of US shale gas and competing new hydrocarbon provinces.

Yet economic reform will encounter opposition from the beneficiaries of rent-seeking in Trinidad and Tobago who gain from the deployment of energy rent to subsidize prices and reduce taxes. The adverse economic consequences include a dependency syndrome, excessive distribution of wealth to the current generation, and unsustainable subsidies. Hitherto, the absence of strong domestic pro-reform political constituencies in Trinidad and Tobago has left the IFIs to take the lead in lobbying for necessary reforms. Yet IFI influence fluctuates: it strengthens during the stabilization programmes and weakens during booms. In this situation, one or more of the dominant political parties needs to construct a political coalition to champion pro-growth policies. The coalition needs to argue the basic case, which is that gas-based development is unsustainable through the long term, while over the short and medium term it subjects the economy to destabilizing revenue fluctuations and neglects the promotion of productivity gains through effective competitive diversification.

Mauritian experience suggests that Trinidad and Tobago needs to pursue a dual track strategy that can benefit from emerging trends in the global economy to promote a dynamic diversified economy that eclipses gas-based industry. First, burgeoning global demand for personalized consumption of high-value goods and services cuts the relative cost of overcoming the friction of distance to major markets. Second, the prospect of participating in these markets is facilitated by the shift from corporate strategies of vertical integration (which hedge risk by internalizing all production within a large integrated company), towards multifirm value chains (which reduce risk by integrating many small but flexible companies, often irrespective of location). Third, Mauritius, like India, has benefited from such trends, partly as a consequence of nationals spending periods of residence overseas and building social networks that facilitate entry into globally linked businesses when nationals return home. Governments can assist such firms by providing macroeconomic stability and an enabling environment offering world-class institutions, infrastructure, and education.

9.4.2 *Achieving Macroeconomic Stability*

Macroeconomic stability is a prerequisite for effective development, especially where economies depend upon rent that is volatile, as in mineral economies. Rent cycling theory suggests that macro stability in mineral economies requires controlled domestic rent absorption and buffers against fluctuations in hydrocarbon revenues. The rent that the domestic economy forgoes by adopting a lower rate of domestic absorption should be sterilized in low-risk offshore assets that deliver a steady financial return. The resulting smaller and more stable domestic rent stream should be deployed efficiently among competing sector neutral investment options, according to the social rate of return. Rent cycling theory suggests that efficiency in allocation is more likely to be achieved where rent is diffused through many economic agents rather than concentrating it on the government and/or a handful of large companies (Artana et al. 2007). Diffuse deployment also helps constrain scope for rent-seeking activity and corruption.

The IMF (2012b) promotes the permanent income hypothesis to determine an appropriate rate of domestic rent absorption. This approach considers the mineral reserves as a finite stock of wealth, which when prudently invested yields a revenue stream that can be sustained indefinitely. The annual yield ratio sets an upper bound to the size of the nonenergy fiscal deficit that can be sustained. Since the revenue stream will fluctuate, any revenue in excess of the sum that can be prudently absorbed is sterilized in offshore funds. The funds also provide scope for incremental adjustment to negative price shocks. The net effect is to achieve a sustainable rate of domestic rent absorption, facilitate economic stabilization, and ease Dutch disease effects so as to encourage private investment in competitive diversification.

For example, the IMF (2012b) conservatively estimated that the hydrocarbon reserves of Trinidad and Tobago would generate sufficient annual revenue to sustain a nonenergy fiscal deficit of 4–7% of nonenergy GDP, depending on assumptions regarding long-term prices and the longevity of the reserves. Yet through 2009–11 the actual nonenergy deficit in public expenditure averaged 18.9% of nonenergy GDP, illustrating government accommodation of rent-seeking. A rules-based system can help governments to curb domestic rent absorption. Section 8.5.3 describes how Alsweilem (2015) outlined such a system to manage the competing claims of current and future generations on the depleting oil reserves of Saudi Arabia. His system allocates revenues among three funds, namely a Savings Fund, a Stabilization Fund, and a Development Fund. The Savings Fund is by far the largest and generates the annual income stream from the depleting assets, including the amount for domestic absorption. The Stabilization Fund buttresses against revenue volatility, releasing revenue to cushion adjustment to downswings and accumulating revenue during revenue upswings for future protection. Finally, the Development Fund is by far the smallest and can be combined with private investment to promote development projects that promise high returns.

The Savings Fund is buttressed against predatory government withdrawals (to boost electoral support, for example) by being designated to assist future generations to meet growing welfare burdens, mainly the pension and health care requirements of an ageing population. It should achieve this without shrinking the capital stock or burdening the younger generation of workers with high support payments. Norway uses its Provident Fund to moderate the domestic absorption of its hydrocarbon rent, although it inserted an escape clause to fund larger deficits under specific emergency circumstances (Gust and Zakharova 2012: 8).

The balance between the interests of current and future generations turns on whether to opt for intergenerational equity or not. Norway operates a 'bird-in-the-hand' approach that requires all rent to accumulate in the fund and sets the permitted annual drawdown to favour future generations by funding pensions. The projected rent stream is adjusted for inflation and set to maintain a constant real sum over time. This means that while the annual drawdown remains constant in real terms, it becomes a steadily smaller ratio of total GDP, provided that nonhydrocarbon GDP growth remains positive.

The transition to a sustainable rate of domestic rent absorption entails shrinking subsidies to energy consumption and to state enterprises. It may also call for increased rates of both direct and indirect taxation to offset the loss of annual rents. The literature suggests that such reforms will encourage greater public scrutiny of government finances (Ross 2001). A left-of-centre coalition might, for example, cushion the social costs for the poorest members of the community that arise from the withdrawal of subsidies by compensating them on a per capita basis for any hardship they incur. The cash-strapped Iranian government provides an example (Bjorvatn et al. 2012): it aimed to eliminate energy subsidies through 2011–15. The subsidies absorbed between one-fifth and two-fifths of total government expenditure, which helped to swell the fiscal deficit. In addition, the subsidies increased damage to the environment by encouraging wasteful consumption of energy (Lechtenbohmer et al. 2010).

Iranian subsidies had been regressive because the richer one-third of the population absorbed 70% of all energy subsidies (Guillaume et al. 2011). The reforms therefore distributed rent on a per capita basis to compensate for the income lost from the withdrawal of energy subsidies. They provided a per capita lump sum for the poorest 70% of the population, which spends a higher share of its income on energy than richer groups. Of the estimated US$60 billion annual saving from removing subsidies, 50% is paid to lower-income families at a rate of US$40 per capita (US$200 for a family of five); 30% is paid to manufacturers impacted by higher energy costs; and 20% compensates the government for its own higher energy costs.

9.4.3 *Establishing an Enabling Environment*

The switch from sectoral targeting to a sector neutral policy requires an enabling environment that encourages both domestic and overseas investors to prosper. Treisman (2002) established that the quality of the institutions and the business environment tend to improve with per capita income. Yet high-rent Trinidad and Tobago invariably ranks well behind low-rent Mauritius despite the latter having a per capita income just two-thirds that of Trinidad and Tobago (Tables 3.1, 4.5, and 7.4). The enabling environment needs to provide world-class institutions, economic infrastructure, and human capital, which might be most efficiently sourced in a special economic zone (Auty 2011a), reversing current policy of scattering activity across Trinidad and Tobago.

With respect to institutions, Table 3.1 reveals an aggregate score of the six indices for Trinidad and Tobago in 2015 of 0.8, compared with 5.1 for Mauritius, where a higher figure indicates higher quality. Moreover, the Mauritian aggregate figure improved from 3.0 in 1996, whereas that of Trinidad and Tobago *fell* from 2.0 even though its per capita income more than doubled in 1996–2015. In 2015 Trinidad and Tobago performed especially poorly in terms of the control of corruption, which declined from 0.9 in 1996 to less than –0.3 in 2014, while for Mauritius the same indicator improved slightly from 0.0 to 0.3. The main improvements in Mauritius occurred in government effectiveness and the regulation burden imposed on businesses. Yet despite clear evidence of bureaucratic inefficiency and implied wasteful rent deployment (Artana et al. 2007), governments in Trinidad and Tobago persist in seeking to expand public intervention.

In terms of business efficiency, Trinidad and Tobago ranks 79th out of 185 countries according to the World Bank (2014) Doing Business Survey, compared with 28th for Mauritius (Table 7.4). Among the ten leading criteria, Trinidad and Tobago performs least well in terms of enforcing contracts, registering property, securing construction permits, and paying taxes. Although Mauritius also lags in registering property and providing construction permits, its remaining eight indices are close to the economy's commendable overall index. A low standard deviation among the ten indices used in the World Bank survey is a characteristic of the higher-ranked countries, as sixth-placed Norway affirms along with 41st place Chile (Table 7.4). By comparison, Brazil underperforms expectations considerably, ranking 120th, little better than India at 140th and Uganda at 150th.

Finally, in the Global Competitiveness Index Trinidad and Tobago ranks 89th and Mauritius 46th (Table 4.5). In comparison, Brazil ranks 75th and Chile 35th. The main concerns of firms in Trinidad and Tobago are institutions, innovation enhancers, and the efficacy of domestic markets. Bureaucratic inefficiency, corruption, a poor work ethic, and crime raise further concerns, whereas firms in Mauritius cite insufficient capacity for innovation as problematic. Crime and corruption were much further down the list of concerns in Mauritius. However, the macroeconomic environment in Trinidad and Tobago was deemed superior, mainly because of the country's lower debt/GDP ratio, higher rate of saving, and smaller budget deficit, all of which were likely to evaporate with the end of the commodity super-cycle.

The greater financial resources available to Trinidad and Tobago from its rent compared with Mauritius have been deployed less efficiently than they might have been. Although heavy investment in major capital projects like roads, schools, and housing boosted infrastructure and stimulated the construction sector, such interventions are not sustainable in themselves. Recurrent expenditure has also increased in tandem with windfall revenues, which may have increased the social safety net but has also swollen dependence on direct government 'handouts' and short-term jobs with little development of skills or encouragement of entrepreneurs. In contrast, Mauritius has managed to upgrade its business environment more successfully and with fewer resources.

The business surveys strongly suggest that Trinidad and Tobago might fare better if it reduced the rate of rent absorption and deployed less rent through government and dispersed more through the private sector. This shift in resources would free the government to focus on aspects of business promotion that private firms cannot manage so well on their own. Such measures include correcting coordination failure and ensuring that markets are competitive. This will give local financial institutions the opportunity to deploy excess liquidity to encourage private investors to diversify the economy.

9.5 Further Research

There is scope to develop additional rent-driven models, notably models to distinguish between the development trajectories of high-rent economies. Baldwin's diffuse staple model is one example, along with a model of concentrated mineral linkages, distinguishing between ore and hydrocarbons. Another subset of models is required for economies with badly distorted initial conditions, like many of the formerly land-rich economies of sub-Saharan

Africa with their trisector structure, comprising a modern sector, an informal sector, and low-productivity agriculture. The specification of such a multi-sector model that is capable of absorbing surplus labour as fast as labour-intensive export manufacturing has done would usefully inform policy in sub-Saharan Africa.

The models should assess the roles of agriculture along with the informal transition sector, manufacturing, and export services in driving economic growth and productivity, establishing their capacity to help absorb both skilled workers and low-income workers in increasingly productive activity. Rodrik (2015) warned, however, that the employment of low-income workers in services is conditional on local demand, which is unlikely to match the rates of job creation achieved by labour-intensive manufactured exports that serve high-growth global demand. Yet just as the expansion of export services in India was not anticipated by most observers, so the diffusion of telecommunications along with dynamic value chains may connect low-income workers to the international economy in ways yet to clearly emerge.

A second area for further research concerns the political dimension of the models, with respect to the evolution of the political state with rising per capita income and elite negotiation of rent-sharing settlements. The fact that the two principal case studies, Mauritius and Trinidad and Tobago, sustained parliamentary democracies has rendered the issue of political evolution a less prominent concern in this study. Within the context of the global economy, however, the two basic rent-driven models predict contrasting political trajectories. The competitive diversification model is expected to pursue endogenous incremental democratization, facilitated by its initial stage as a developmental political state and disciplined policies that sustain rapid per capita GDP growth. Drawing upon Olson (2000), we hypothesize that the low-rent regime may start as a benevolent autocracy, which passes through a diffusing oligarchy (that erodes the power of the elite) and into a democracy that is consensual rather than polarized (due to successful economic growth).

The political trajectory of the staple trap model is predicted to be more erratic, starting as a predatory autocracy, or quickly reverting to that state as a result of political unrest, which evolves into a concentrated oligarchy. In this case, democratization is most likely to result from a growth collapse and to require external assistance for its establishment. The process is therefore likely to be abrupt and vulnerable to regression. Zak and Feng (1999, 2003) suggested that transitions to democracy can occur if economic growth falters. Przeworski et al. (2000) claimed that rising income does not affect the likelihood of transition to democracy, but it does reduce the probability of regression. This is because the gains from a shift to democracy attenuate at high-income levels as the marginal utility of redistribution gains declines, whereas losses from associated destruction of capital stock (due to violence) strengthen with rising incomes. However, Boix and Stokes (2003) and Epstein et al. (2004) convincingly challenged Przeworski et al. (2000). Acemoglu and Robinson (2012) stressed the interaction of elites and the low-income majority in deploying extractive and inclusive institutions to shape the evolving political economy.

Finally, there is scope to apply the two basic models to case study countries. South Africa provides an interesting example (Nattrass 1988; Bhorat et al. 2014). From 1925 white-dominated governments sought to privilege white workers by overriding the economy's emerging comparative advantage in labour-intensive activity and forcing industrialization by import substitution. They deployed mostly regulatory rent, generated by raising trade barriers and repressing black wages, along with foreign exchange from gold exports. The economy traced a staple trap trajectory that created insufficient jobs, failed to achieve competitive diversification, and spawned a protracted growth collapse during 1975–99. Although the growth collapse consolidated a comparative advantage in cheap labour, persistence with industrial policy risks prolonging rent-seeking by big business, unions, and government. Rather, the development strategy should promote competitive diversification via export-led growth to eliminate a chronic labour surplus. This is what was expected from the African National Congress (ANC) government when it was elected in 1994, but instead the inertia of rent-seeking within the political system led to state capture (Bhorat 2017).

Interesting as it is, rent-seeking in South Africa is rivalled by the research opportunities thrown up by, for example, the impact of the rent curse on the Russian Federation (Gaddy and Ickes 2010), Iran (Esfahani and Taheripour 2002), and Venezuela (Hausmann and Rodriguez 2014). The ultimate objective of such case studies is to distil them into an insightful synthesis of the political economy of economic development. Nor have the advanced economies evaded malign rent-seeking activity: Lindsey and Teles (2017) analysed the political processes by which wealthy Americans use their wealth to influence politicians to legislate in order to create rents that further enrich the wealthy, while decelerating economic growth and heightening income inequality.

References

Acemoglu, D. (2002) Technical change, inequality, and the labour market. *Journal of Economic Literature* 40(1), 7–72.

Acemoglu, D. and Robinson, J. (2008) Persistence of power, elites and institutions. *American Economic Review* 98(1), 267–93.

Acemoglu, D. and Robinson, J. (2012) *Why Nations Fail: The Origins of Power, Prosperity, and Poverty*. London: Profile Books.

Acemoglu, D., Johnson, S., and Robinson, J. (2001) The colonial origins of comparative development: an empirical investigation. *American Economic Review* 91(1), 1369–401.

Acemoglu, D., Johnson, S., and Robinson, J. (2002) Reversal of fortune: geography and institutions in the making of the modem world income distribution. *Quarterly Journal of Economics* 117, 1231–94.

Adamson, A.H. (1972) *Sugar Without Slaves: The Political Economy of British Guiana 1838–1904*. New Haven, CT: Yale University Press.

Ahluwalia, Isher J. (1991) *Productivity and Growth in Indian Manufacturing*. New Delhi: Oxford University Press.

Alesina, A., Spolaore, E., and Wacziarg, R. (2005) Trade, growth and size of countries. In: Aghion, P. and Durlauf, S.N. (eds) *Handbook of Economic Growth*, Volume 1B. Amsterdam: Elsevier, 1499–542.

Alexeev, M. and Conrad, R. (2009) The elusive curse of oil. *Review of Economics and Statistics* 91(3), 586–98.

Alouini, O. and Hubert, P. (2012) *Country Size, Economic Performance and Volatility*. Brussels: European Commission.

Al-Sheikh, H. and Erbas, S.N. (2016) The oil curse and labour markets. In: Elbadawi, I. and Selem, H. (eds) *Understanding and Avoiding the Resource Curse in Resource-Rich Arab Countries*. Cambridge: Cambridge University Press, 149–86.

Alsweilem, K.A. (2015) *A Stable and Efficient Fiscal Framework for Saudi Arabia: The Role of Sovereign Funds in Decoupling Spending from Oil Revenue and Creating a Permanent Source of Income*. Cambridge, MA: Centre for International Development.

Ammam, E. and Baer, W. (2013) Brazil as an emerging economy: a new economic miracle? *Revista de Economia Politica* 32(3), 412–23.

Amin, M. and Mattoo, A. (2008) Human capital and the changing structure of the Indian economy. Policy Research Working Paper 4576. Washington, DC: World Bank.

Amsden, A.H. (1992) *Asia's Next Giant: South Korea and Late Industrialization*. Oxford: Oxford University Press.

References

Anand, R., Mishra, S., and Spatafora, N. (2012) Structural transformation and the sophistication of production. IMF Working Paper 12/59. Washington, DC: IMF.

Anderson, K. and Masters, W.A. (2009) *Distortions to Agricultural Incentives in Africa.* Washington, DC: World Bank.

Artana, D., Bour, J.L., and Navajas, F. (2006) Designing fiscal policy to achieve development. In: Rojas-Suarez, L. and Elias, C. (eds) *Policy Projections for Trinidad and Tobago: From Growth to Prosperity.* Washington, DC: IADB, 25–64.

Artana, D., Auguste, S., Moya, R., Sookram, S., and Watson, P. (2007) *Trinidad and Tobago: Economic Growth in a Dual Economy.* Washington, DC: IADB.

Askari, H. Bazzari, M., and Tyler, W. Policies and economic potential in the countries of the Gulf Cooperation Council. In: Shafik, N. (ed.) *Economic Challenges Facing Middle Eastern and North African Countries.* London: Macmillan Press.

Auty, R.M. (1973) Factory size and economies of scale in the Commonwealth Caribbean Sugar Industry 1930–71. Unpublished PhD thesis. London: University College London.

Auty, R.M. (1976) Caribbean sugar factory size and survival. *Annals of the Association of American Geographers* 66(1), 76–88.

Auty, R.M. (1990) *Resource-Based Industrialization: Sowing the Oil in Eight Exporting Countries.* Oxford: Clarendon Press.

Auty, R.M. (1992) The macro impacts of Korea's heavy industry drive re-evaluated. *Journal of Development Studies* 29, 24–48.

Auty, R.M. (1993) *Sustaining Development in Mineral Economies: The Resource Curse Thesis.* London: Routledge.

Auty, R.M. (1994a) Industrial policy reform in six large NICs: the resource curse thesis. *World Development* 22, 11–26.

Auty, R.M. (1994b) *Economic Development and Industrial Policy: Korea, Brazil, Mexico, India and China.* London: Mansell.

Auty, R.M. (1995) Industrial policy capture in Taiwan and South Korea. *Development Policy Review* 13, 195–217.

Auty, R.M. (1997) Competitive industrial policy and macro performance: has South Korea outperformed Taiwan? *Journal of Development Studies* 32, 445–63.

Auty, R.M. (2001) *Resource Abundance and Economic Development.* Oxford: Clarendon University Press.

Auty, R.M. (2007) Patterns of rent-extraction and deployment in developing countries: implications for governance, economic policy and performance. In: Mavrotas, G. and Shorrocks, A. (eds) *Advancing Development: Core Themes in Global Economics.* London: Palgrave, 555–77.

Auty, R.M. (2009) Natural resource rent cycling outcomes in Botswana, Indonesia and Venezuela. *International Social Science Journal* 195, 33–44.

Auty, R.M. (2010) Elites, rent cycling and development: adjustment to land scarcity in Mauritius, Kenya and Cote d'Ivoire. *Development Policy Review* 28(4), 411–33.

Auty, R.M. (2011) Early reform zones: catalysts for dynamic market economies in Africa. In: Farole, T. and Akinci, G. (eds) *Special Economic Reform Zones: Progress, Emerging Challenges and Future Prospects.* Washington, DC: World Bank, 196–205.

Auty, R.M. (2016a) Will oil rent derail Uganda's preferred labour-intensive development trajectory? Lancaster Environment Centre Working Paper. Lancaster: Lancaster University.

Auty, R.M. (2016b) How fluctuating rent streams shaped Rwanda's post-independence political economy. Lancaster Environment Centre Working Paper. Lancaster: Lancaster University.

Auty, R.M. (2017a) Natural resources and small island economies: Mauritius and Trinidad and Tobago. *Journal of Development Studies* 53(2), 264–77.

Auty, R.M. (2017b) Land-rich Uganda's false start on economic development. Lancaster Environment Centre Working Paper. Lancaster: Lancaster University.

Auty, R.M. and Gelb, A.H. (1986) Oil windfalls in a small parliamentary democracy: their impact on Trinidad and Tobago. *World Development* 14, 1161–75.

Auty, R.M. and Pontara, N. (2008) A dual track strategy for managing Mauritania's projected oil rent. *Development Policy Review* 26(1), 59–77.

Baahiigwa, G., Rigby, D., and Woodhouse, P. (2005) Right target, wrong mechanism? Agricultural modernization and poverty reduction in Uganda. *World Development* 33(3), 481–96.

Baissic, C. (2011) Planned obsolescence? Export processing zones and structural reform in Mauritius. In: Farole, T. and Akinci, G. (eds) *Special Economic Zones: Progress, Emerging Challenges and Future Directions*. Washington, DC: World Bank, 227–44.

Baldwin, R.E. (1956) Patterns of development in newly settled regions. *Manchester School of Social and Economic Studies* 24, 161–79.

Bardham, P. (1984) *The Political Economy of Development in India*. New York: Columbia University Press.

Bauer, P.T. and Yamey, B.S. (1957) *The Economics of Under-Developed Countries*. Cambridge: Nisbet.

Beckford, G.L. (1972) *Persistent Poverty: Underdevelopment in Plantation Economies of the Third World*. Oxford: Oxford University Press.

Bell, C. and Rousseau, P.L. (2001) Post-indepedence India: a case of finance-led industrialization? *Journal of Development Economics* 65(1), 153–75.

Benin, S. and Nin-Pratt, A. (2016) Inter-temporal trends in agricultural productivity. In: Benin, S. (ed) *Agricultural Productivity in Africa: Trends, Patterns, and Determinants*. Washington, DC: IFPRI, 25–104.

Bergsman, J. (1970) *Brazil's Industrialization and Trade Policies*. London: Oxford University Press.

Best, L. (1968) Outline of a model of pure plantation economy. *Social and Economic Studies* 17(3), 283–326.

Bevan, D., Collier, P., and Gunning, J.W. (1987) Consequences of a commodity boom in a controlled economy: accumulation and redistribution in Kenya. *World Bank Economic Review* 1, 489–513.

Bevan, D., Collier, P., and Gunning, J. (1999) *The Political Economy of Poverty, Equity and Growth: Nigeria and Indonesia*. Washington, DC: World Bank.

Bhorat, H. (2017) *Betrayal of the promise: how South Africa is being stolen*. State Capacity Research Project. Stellenbosch: Stellenbosch University.

Bhorat, H., Hirsch, A., Kanbur, R., and Ncybe, M. (2014) Economic policy in South Africa—past, present and future. In: Bhorat, H., Hirsch, A., Kanbur, R., and Ncybe, M. (eds) *The Oxford Companion to the Economics of South Africa*. Oxford: Oxford University Press, 1–25.

Binswanger-Mkhize, H.P. (2012) *The role of agriculture in structural transformation*. WCAO Thematic Note 02. Washington, DC: IFPRI.

Binswanger-Mkhize, H.P. and Savastano, S. (2018) African agriculture is intensifying—but not by much. In: Christiaensen, L. and Demery, L. (eds) *Agriculture in Africa: Telling Myths from Facts*. Washington, DC: World Bank, 95–103.

Bisat, A., El-Arian, M., and Helbing, T. (1997) Growth investment and saving in the Arab countries. IMF Working Paper WP97/85. Washington, DC: IMF.

Bjorvatn, K., Farzanegan, M.R., and Schneider, F. (2012) Resource curse and power balance: evidence from oil-rich countries. *World Development* 40(7), 1308–16.

Bloom, D.E. and Williamson, J.G. (1998) Demographic transitions and economic miracles in emerging Asia. *World Bank Economic Review* 12, 419–55.

Blouet, B.W. and Blouet, O.M. (1982) *Latin America and the Caribbean: A Regional Survey*. Chichester: John Wiley and Sons.

Boix, C. and Stokes, S.C. (2003) Endogenous democratization. *World Politics* 55(3), 517–45.

Boltho, A. and Weber, M. (2009) Did China follow the East Asian Model? *European Journal of Comparative Economics* 6(2), 267–86.

Boone, P. (1996) Politics and the effectiveness of foreign aid. *European Economic Review* 89(1), 22–46.

Borchert, I. and Mattoo, S. (2009) The crisis-resilience of services trade. Policy Research Working Paper 4917. Washington, DC: World Bank.

Bosker, M. and Garretsen, H. (2010) New economic geography and services. In: Ghani, E. (ed.) *The Service Revolution in South Asia*. New Delhi, Oxford University Press, 147–77.

Bosworth, B. and Collins, S.M. (2008) Accounting for growth: comparing China and India. *Journal of Economic Perspectives* 22(1), 45–66.

Bosworth, B. and Maertens, A. (2010) Economic growth and employment generation: the role of the service sector. In: Ghani, E. (ed.) *The Service Revolution in South Asia*. New Delhi, Oxford University Press, 103–46.

BP (2017) *BP Statistical Review of World Energy 2017*. London: British Petroleum.

Braumann, B. (1997) Unemployment persistence and capital shortage: the case of Trinidad and Tobago. IMF Working Paper 97/77. Washington, DC: IMF.

Bruegel (2017) Real effective exchange rates for 178 countries: a new database. http://bruegel.org/publications/datasets/real-effective-exchange-rates-for-178-countries-a-new-database.

Brunnschweiler, C.N. (2008) Cursing the blessings? Natural resource abundance, institutions and economic growth. *World Development* 36(3), 399–49.

Buera, F.J. and Kaboski, J.P. (2012) The rise of the service economy. *American Economic Review* 102(6), 2540–69.

Cashin, P. and McDermott, C.J. (2002) The long-run behaviour of commodity prices: small trends and big variability. *IMF Staff Papers* 49(2), 175–98.

Cashin, P., Liang, H., and McDermott, C.J. (2000) How persistent are shocks to world commodity prices? *IMF Staff Papers* 47, 177–217.

Castaldi, C. Cimoli, M., Correa, N., and Dosi, G. (2008) Technological learning, policy regimes and growth: long-term patterns and some specificities of the 'globalised' economy. In: Cimoli, M., Dosi, G., and Stiglitz, J.E. (eds) *Industrial Policy and Development*. Oxford: Oxford University Press, 39–75.

Castley, R. (1997) *Korea's Economic Miracle: The Crucial Role of Japan*. London: Palgrave/ Macmillan.

Castro, A. (2009) The impact of public policies in Brazil along the path from semi-stagnation to growth in a Sino-centric market. In: Cimoli, M., Dosi, G., and Stiglitz, J.E. (eds) *Industrial Policy and Development*. Oxford: Oxford University Press, 257–76.

Cavalcanti, T., Mohaddes, K., and Raissi, M. (2011) Growth, development and natural resources: new evidence using heterogeneous panel analysis. *Quarterly Review of Economics and Finance* 51, 1305–18.

Central Bank of Trinidad & Tobago (2009) *Annual Employment Statistics: Trinidad and Tobago*. Port of Spain: Central Bank of Trinidad & Tobago.

Central Bank of Trinidad & Tobago (2014) *Annual Economic Survey 2013*. Port of Spain: Central Bank of Trinidad & Tobago.

Chalk, N.A., Fennell, S., Wilson, J.F., El-Erian, M.A., and Kireyev, A. (1997) Kuwait: from reconstruction to accumulation for future generations. IMF Occasional Paper 150. Washington, DC: IMF.

Chalmin, P. (1990) *The Making of a Sugar Giant: Tate and Lyle 1959–1989*. London: Harwood Academic Publishers.

Chenery, H.B. (1981) Restructuring the world economy. *Foreign Affairs* 59, 1102–20.

Chenery, H.B. and Syrquin, M. (1975) *Patterns of Development 1950–70*. Washington, DC: World Bank.

Cherif, R. and Hasanov, H. (2016) Soaring of the Gulf falcons. In: Cherif, R., Hasanov, F., and Zhu, M. (eds) *Breaking the Oil Spell: The Gulf Falcons' Path to Diversification*. Washington, DC: IMF, 3–46.

Chernoff, B. and Warner, A.M. (2002) *Sources of Fast Growth in Mauritius: 1960–2003*. Cambridge, MA: Harvard Centre for International Development.

Cho, Y.J. (1996) Government intervention, rent distribution and economic development in Korea. In: Aoki, M., Kim, H., and Okuno-Fujiwara, M. (eds) *The Role of Government in East Asian Economic Development*. Oxford: Clarendon Press, 208–232.

Clarke, T. (2011) The sustainability of Trinidad and Tobago's economic growth: an assessment of the implications of green national accounting. Jamaica Institute of Environmental Professionals Fifth Biennial Conference, Kingston, 6–8 June.

Collier, P. (2006) Is aid oil? An analysis of whether Africa can absorb more aid. *World Development* 34, 1482–97.

Collier, P. and Hoeffler, A. (2009) Testing the neo-con agenda: democracy in resource-rich societies. *European Economic Review* 53, 293–308.

Corbo, V. and de Melo, J. (1987) Lessons from the southern cone policy reforms. *World Bank Researach Observer* 2, 111–42.

Cuddington, J. (1989) Commodity price booms in developing countries. *World Bank Research Observer* 4, 143–65.

References

Das, D.K., Eroban, A.A., Aggarwal, S., and Sengupta, S. (2013) *Revisiting the Service-Led Growth in India: Understanding India's Service Sector Productivity Growth*. Sydney: University of New South Wales.

Datt, G. (2016) *Indian Economy*. New Delhi: S. Chand Publishing.

D'Costa, A.P. (2006) Exports, university–industry linkages, and innovation challenges in Bangalore, India. Policy Research Working Paper 3887. Washington, DC: World Bank.

Deacon, R. (2011) The political economy of the natural resource curse: a survey of theory and evidence. *Foundations and Trends in Microeconomics* 7(2), 111–208.

de Brauw, A., Mueller, V., and Lee, H.L. (2014) The role of rural–urban migration in the structural transformation of sub-Saharan Africa. *World Development* 63, 33–42.

Dehejia, R. and Panagariya, A. (2014) Trade liberalization in manufacturing and accelerated growth in services in India. NBER Working Paper 19923, Cammbridge, MA: National Bureau of Economic Research.

De la Cruz, J.A. and Riker, D. (2012) Product space analysis of the exports of Brazil. Working Paper 2012-06A. Washington, DC: US International Trade Commission.

Demas, W.G. (1965) *The Economics of Development in Small Countries*. Montreal: McGill University Press.

Dev, S. Mahendra (1993) On-agricultural employment in rural India: evidence at a disaggregate level. In: Visaria, P. and Basant, R. (eds) *Non-Agricultural Employment in India: Trends and Prospects*. New Delhi: Sage Publications.

de Vries, G., Timmer, M., and de Vries, K. (2013) Structural transformation in Africa: static gains, dynamic losses. GGDC Research Memorandum 136. Groningen: Groningen Growth and Development Centre, University of Groningen.

Dhanda, K.S. (2004) Labour and place in Barbados, Jamaica and Trinidad. *New West Indian Guide* 75(3), 229–56.

Diao, X. and McMillan, M. (2014) Towards understanding economic growth in Africa: a reinterpretation of the Lewis model. IFPRI Discussion Paper 01380. Washington, DC: IFPRI.

Diao, X., Harttgen, K., and McMillan, M. (2017) The changing structure of Africa's economies. NBER Working Paper 23021. Cambridge, MA: National Bureau of Economic Research.

Di John, J. (2011) Is there really a resource curse: a critical review of theory and evidence. *Global Governance* 17(2), 167–84.

Diop, N. and de Melo, J. (2016) Dutch disease in the services sector. In: Elbadawi, I. and Selim, H. (eds) *Understanding and Avoiding the Resource Curse in Resource-Rich Arab Countries*. Cambridge: Cambridge University Press.

Djankov, S., Hart, O., McLiesh, C., and Shleifer, A. (2006) Debt enforcement around the world. Working Paper 12807. Cambridge, MA: NBER.

Dornbusch, R. and Edwards, S. (1994) *The Macroeconomics of Populism in Latin America*. Chicago Il: Universsity of Chicago Press.

Duarte, M. and Restuccia, D. (2010) The role of structural transformation in aggregate productivity. *Quarterly Journal of Economics* 125(1), 129–73.

Dumont, R. (1966) *False Start in Africa*. London: Andre Deutsch.

Eberhardt, M. and Vollrath, D. (2014) Agricultural technology and structural change. CSAE Working Paper WPS 2014/21. Oxford: CSAE.

Echevarria, C. (1997) Changes in sectoral composition associated with economic growth. *International Economic Review* 38: 431–52.

Economist (1980) India's private sector: red tape, black money and white hope. *The Economist* 11 October, 79–80.

Economist (2000) Trinidad: pandaymonium. *The Economist* 7 December.

Economist (2005) The next wave: India's IT and remote-service industries just keep on growing. *The Economist* 12 November, 57–8.

Economist (2009) Brazil takes off. *The Economist* 12 November.

Economist (2013) Report on outsourcing and offshoring. *The Economist* 19 January.

Economist (2016) A green revolution: briefing African agriculture. *The Economist* 12 March, 23–5.

Economist (2017) Sewing cloth still needs human hand, but for how much longer? *The Economist* 24 August.

Economist (2018) Politicians' battle against Korean conglomerates hit a snag. The *Economist* 26 April.

Eichengreen, B. and Gupta, P. (2011) The service sector as India's road to economic growth. NBER Working Paper 16757. Cambridge, MA: National Bureau of Economic Research.

Eichengreen, B. and Gupta, P. (2013) The real exchange rate and export growth: are services different? Bank of Korea Working Paper 2013–17. Seoul: Bank of Korea.

Eichengreen, B., Park, D., and Shin, K. (2013) Growth slowdowns redux: new evidence on the middle-income trap. NBER Working Paper 18673. Cambridge, MA: National Bureau of Economic Research.

Elbadawi, I. and Kaltani, L. (2016) Real exchange rates and export performance in oil-dependent Arab economies. In: Elbadawi, I. and Selim, H. (eds) *Understanding and avoiding the oil curse in resource-rich Arab economies*. Cambridge: Cambridge University Press, 44–81.

El-Katiri, L. (2016) Oil's fall is a challenge for Gulf economies, but also an opportunity. *Harvard Business Review* 7 March.

Energy Chamber (2011) The Year in Energy. *Business Guardian* 16, Week Five, December.

Energy Chamber (2013) Energy: The Year in Review. *Business Guardian* 18, Week One, January.

Engerman, S. and Sokoloff, K. (2012) *Economic Development in the Americas Since 1500: Endowments and Institutions*. New York: Cambridge University Press.

Epstein, D.L., Bates, R., Goldstone, J., Kristensen, I., and O'Halloran, S. (2004) Democratic transitions. CID Working Paper 101. Cambridge, MA: Centre for International Development.

Esfahani, H.S. and Taheripour, F. (2002) Hidden public expenditures and the economy in Iran. *International Journal of Middle East Studies* 34, 691–718.

Ferrantino, M.J. and Taglioni, D. (2014) Global value chains in the current trade slowdown. Economic Premise 137. Washington, DC: World Bank.

Ffrench-Davies, R. (2014) Is Chile a model for economic development? Working Paper 392. Santiago: Department of Economics, University of Chile.

Financial Services Commission (2013) *Mauritius International Finance Centre: Statistics and Surveys*. Basseterre: Ministry of Finance and Development.

Financial Times (1994a) Mauritius: survey. *Financial Times*.

Financial Times (1994b) Africa: Mauritius. *Financial Times* 13 September.

Financial Times (2013) Mauritius: survey. *Financial Times*.

Findlay, R. and Wellisz, S. (1993) *The Political Economy of Poverty, Equity and Growth: Five Small Open Economies*. Washington, DC: World Bank.

Firpo, S. and Pieri, R. (2017) Structural change, productivity growth and trade policy in Brazil. In: McMillan, M.S., Rodrik, D., and Sepúlveda, C. (eds) *Structural Change, Fundamentals, and Growth: A Framework and Case Studies*. Washington, DC: International Food Policy Research Institue (IFPRI), 267–92.

Flaaen, A., Ghani, E., and Mishra, S. (2013) How to avoid middle income traps: evidence from Malaysia. World Bank Policy Research Working Paper 6427. Washington, DC: World Bank.

Fox, F., Senbet, L.W., and Simbanegavi, W. (2016) youth employment in sub-saharan africa: challenges, constraints and opportunities. *Journal of African Economies* 25 (Suppl 1), 3–15.

Frankel, J.A. (2012) The natural resource curse: a survey of diagnoses and some prescriptions. In: Arezki, R., Pattillo, C.A., Quintyn, M., and Zhu, M. (eds) *Commodity Price Volatility and Inclusive Growth in Low-Income Countries*. Washington, DC: IMF, 7–34.

Fuglie, K. and Wang, S.L. (2012) Productivity growth in global agriculture shifting to developing countries. *Choices* 4, 1–7.

Furlonge, H.I. and Kaiser, M. (2010) Overview of natural gas sector developments in Trinidad and Tobago. *International Journal of Energy Sector Management* 4(4), 535–54.

Gaddy, C.G. and Ickes, B.W. (2010) Russia and the financial crisis. *Eurasian Geography and Economics* 51(3), 281–311.

Geertz, C. (1963) *Agricultural Involution: The Process of Ecological Change in Indonesia*. Berkeley, CA: University of California Press.

Gelb, A. and Associates (1988) *Oil Windfalls—Blessing or Curse?* Oxford: Oxford University Press.

Gelb, A.H., Knight, J., and Sabot, R. (1991) Public sector employment, rent seeking and economic growth. *Economic Journal* 101: 1186–99.

Gelb, A.H., Meyer, C.J., and Ramachandran, V. (2014) Development as diffusion: manufacturing productivity and sub-Saharan Africa's missing middle. CGD Working Paper 357. Washington, DC: Centre for Global Development.

Gelb, A.H., Meyer, C.J., Wadwha, V., and Ramachandran, D. (2017) Can Africa be a manufacturing destination? Labour costs in comparative perspective. CGD Working Paper 466. Washington, DC: Centre for Global Development. https://www.cgdev.org/publication/can-africa-be-manufacturing-destination-labor-costs-comparativeperspective.

Gerelmaa, L. and Kotani, K. (2016) Further investigation of natural resources and economic growth: do natural resources depress economic growth? *Resources Policy* 50, 312–21.

Ghanem, H. (1999) The Ivorian cocoa and coffee boom of 1976–80: the end of a miracle? In: Collier, P., Gunning, J.W., and Associates (eds) *Trade Shocks in the Developing Countires: Volume I Africa*. Oxford: Oxford University Press, 142–62.

Ghani, E., Goswami, A.G., and Kharas, H. (2012) Service with a smile. Economic Premise 96. Washington, DC: World Bank.

Girvan, N. (1971) *Foreign Capital and Economic Underdevelopment in Jamaica*. Old Woking: Unwin and Institute of Social and Economic Research University of the West Indies.

Giuliano, P. and Ruiz-Arranz, M. (2009) Remittances, financial development and growth. *Journal of Development Economics* 90(1), 144–52.

Glaeser, E.L., La Porta, R. Lopes-de-Silanes, F. and Shleifer, A. (2004) Do institutions cause growth? *Journal of Economic Growth* 9(3), 271–303.

Googoolye, Y. (2012) *Mauritius: A Regional Financial Services Hub*. Pointe aux Piments: Mauritian Management Association.

Goswami, A.G., Mattoo, A., and Saez, E. (2012) *Exporting Services: A Developing Country Perspective*. Washington, DC: World Bank.

Grabowski, R. (2015) Agriculture, labour-intensive growth and structural change: East Asia, Southeast Asia and Africa. *Development Journal of the South* 1.

Graham, E. and Floering, I. (1984) *The Modern Plantation in the Third World*. London: Croom Helm.

Greenaway, D. and Chong, H.N. (1988) Industrialisation and macroeconomic performance in developing countries under alternative trade strategies. *Kyklos* 41, 419–35.

Greenaway, D. and Lamusse, R. (1999) Private and public sector responses to the 1972–75 sugar boom in Mauritius. In: Collier, P., Gunning, J.W., and Associates (1999) *Trade Shocks in Developing Countries. Volume I Africa*. Oxford: Oxford University Press, 207–25.

Gust, C. and Zakharova, D. (2012) Strengthening Russia's fiscal framework. IMF Working Paper 12/076. Washington, DC: IMF.

Gwynne, R.N. (1985) *Industrialization and Urbanization in Latin America*. London: Croom Helm.

Haig, R.M. (1926) Toward an understanding of the metropolis. *Quarterly Journal of Economics* 41, 179–208.

Hallward-Driemeier, M. and Nayyar, G. (2017). Trouble in the making? The future of manufacturing-led development. Washington, DC: World Bank Publication 27946.

Harding, R. (2017) Manufacturing flocks to new corners of Asia. *Financial Times* 8 August.

Harvey, R. (1980) Chile's counter-revolution: a survey. *The Economist* Supplement 2 February.

Hausmann, R. and Rodriguez, F.R. (2014) *Venezuela Before Chavez: Anatomy of an Economic Collapse*. Philadelphia: Pennsylvania State Press.

Hausmann, R. (2008) In search of the chains that hold Brazil back. Working Paper RWP08-061. Cambridge MA: John F. Kennedy School of Government.

Hausmann, R., Hwang, J., and Rodrik, D. (2007) What you export matters. *Journal of Economic Growth* 12(1), 1–25.

Hausmann, R. and Klinger, B. (2007) The structure of the product space and the evolution of comparative advantage. CID Working Paper 146. Cambridge, MA: Harvard Centre for International Development.

Henry, C.M. (2016) The riddle of diversification. In: Cherif, R., Hassanov, F., and Zhu, M. (eds) *Breaking the Oil Spell: The Gulf Falcons' Path to Diversification*. Washington, DC: IMF, 47–62.

Holcombe, R. (2013) South Korea's economic future: industrial policy, or economic democracy? *Journal of Economic Behaviour and Organization* 88(C), 3–13.

IADB (2009) *Country Program Evaluation: Trinidad and Tobago 2000–08*. Washington, DC: IADB.

IADB (2016) Inter-American Development Bank annual report 2015: the year in review. Washington, DC: IADB.

IMF (1999) Trinidad and Tobago: selected issues and statistical appendix. IMF Staff Country Report 99/67. Washington, DC: IMF.

IMF (2002) Mauritius: selected issues and statistical appendix. IMF Staff Country Report 02/144. Washington, DC: IMF.

IMF (2003) A Tale of two giants: India's and China's experience with reform and growth. Washington, DC: IMF.

IMF (2005a) Trinidad and Tobago: selected issues. IMF Staff Country Report 05/06. Washington, DC: IMF.

IMF (2005b) Mauritius: challenges of sustained growth. IMF Special Issues. Washington, DC: IMF.

IMF (2007) Trinidad and Tobago: selected issues. IMF Staff Country Report 07/08. Washington, DC: IMF.

IMF (2008) India: selected issues. IMF Staff Country Report 08/52. Washington, DC: IMF.

IMF (2009) Trinidad and Tobago: article IV consultation—staff report. IMF Staff Country Report 09/78. Washington, DC: IMF.

IMF (2012a) Trinidad and Tobago: selected issues. IMF Staff Country Report 12/128. Washington, DC: IMF.

IMF (2012b) Trinidad and Tobago: article IV consultation—staff report. IMF Staff Country Report 12/127. Washington, DC: IMF.

IMF (2013a) Caribbean small states: challenges of high debt and low growth. IMF Working Paper 13. Washington, DC: IMF.

IMF (2013b) Trinidad and Tobago: selected issues. IMF Staff Country Report 13/306. Washington, DC: IMF.

IMF (2016) Economic diversification in the oil-exporting Arab countries. Working Paper of the Annual Meeting of the Arab Ministers of Finance. Washington, DC: IMF.

IMF (2017) Saudi Arabia: selected issues. IMF Staff Country Report 17/317. Washington, DC: IMF.

Isham, J., Pritchett, L., Woolcock, M., and Busby, G. (2005) The varieties of resource experience: how natural resource export structures affect the political economy of economic growth. *World Bank Economic Review* 19(1), 141–64.

Jahan, S., and Wang, K. (2013) A big question on small states. *Finance and Development* 50 (3).

Johnson, E.A.J. (1970) *The Organization of Space in Developing Countries*. Cambridge, MA: Harvard University Press, 21–7.

Johnson, H. (1972) The origins and early development of cane farming in Trinidad, 1882–1906. *Journal of Caribbean History* 5, 46–74.

Johnston, B.F. and Mellor, J.W. (1961) The role of agriculture in economic development. *American Economic Review* 60, 566–93.

Jorgensen, O.H. (2013) Efficiency and equity implications of oil windfalls in Brazil. World Bank Policy Working Paper 6597. Washington, DC: World Bank.

Joseph, A. and Troester, W. (2013) Can the Mauritian Miracle continue? The role of financial and ICT services as prospective growth drivers. Working paper 01/2013. Berlin: HTW.

Karl, T.L. (1997) *The Paradox of Plenty: Oil Booms and Petro-States*. Berkeley: University of California Press.

Keefer, P. (2007) Clientelism, credibility and policy choices of young democracies. *American Journal of Political Science* 51(4), 804–21.

Khan, A.R. (1972) *The Economy of Bangladesh*. Basingstoke: Macmillan.

Khan, M. (2000) Rent-seeking as process. In: Khan, M.H. and Jomo, K.S. (eds) *Rents, Rent-Seeking and Economic Development: Theory and Evidence in Asia*. Cambridge: Cambridge University Press, 70–144.

Krueger, A.O. (1992) *The Political Economy of Agricultural Pricing Policy: A Synthesis*. Washington, DC: World Bank.

Krueger, A.O. and Tuncer, B. (1982) An empirical test of the infant industry argument. *American Economic Review* 72, 1142–52.

Kuznets, P.W. (1988) An East Asian model of economic development. *Economic Development and Cultural Change* 36(3 Suppl), 11–43.

Kuznets, S. (1971) *Economic Growth of Nations*. Cambridge, MA: Harvard University Press.

Lal, D. (1983) *The Poverty of Development Economics*. London: Institute of Economic Affairs.

Lal, D. (1988) *The Hindu Equilibrium. Volume 1*. Oxford: Clarendon Press.

Lal, D. (1995) Why growth rates differ. The political economy of social capability in 21 developing countries. In: Koo, B.H. and Perkins, D.H. (eds) *Social Capability and Long-Run Economic Growth*. Basingstoke: Macmillan, 310–27.

Lal, D. (2005) *The Hindu Equilibrium: India 1500 BC to 2000 AD*. Oxford: Oxford University Press.

Lal, D. and Myint, H. (1996) *The Political Economy of Poverty, Equity and Growth*. Oxford: Clarendon Press.

Lange, G.-M., Wodon, Q., and Carey, K. (2018) *The Changing Wealth of Nations 2018: Building a Sustainable Future*. Washington, DC: World Bank.

Lau, L.J., Qian, Y., and Roland, G. (2000) Reform without losers: an interpretation of China's dual track approach to transition. *Journal of Political Economy* 108(1), 120–43.

Lechtenbohmer, S. Prantner, M., Siefreid, D., et al. (2010) *Energy Price Reform in Iran*. Wuppertal: Wuppertal Institute for Climate.

References

Lederman, D. and Maloney, W.F. (2007) *Natural Resources: Neither Curse nor Blessing*. Palo Alto, CA: Stanford University Press.

Lee, M. and Gueye, C.A. (2014) Do resource windfalls improve the standard of living in Sub-Saharan african countries? Evidence from a panel of countries. IMF Working Paper 15/83. Washington, DC: IMF.

Lewis, W.A. (1954) Economic development with unlimited supplies of labour. *Manchester School of Social and Economic Studies* 22, 139–91.

Lewis, W.A. (1978) *Growth and Fluctuations 1870–1913*. London: Allen and Unwin.

Lewis, W.A. (1979) The dual economy revisited. *Manchester School of Social and Economic Studies* 47(3), 211–99.

Li, S., and Zhang, W. (2000) The road to capitalism: competition and institutional change in China. *Journal of Comparative Economics* 28, 269–92.

Lim, W. (2000) *The origin and evolution of the Korean economic system*. Working Paper. Seoul: Korean Development Institute.

Lindsey, B. and Teles, S.M. (2017) *The Captured Economy*. Oxford: Oxford University Press.

Lipton, M. (1968) *Urban Bias and Agricultural Planning*. Brighton: Institute of Development Studies, University of Sussex.

Lipton, M. (1977) *Why Poor People Stay Poor: Urban Bias in World Development*. London: Temple Smith.

Lisboa, M.B. and Latif, Z.A. (2013) Democracy and growth in Brazil. Working Paper 311/2013. Sao Paulo: INSPER.

Lizzeri, A. and Persico, N. (2004) Why did the elites extend the suffrage? Democracy and the scope of government with application to Britain's Age of Reform. *Quarterly Journal of Economics* 119(2), 707–65.

Londono, J.L. (1996) *Poverty, Inequality and Human Capital Development in Latin America*. Washington, DC: World Bank.

Loungani, P., Mishra, S., Papageorgiou, C., and Wang, K. (2017) World trade in services: evidence from a new dataset. IMF Working Paper 17/77. Washington, DC: IMF.

Lundgren, C.J., Thomas, A.H., and York, R.C. (2013) *Boom, Bust or Prosperity: Managing Sub-Saharan Africa's Natural Resource Wealth*. Washington, DC: IMF.

Macmillan, A. (1914) *Mauritius Illustrated*. London: Asian Educational Services.

Maddison, A. (1992) *The Political Economy of Poverty, Equity and Growth: Brazil and Mexico*. Washington, DC: World Bank.

Maddison, A. (2007) *Contours of the World Economy 1–2030 AD*. Oxford: Oxford University Press.

Maddison, A. (1995) *Monitoring the World Economy 1820–1992*. Paris: OECD.

Marfin, M. and Bosworth, B. (1994) Saving, investment and economic growth. In: Bosworth, B., Dornbusch, R., and Laban, R. (eds) *The Chilean Economy: Lessons and Challenges*. Washington, DC: The Brookings Institution.

Massol, O. and Banal-Estanol, A. (2014) Export diversification and resource-based industrialisation: the case of natural gas. *European Journal of Operational Research* 237(3), 1067–82.

Matsuyama, K. (1992) Agricultural productivity, comparative advantage, and economic growth. *Journal of Economic Theory* 58(2), 317–34.

McGuire, G. (2014) Contracts and pricing in Trinidad and Tobago. In: Boopsingh, T.M. and McGurire, G. (eds) *From Oil to Gas and Beyond: A Review of the Trinidad and Tobago Model*. Latham, MD: University Press of America, 112–39.

McKinsey (2012) *Manufacturing the Future: The Next Era of Global Growth and Innovation*. New York: McKinsey Global Institute.

McKinsey (2016) *Lions on the Move II: Realising the Potential of Africa's Economies*. New York: McKinsey Global Institute.

McMillan, M. (2012) Global patterns of structural change. WCAO Thematic Note 02. Washington, DC: IFPRI.

McMillan, M., Rodrik, D., and Verduzco-Gallo, I. (2014) Globalization, structural change and productivity growth, with an update on Africa. *World Development* 63, 11–32.

McMillan, M., Rodrik, D., and Sepulveda, C. (2016) *Structural Change, Fundamentals and Growth: A Framework and Case Studies*. Washington, DC: IFPRI.

Mehlum, H., Moene, K., and Torvik, R. (2006) Institutions and the resource curse. *Economic Journal* 116(508), 1–20.

Meighoo, K. (2008) Ethnic mobilisation versus ethnic politics: understanding ethnicity in Trinidad and Tobago politics. *Commonwealth and Comparative Politics* 46(1), 101–27.

Mellor, J.W. (1976) *The New Economics of Growth: A Strategy for India and the Developing World*. Ithaca: Cornell University Press.

Mellor, J.W. (1995) *Agriculture on the Road to Industrialisation*. Baltimore, MD: Johns Hopkins University Press.

Mendes, M. (2014) *Inequality, Democracy and Growth in Brazil*. Cambridge, MA: Academic Press.

Ministry of Finance (1980) *Accounting for the Petrodollar*. Port of Spain: Ministry of Finance.

Ministry of Finance (1989) *National Statistics of Chile 1985–89*. Santiago: Ministry of Finance.

Mishra, S., Lundstrom, S., and Annand, R. (2012) Service export sophistication and economic growth. CEPR Vox 050412. London: CEPR. http://www.voxeu.org/article/service-export-sophistication-and-economic-growth.

Mitchell, D. (2005) Sugar in the Caribbean: adjusting to eroding preferences. World Bank Policy Working Paper 3802. Washington, DC: World Bank.

Mohammad, S. and Whalley, J. (1984) Rent seeking in India: its costs and policy significance. *Kyklos* 47, 387–413.

Montalvo, J.G. and Reynal-Querol, M. (2005) Ethnic diversity and economic development. *Journal of Development Economics* 76, 293–323.

Morande, F.G. (1996) Savings in Chile: what went right? Research Department Publication 4030. Washington, DC: Inter-American Development Bank.

Mottley, W. (2008) *Trinidad and Tobago Industrial Policy 1959–2008: A Historical and Contemporary Analysis*. Kingston, Jamaica: Ian Randle Publishers.

Murphy, K.L., Shleifer, A., and Vishny, R.W. (1989) Industrialization and the big push. *Journal of Political Economy* 97, 1003–26.

Nattrass, J. (1988) *The South African Economy*: Its Growth and Change. Cape Town: Oxford University Press.

Ndulu, B.J., O'Connell, S.A., Bates, R.H., Collier, P., and Soludo, C.C. (eds) (2008) *The Political Economy of Economic Growth in Africa 1960–2000: Volume 1*. Cambridge: Cambridge University Press.

Niddrie, D.L. (1983) The Caribbean. In: Blakemore, H. and Smith, C.T. (eds) *Latin America and the Caribbean: Geographical Perspectives*. London: Methuen, 77–132.

Noland, M. and Pack, H. (2003) *Industrialization in an Era of Globalization: Lessons from Asia*. Washington, DC: Institute for International Economics.

North, D.C. (1955) Location theory and regional economic growth. *Journal of Political Economy* 63(3), 243–58.

North, D., Wallis, J., Webb, S., and Weingast, B. (2009) *Violence and Social Orders: A Conceptual Framework for Interpreting Recorded Human History*. Cambridge: Cambridge University Press.

North-Coombes, M.D. (1988) Struggles in the cane fields: small growers in Mauritius 1921–37. In: Albert, W. and Graves, A. (eds) *The World Sugar Economy in War and Depression*. London: Routledge, 194–208.

Noyelle, T. (1986) Revitalising the industrial city. *Annals of the American Academy of Political and Social Science* 488, 9–17.

OECD (2017) *Statistics on Resource Flows to Developing Countries*. Paris: OECD. http://www.oecd.org/dac/stats/statisticsonresourceflowstodevelopingcountries.htm.

Olson, M. (2000) *Power and Prosperity*. New York: Basic Books.

Owolabe, K. (2007) Politics, institutions and ethnic voting in plural societies: comparative lessons from Trinidad and Tobago, Guyana and Mauritius. Working Paper. South Bend, IN:University of Notre Dame.

Page, J. (2012) Can Africa industrialize? *Journal of African Economies* 21 (Special issue 2), ii86–124.

Pang, E.F. and Lim, L.Y.C. (2015) Labour productivity and Singapore's development model. *Singapore Economic Review* 60 (3), 1550033-0-30.

Palma, J.G. (2011) Why has productivity growth stagnated in most Latin American countries since the neo-liberal reforms? In: Ocampo, J.A. and Ros, J. (eds) *The Oxford Handbook of Latin American Economies*. Oxford: Oxford University Press, 568–607.

Palmer, D.W. and Pemberton, C.A. (2007) An estimation of the efficient size of sugarcane enterprises in Trinidad. *Farm and Business: Journal of the Caribbean Agro-Economic Society* 7(1) 1–16.

Panagariya, A. (2005) Agricultural liberalization and the least developed countries: six fallacies. *The World Economy* 28(9), 1277–99.

Park, Y.C. (1986) Foreign debt, balance of payments and growth prospects: The Republic of South Korea. *World Development* 14, 1019–58.

Perkins, D. and Syrquin, M. (1989) Large countries: the influence of size. In: Chenery, H. and Srinivasan, T.M. (eds) *Handbook of Development Economics Vol 2*. Amsterdam: North Holland, 1691–753.

Petreski, A. and Wong, S.A. (2014) Dutch disease in Latin American countries: de-industrialization, how it happens, and the role of China. MPRA Paper 57056. Munich: University Library of Munich.

Pissarides, C. and Veganzones-Varoudakis, M.-A. (2007) Labor markets and economic growth in the MENA region. In: Nugent, J.B. and Pesaran, M.H. (eds) *Explaining Growth in the Middle East. Contributions to Economic Analysis*. Amsterdam: Elsevier.

Prebisch, R. (1950) *The economic development of Latin America and its principal problems*. Santiago: ECLA.

Przeworski, A., Alvarez, M.E., Cheibub, J.A., and Limongi, F. (2000) *Democracy and Development: Political Institutions and Well-being in the World 1950–1990*. Cambridge: Cambridge University Press.

Pyo, H. (1989) Export-led growth, domestic distortions and trade liberalisation: the Korean experience during the 1980s. *Journal of Asian Economics* 1(2), 225–47.

Racha, S. (2001) From oil to natural gas: prospects and challenges for the Trinidad and Tobago economy. Mimeo, Port of Spain: Central Bank of Trinidad & Tobago.

Radelet, S. (2016) Africa's rise—interrupted? *Finance and Development* 53(2), 1–6.

Rahman, A.H. (1992) Structural adjustment and macroeconomic performance in Bangladesh in the 1980s. *Bangladesh Development Studies* 20, 89–125.

Raiser, M., Schaffer, M., and Schuchardt, J. (2004) Benchmarking structural change in transition. *Structural Change and Economic Dynamics* 15, 47–81.

Rajan, R.G. and Subramanian, A. (2011) Aid, Dutch disease and manufacturing growth. *Journal of Development Economics* 94(1), 106–18.

Rajapatirana, S. (2001) *Post trade liberalization policies and institutional challenges in Latin America and the Caribbean*. Washington, DC: World Bank.

Robinson, J.A., Torvik, R., and Verdier, J. (2006) Political foundations of the resource curse. *Journal of Development Economics* 79, 447–68.

Rodrik, D. (1999) *The New Global Economy and Developing Countries: Making Openness Work*. London: Overseas Development Council.

Rodrik, D. (2001) Development strategies for the next century. In: Pleskovic, B. and Stern, N. (eds) *Annual World Bank Conference on Development Economics 2000*. Washington, DC: World Bank.

Rodrik, D. (2016) Premature deindustrialization, *Journal of Economic Growth*, Springer, 21(1), 1–33.

Rodrik, D. (2018) An African growth miracle? *Journal of African Economies* 27 (1–1), 1–18.

Rojas-Suarez, L., Elias, C. Jaramillo, F., and Artana, D. (2006) *From Growth to Prosperity: Policy Perspectives for Trinidad and Tobago*. Washington, DC: IADB.

Ross, M. (2001) Does oil hinder democracy? *World Politics* 53(3), 325–61.

Rumult, R.P. (1974) *Strategy, Structure and Economic Performance*. Boston, MA: Harvard Business School Press.

Sacerdoti, E., El-Masry, G., Khandelwal, P., and Yao, Y. (2002) Mauritius: challenges of sustained growth. IMF Working Paper 02/189. Washington, DC: IMF.

Sachs, J.D. (1989) Social conflict and populist policies in Latin America. NBER Working Paper 2897. Cambridge, MA: Natinal Bureau of Economic Research.

Sachs, J.D. and Warner, A.M. (1997) *Natural Resource Abundance and Economic Development*. Cambridge, MA: Harvard Institute for International Development.

Sachs, J.D. and Warner, A.M. (1999) Natural resource intensity and economic growth. In: Mayer, J., Chambers, B., and Farooq, A. (eds) *Development Policies in Natural Resource Economies*. Cheltenham: Edward Elgar, 13–38.

Schlumberger, O. (2008) Structural reform, economic order and development: patrimonial capitalism. *Review of International Political Economy* 15(4), 622–49.

Schmidt-Hebbel, K. (2006) Chile's economic growth. *Cuadernos de Economia* 43.

Seers, D. (1964) The mechanism of an open petroleum economy. *Social and Economic Studies* 13(2), 233–42.

Segura, A. (2006) Management of oil wealth under the permanent income hypothesis: the case of Sao Tome and Principe. IMF Working Paper 06/103. Washington, DC: IMF.

Serageldin, I. and Grootaert, C. (2000) Defining social capital: an integrating view. In: Picciotto, R. and Wiesner, E. (eds) *Evaluation and Development: The Institutional Dimension*. New Brunswick, NJ: Transaction Publishers, 203–17.

Sergeant, K., Racha, S., and John, M. (2002) The Petroleum Sector: Case of Trinidad and Tobago. Trends, Policies and Impact 1985–2000. Santiago: CEPAL.

Sharpley, J. and Lewis, S. (1990) The manufacturing sector in the mid-1980s. In: Riddell, R.C. (ed.) *Manufacturing Africa*. London: James Currey, 206–41.

Shepherd, C.Y. (1929) The sugar industry of the British West Indies and British Guiana with special reference to Trinidad. *Economic Geography* 5(2), 149–75.

Siamwalla, A. (1995) Land-abundant agricultural growth and some of its consequences: Thailand. In: Mellor, J.W. (ed.) *Agriculture on the Road to Industrialisation*. Baltimore, MD: Johns Hopkins University Press, 23–66.

Singer, H.W. (1950) The distribution of gains from investing and borrowing countries. *American Economic Review Papers and Proceedings* 40, 473–75.

Singh, K. and Bery, S. (2005) India's growth experience. In: Tseng, W. and Cowen, D. (eds) *India and China's Recent Experience with Reform and Growth*. Washington, DC: IMF, 23–58.

Sirageldin, I. and Al-Ebraheem, Y. (1999) Budget gap, resource deficit and human resource development in oil economies. In: Sirageldin, I. (ed.) *Population and Development in the Middle East and North Africa: Challenges for the Twenty-First Century*. Baltimore, MD: Johns Hopkins University.

Smith, I. (1976) Can the West Indies sugar industry survive? *Oxford Bulletin of Economics and Statistics* 38(2), 125–40.

Sookraj, R. (2011) The closing of Caroni 1975 Ltd. *R-Evolutionary* 2(7), 1–4.

Stauffer, T.R. (1975) *Energy-Intensive Industries in the Persian/Arabian Gulf: A New Ruhr without Water?* Cambridge, MA: Harvard Centre for Middle Eastern Studies.

Stern, J.J. (1990) Industrial targeting in Korea. HIID Discussion Paper 343. Cambridge, MA: HID.

Stern, J.J., Kim, J.-H., Perkins, D.H., and Yoo, Y.-H. (1995) *Industrialization and the State: The Korean Heavy and Chemical Industry Drive*. Cambridge, MA: Harvard Institute for International Development.

Stevens, P. (2003) Resource impact: curse or blessing? A literature survey. *Journal of Energy Literature* 9(1), 3–42.

Stiglitz, J.E. (1995) Social absorption capability and innovation. In: Koo, B.H. and Perkins, D.H. (eds) *Social Capability and Long-Term Economic Growth*. Basingstoke: Macmillan, 48–81.

Stiglitz, J. and Kanbur, R. (2015) Dynastic inequality, mobility and equality of opportunity. CEPR Discussion Paper 10542. London: Centre for Economic Policy Research.

Subramanian, A. (2009) The Mauritian success story and its lessons. UNU/WIDER Research Paper 2009/36. Helsinki: UNU/WIDER.

Subramanian, A. and Roy, D. (2003) Who can explain the Mauritian miracle? Meade, Romer, Sachs or Rodrik? In: Rodrik, D. (ed.) *In Search of Prosperity: Analytic Narratives of Economic Growth*. Princeton, NJ: Princeton University Press, 205–43.

Sudama, T. (1979) The model of the plantation economy: the case of Trinidad and Tobago. *Latin American Perspectives* 6(1), 65–83.

Sundberg, M. and Gelb, A.H. (2006) Making aid work. *Finance and Development* 43(4).

Svensson, J. (2000) Foreign aid and rent-seeking. *Journal of International Economics* 51, 437–61.

Syed, M. and Walsh, J.P. (2012) The tiger and the dragon. *Finance and Development* 49(3), 36–9.

Syrquin, M. (1986) Productivity growth and factor reallocation. In: Chenery, H.B., Robinson, S., and Syrquin, M. (eds) *Industrialization and Growth: A Comparative Study*. New York: Oxford University Press, 229–62.

Syrquin, M., and Chenery, H.B. (1989) Patterns of development, 1950 to 1983. World Bank Discussion Paper 41. Washington, DC: World Bank.

Teravaninthorn, S. and Raballand, G. (2009) *Transport Prices and Costs in Africa: A Review of the International Corridors*. Washington, DC: World Bank.

Timmer, C.P. (2008) The agricultural transformation. In: Chenery, H.C. and Srinivasan, N. (2008) *Handbook of Development Economics. Volume 1*. Amsterdam: North Holland, 275–331.

Timmer, C.P. (2012) The mathematics of structural transformation. WCAO Thematic Note 02. Washington, DC: IFPRI.

Tollison, R.D. (1982) Rent-seeking: a survey. *Kyklos* 35(4), 575–602.

Tomich, T.P., Kilby, P., and Johnston, B.F. (1995) *Transforming Agrarian Economies: Opportunities Seized and Opportunities Missed*. Ithaca: Cornell University Press.

Torres, N., Afonso, O., and Soares, I. (2013) A survey of literature on the resource curse: critical analysis of the main explanations, empirical tests and resource proxies. CEFUP Working Paper 2013–02. Porto: Centro de Economia e Financas, University of Porto.

Treisman, D. (2002) The causes of corruption: a cross-national study. *Journal of Public Economics* 76(3), 399–458.

Ungor, M. (2011) De-industrialization of the riches and the rise of China. Meeting Papers 740. Society for Economic Dynamics, Ghent 7–9 July.

Ungor, M. (2017) Productivity growth and labour reallocation: Latin America versus East Asia. *Review of Economic Dynamics* 24, 25–42.

US Congress (2011) *The Economy of Trinidad and Tobago*. Washington, DC: US Congress.

Vandermoortele, N. and Bird, K. (2011) *Progress in Economic Conditions in Mauritius: Success Against the Odds*. London: Overseas Development Institute.

van der Ploeg, F. and Poelhekke, S. (2009) Volatility and the natural resource curse. *Oxford Economic Papers* 61(4), 727–60.

van de Walle, N. (1999) *African Economies and the Politics of Permanent Crisis, 1979–1999*. Cambridge University Press: Cambridge.

Velculescu, D. and Rizavi, S. (2005) Trinidad and Tobago: the energy boom and proposals for a sustainable fiscal policy. IMF Working Paper 05/197. Washington, DC: IMF.

Walton, J. (1975) Internal colonialism: problems of definition and measurement. In: Cornelius, W.A. and Truebood, F.A. (eds) *Urbanization and Inequality: The Political Economy of Urban and Rural Development in Latin America*. London: Sage, 29–50.

Warner, A. (2015) Natural resource booms in the modern era: is the curse still alive? IMF Working Paper 15/237. Washington, DC: IMF.

Winters, L.A. and Yusuf, S. (2007) *Dancing with Giants: China, India and the Global Economy*. Washington, DC: World Bank.

Wood, A., and Berge, K. (1997) Exporting manufactures: human resources, natural resources, and trade policy. *Journal of Development Studies* 34: 35–59.

Woolcock, M. and Narayan, D. (2000) Social capital: implications for development theory, research and policy. *World Bank Research Observer* 15(2), 225–49.

World Bank (1968) *AF-80: Current Economic Position and Prospects of Mauritius*. Washington, DC: World Bank.

World Bank (1987) Kenya: industrial sector policies for investment and export growth. Report 6711-KE. Washington, DC: World Bank.

World Bank (1989) *World Tables 1988–89*. Baltimore, MD: Johns Hopkins University Press.

World Bank (1993) *The East Asian Miracle: Economic Growth and Public Policy*. New York: Oxford University Press.

World Bank (1999) Country assistance strategy for the government of Trinidad and Tobago. Report 19052TR. Washington, DC: World Bank.

World Bank (2004) *Beyond Economic Growth: An Introduction to Sustainable Development*. Washington, DC: World Bank.

World Bank (2006) *Where Is the Wealth of Nations?* Washington, DC: World Bank.

World Bank (2009a) *From Privilege to Competition: Unlocking Private-Led Growth in MENA*. Washington, DC: World Bank.

World Bank (2009b) *The Service Revolution in South Asia*. Washington, DC: World Bank.

World Bank (2011) *The Changing Wealth of Nations: Measuring Sustainable Development in the New Millennium*. Washington, DC: World Bank.

World Bank (2012) Are natural resources bad for growth? *Africa's Pulse* 6 (2), 17–20.

World Bank (2013) *Unlocking Africa's Agricultural Potential: An Action Agenda for Transformation*. Washington, DC: World Bank.

World Bank (2014) *World Bank Doing Business 2015*. Washington, DC: World Bank.

World Bank (2017a) *World Development Indicators 2017*. Washington, DC: World Bank.

World Bank (2017b) *Bangladesh: Development Update*. Washington, DC: World Bank.

World Economic Forum (2016) *Global Competitiveness Report 2014–15*. Geneva: World Economic Forum.

World Economic Forum (2016) *Global Competitiveness Report 2015–16*. Geneva: World Economic Forum.

World Travel and Tourism Council (2012) *Travel and Tourism: Economic Impact 2012, Mauritius*. London: World Travel and Tourism Council.

Yoo, J.-H. (1990) The industrial policy of the 1970s and the evolution of the manufacturing sector in Korea. Working Paper 9017. Seoul: Korean Development Institute.

Yueng, L.L.K. (1998) *The Economic Development of Mauritius since Independence*. Sydney: University of New South Wales.

Zak, P.J. and Feng, Y. (1999) Determinants of demographic transitions. *Journal of Conflict Resolution* 43, 162–77.

Zak, P.J. and Feng, Y. (2003) A dynamic theory of the transition to democracy. *Journal of Economic Behavior and Organization* 52, 1–25.

Index

Note: Tables are indicated by an italic *t* following the page number.

Index

Index